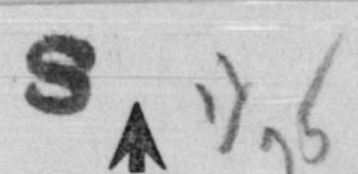

FRANK LLOYD WRIGHT ON ARCHITECTURE

For half a century Frank Lloyd Wright, now 76, has led a singularly active life as architect, thinker and teacher. Yet in all these years this is the first attempt which has been made to collect all his writings in order to provide a guidebook to the development and thinking of America's greatest architect.

Here is a book which should be read by everyone who is interested in building: by those who are going to build homes, by architects, by everyone who wants to know for his own enjoyment the secret of the modern luxury and elegance of natural materials, of free-and-easy living spaces and fresh proportions. From the spicy pen of America's master builder come the richly suggestive formulas to vitalize our new architecture and brighten our daily life.

FRANK LLOYD WRIGHT ON ARCHITECTURE
Selected Writings 1894-1940
Edited with an Introduction by Frederick Gutheim

AN AUTOBIOGRAPHY
Four books in one volume

IN THE NATURE OF MATERIALS
The Buildings of Frank Lloyd Wright
By Henry-Russell Hitchcock

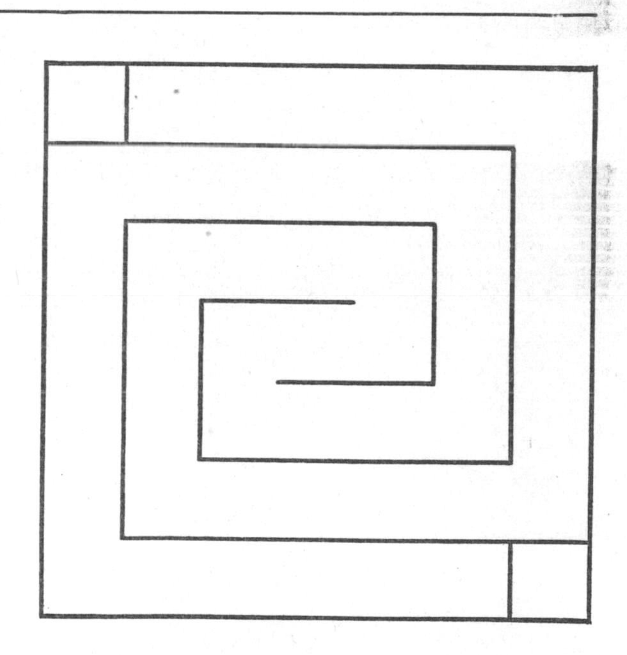

FRANK LLOYD WRIGHT

SELECTED WRITINGS 1894-1940 · Edited with an Introduction by FREDERICK GUTHEIM

DUELL, SLOAN AND PEARCE
NEW YORK 1941

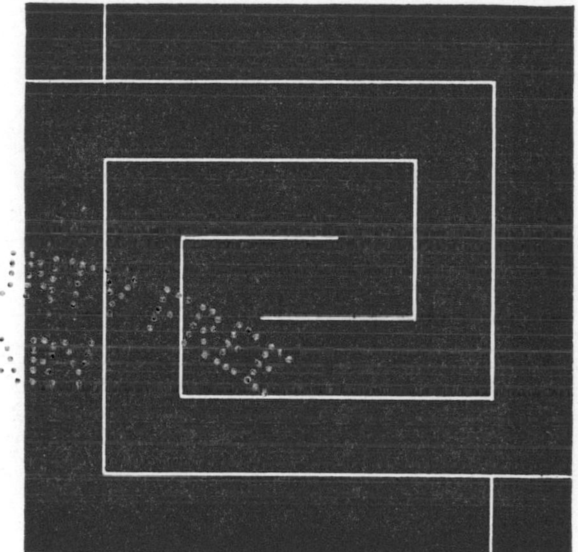

ON ARCHITECTURE

L B

Seventh Printing

PRINTED IN THE UNITED STATES OF AMERICA

FOR POLLY

Contents

Preface

When I first considered the collection and arrangement of the selected writings of Frank Lloyd Wright in one volume I was aware of the existence of a great mass of published and unpublished material. As my work progressed I began to realize how much more extensive was this literature than I had originally supposed. While the selections printed here are but a small part of Wright's literary effort, a work which must be considered of increasing importance, I am confident that they are fully representative of the much larger body of material from which they have been drawn. Each selection has been carefully chosen to preserve the spirit of the original context. For the occasional student whose necessities dictate reference to the original, the references in the head and the attached bibliography will be helpful.

A word or two on the arrangement of the material may be useful. A strict chronological order has been adhered to throughout, save in the one case where it was necessary to depart from this policy in order to throw the two essays "In the Cause of Architecture" into a closer relationship. As a companion volume to *An Autobiography* and *In the Nature of Materials,* this arrangement has certain practical advantages to the reader. It further aids in the solution of my principal editorial problem: to make a readable unity of what was in the beginning, and necessarily still remains in a few places, closely edited pieces of unrelated material.

Working principally with the original manuscripts, which usually carry the dates of their composition, I have taken advantage of this unique opportunity to use these dates—which in many cases are considerably in advance of the publication dates—as the basis for arrangement. In the headings of each selection the first date is the date of composition, and in the case of published material the date published is given in the credit line. The manuscript files at Taliesin have passed through two fires and the problem of identifying and dating certain manuscripts has presented certain difficulties. While I cannot be certain in every case, the dates given do not conflict with reasonable assumptions based on both external and internal evidence. At the worst there may be some error in the order of selections within any given year. I have avoided using material from books still in print or in the process of revision, but save for this restraint I have read and used every piece of Wright material that might contribute to this book.

In the search for the more elusive items I have been indebted to the suggestions made by many friends and admirers of Frank Lloyd Wright; to Mr. and Mrs. Rudolf Mock, Mr.

Eugene Masselink, Mr. Henry Klumb, Mr. William F. Deknatel and Mr. Julian E. Berla I owe additional thanks for criticisms and suggestions regarding individual selections. The index has been prepared with intelligence and professional skill by Mrs. Eric S. Purdon. I wish also to express my thanks to the Museum of Modern Art for the opportunity to check my own lists against the Wright bibliography prepared by their staff, and to Grant Carpenter Manson for further help in the preparation of the bibliography.

Many of these selections have been published elsewhere. Some of them stand here as monuments to the foresight and appreciation of great editors. I think particularly of the editor of the *Ladies' Home Journal,* who commissioned Wright to prepare plans of houses and articles as early as 1901; of the editor of the *Architectural Record* who printed in 1908 an article that at that time must have taken editorial courage to publish; of a later editor of the *Architectural Record* who in 1927—in the darkest eclipse of Wright's fame—commissioned the series of articles "In the Cause of Architecture: The Nature of Materials." Publications of independence, courage and initiative such as these deserve more than my gratitude for the permission to reprint material originally published in their pages. While on this theme it may be well to point out courage in a far more welcome and more surprising place—The Art Institute of Chicago—which in fair weather and foul stood by one of the brightest stars in the Chicago galaxy.

Although each selection carries in its title the name of the article and the place printed, I wish also to thank here the publishers of the following magazines for permission to reprint material by Frank Lloyd Wright: the *Architectural Forum, Liberty,* the *Saturday Review of Literature, Physical Culture,* the *Architect's Journal,* the *Architectural Review* and the *Ladies' Home Journal.* I wish also to thank the Princeton University Press for permission to reprint selections from the Kahn Lectures for 1930, published by them under the title *Modern Architecture,* and to the Art Institute of Chicago for permission to reprint selections from *Two Lectures on Architecture.*

My debt to Frank Lloyd Wright is greatest. Without his active cooperation this work could not have been undertaken. With complete respect for the historical value of this un-retouched picture of past opinions—with which he may differ today—he has patiently and promptly read and authenticated these selections. Those who know his active and questing mind will best understand the monumental restraint thus exercised.

FREDERICK GUTHEIM

Introduction

In presenting this volume to its readers I would like to make clear its purpose; for, simple as it is, I hardly believe it will be obvious. As an architect Frank Lloyd Wright's work has become known to many throughout the world, but one may well question the extent to which it has been understood or properly appreciated whether in the United States or —a *volte-face* of architectural criticism—still less abroad. He has not been fortunate in his critics, few of whom have enjoyed opportunities for the comprehensive study of his truly global endeavors, and many of whom have fobbed off on their readers glib platitudes based on their examination of plans and photographs, rather than experience. Whether these have been encomiums or condemnations is of small consequence: they have not advanced any helpful understanding of Wright's architecture.

Now to an extraordinary degree, and with great zeal, Wright has always been at pains to make clear what his architectural intentions have been. He may also claim serious consideration as an architectural critic. This articulateness was perhaps implicit in his pioneering work. But it is in the light of these confessed aims that one may arrive at a proper understanding of his work. This is not to say that his buildings do not have their own independent existence as facts, and that we may enjoy them individually for their own qualities. That is true of all works of art. But criticism and appreciation are two different things. If we are to understand the buildings and their creator, I believe it must be in the full light of such passages as have been gathered together into this book, most of which are here printed for the first time.

For those who have read, or who will read in its new edition, Frank Lloyd Wright's *An Autobiography*, the material of this volume (with the exception of one essay) has been arranged in strict chronological order. While other forms of organization would have thrown certain aspects of his life and work into sharper relief, they would not have underlined what is to me this book's most striking revelation: the superb quality of intellectual growth, the astonishing relation of the man to his times, and the premonitions and incredibly independent foresight of this almost timeless ever-modern personality. So fast have modern changes come about that few among us can capture the milieu of that last decade of the nineteenth century, the crucible in which Wright first formed that deeply spiritual architectural philosophy whose forms in the ensuing half century have spread over the entire world with epidemic rapidity.

As this book opens the clop-clop of horses' hoofs still sound in the streets of Chicago; the broker lives happily in his Gothick cottage in the suburbs; the shanty slums of the West Side are still under construction; bustles and picture hats are in fashion, and every be-ferned parlor covers its floors twice and its windows three times before it can be considered properly fitted out. From these oddly guileless and contented surroundings, the splintered relics of which Chicago has unaccountably preserved, came the strange earnest voice of a young architect. In his Prince Albert coat he addresses the perfumed ladies of the Chicago Women's Club—and he speaks in language so revolutionary that it could scarcely have been understood. "It was so beautiful, Mr. Wright," the ladies burbled—as scarcely earlier they had burbled to Oscar Wilde. He speaks at Hull House, to engineers, to architects, to the D.A.R., at the Art Institute. But nowhere is there evidence, internal or external, that these messages had been received. Yet, as if from some subterranean, impersonal, non-literary source, the magic ideas poured forth, took form and began their revolutionary career. Before 1908 the foundations of this philosophy were in, the walls were up and the roof was on; its scope, limits and character could all be seen. These ideas were consciously organized as a unified doctrine in 1908 in one of the most remarkable essays of this collection, "In the Cause of Architecture," which has stood since, a lonely, splendid beacon in the architectural literature of its day.

To his profession Wright addressed this essay of 1908, and he printed it in the *Architectural Record*. Its leading ideas he amplified in the introduction to that sumptuous record of his collected early work, *Ausgeführte Bauten und Entwürfe*. He defended them from their enemies—and more from their friends—in a subsequent paper printed in 1914. But this consolidation of his thought, as nearly a systematic formal presentation of his architectural ideas then as we have, written with the authority of success, struck the architectural profession a glancing blow. Unluckily its moving words did not succeed in persuading the architects of that day to forsake their eclecticism; at best—or worst—it merely furnished their library-jaded imaginations with fresh forms to plunder. Luckily, this formulation—premature, as we now see—did not succeed for long in persuading its author of the impermeable logic of his own convictions. He had not built a roof under which to seek shelter, but a platform on which to take his stand.

Out of the years of flux—of personal tragedy, spiritual upheaval, travel; of world war and disorganization; of building experiment; tortured and scarred on the merciless rack of journalism; victimized by disloyalty, hatred, jealousy—out of these sordid times so well recorded in *An Autobiography,* to the architect came fresh applications of old principles, new uses for the great tradition, ideas which broke through old forms. In the enigmatic circumstances of these years are embedded many strange acts, strange buildings, strange writings. In every long, significant creative life such periods commonly appear—to the consternation of critics. How else can one explain the Porta Pia in Michelangelo's architecture, or the Pietà Rondanini in his sculpture? How else explain the twenty-year hiatus in the *Education of Henry Adams?* How else explain *Clavigo* in the work of Goethe?

The emergence of modern architecture in Europe, heralded by the writings of its champions Le Corbusier and Gropius, and unveiled to the United States in 1931 as "the International Style," was nearly as challenging to Wright as his own earlier influence had been to the Europeans. Perverted, as he believed it, the new style was producing men and buildings more profoundly significant than those of the eclectic academicians against whom alone he had previously measured himself. It was a positive and stimulating challenge, and in these pages one can see that to its influence is due much subsequent clarification of Wright's earlier ideas. His immediate reaction was instantaneous and clear: he regarded these new forms as exploitations of his own work. He strongly condemned them as two-dimensional cardboard caricatures. He censured the falsely academic effort to make an easy formula for success out of fragments of his own principles. He sprayed their creators with invective and ridicule, and kicked their architectural achievements off his doorstep. But the line between their work and his was harder to define than the line between traditional eclecticism and organic architecture, and imposed the responsibility of further definition of his own aims. To this necessity we owe much of the material in this section.

As the flush of building activity returned from 1935 on, the architect began to build again in his old volume. A new and juster fame was softly replacing the old notoriety. He was again surrounded by eager apprentices. In the writings of this time a more philosophical note begins to emerge, veining the old acrimonious disputes with wit and mellow wisdom. The final section of this book shows us Frank Lloyd Wright as educator, carrying the responsibilities of the Taliesin Fellowship, lecturing in Russia, Brazil, England and throughout the United States, preaching the necessity of such a fundamental reorganization and rebuilding as Broadacre City if democracy is to be realized; but always building, building, building.

As I have worked over these selections, this simple pattern has emerged. That it corresponds in its general divisions to the story told in *An Autobiography* is perhaps inevitable, but I suspect the more surprising thing is its correspondence to the architectural work of these periods. We see here underlined what has always been true and, despite logic and common sense, has too often been ignored—the essential and underlying unified character of all aspects of Wright's life and work. This fact I do not propose to discuss at length or in critical detail, because the necessary apparatus of plates and illustrations is lacking, and there are matters of greater importance to the present volume to be considered.

In one important respect this book makes a discovery. Of all the pieces of folk-lore that have grown up through constant repetition, one of the most adhesive in people's minds is the fiction that Wright was neglected at home, warmly acclaimed abroad and that his influence at home has been mainly felt after this sea voyage. This ingenious theory, I am persuaded, is one way of pretending that the true essence of Frank Lloyd Wright is that fragment of him which passed through the European filter. I submit that Frank Lloyd Wright is no neglected figure in America, but far from it; his career has been more successful than that of almost any great architect in our history. At nineteen he was at work in the office of the greatest architect of his time; two years later he was chief draftsman, the best paid of any in the city of Chicago; before he was twenty-five he had built half a dozen buildings of his own, and dozens of others for Sullivan and Adler. He was independent at twenty-five, forging his own career. At thirty-two he was a national name: his buildings were known—dozens of them; he was a powerful influence; his work had been exhibited, illustrated, written about; he contributed to national magazines. These facts hardly fit the "artist-starving-in-the-garret" myth. No man can build three hundred important buildings and be considered neglected, and no architect who has had the local, national and international réclame of Frank Lloyd Wright for at least the last thirty-five years can be thought ignored. If some of these facts may be deduced from the buildings and *An Autobiography* they must be immeasurably strengthened by the material of this book, which is the record not of the appreciation of a handful of exceptional clients, but of fame and popularity in the eyes of millions.

The plain fact is that Europe "discovered" Frank Lloyd Wright in 1908 when Ashbee and Kuno Francke visited Chicago, and more particularly in 1910 when the Wasmuth monograph was published, placing on the drafting boards of the world the plans and perspectives of Wright's principal work to that date. And yet all European architects really understand after 30 years is his ground plan and the profile of the prairie house. To eyes and minds filled with *das neue Sachlichkeit* the lyric work of Frank Lloyd Wright could have little more to say. They analyzed his work, picking from it those elements which could be understood in two dimensions, or which fitted their current problems and the existing proprieties governing their solution. Almost any page of this book will show how much Wright had to contribute to these preoccupations—and how small a fragment of Wright this contribution was. All that Europe could learn or has learned of the work of Frank Lloyd Wright might have been contained in an exhibition of the Larkin building and any one of the scores of prairie houses.

In one further aspect this book contains new food for thought. The nature of the architectural commissions with which he has been presented has obscured whole strata of Wright's architectural philosophy. It is impossible to deduce from his buildings the range of his economic, sociological and humanitarian interests, for the opportunity to display these in constructing low-cost housing, hospitals, public buildings, recreation centers, or other buildings characteristic of such purposes has not yet been his. Those who have studied his unbuilt projects, filed away in hundreds of drawings, alone can realize the years of effort that have been spent on such building types. This difficulty has made it possible for glib superficiality to talk easily of Wright as a romantic escapist who would create a world in which a subsistence farm peasantry and a stratified factory proletariat would fill the gaps between his feudal country houses. But how can anyone who reads the moving lines in this collection have the slightest doubt that Wright is not aware of, concerned with, and contributing significantly to the solution of the most pressing problems in the world today, domestic, foreign and ideological?

In the few remaining lines of this introduction I propose to show that while nearly every other great architect of our times has been seduced by new means of building and consequently entrapped in sordid instrumentalism, whether of function or construction—what Wright calls using the machine to make buildings that look like pieces of machinery—this master has followed an instinctive, I will not say unerring, path in the direction of architecture's purest and most ultimate ends: the exploration of scale and proportion, the architectural organization and expression of space, the fresh expression of materials, the enhancement of lyric construction, the development of new and significant forms, and always the humanization and psychological enhancement of beautiful buildings. To say this is not to deny his great and more usually recognized accomplishments in siting, the ground plan, construction and functional design generally; but only to place emphasis where it must ultimately belong, not in the values of our age, but of all time. For it is certainly the unique characteristic of this artist-engineer, as well as his most enduring legacy, that in an age of diseased eclecticism which denied architecture he remained true to its high ideals. Faced by the eclectic space-merchants at one extreme, and the form-follows-function mechanists at the other, Wright dared to be an architect.

If it is true that in Wright's words and work we hear the harsh, practical voice of the spirit of the age, it is no less true that his genius transcends these temporal bounds and, because of it, in his architecture the heavenly voices of timeless art are also heard. The enchantment of his greatest structures cannot be explained by any functional analysis, and the man who would be content with any such explanation would be hardly better off than the Yankee farmer who got a few crusty apples while Thoreau got the view. Architecture which denies aesthetics is like food in capsule form. Alas for those who seek simple answers, the solution of Wright's architecture lies deep in the riddle of his personality: the explanation of the charm of his buildings lies deep in aesthetics, not construction or technique. These two depths may be fully plumbed but it is not now likely to be the work of our troubled generation.

1894-1908: Declaration of Faith

1894: Architecture and the Machine

TO THE UNIVERSITY GUILD, EVANSTON, ILL.

The year previous to this speech Wright had left the office of Adler and Sullivan, where he had worked for six years, and began the independent practice of architecture. His first building, the Winslow House, was constructed in that year, exemplifying the ideas expressed in this speech.

Environment. The more true culture a man has, the more significant his environment becomes to him.

Useful Things. Avoid all things which have no real use or meaning, and make those which have especially significant, for there is no one part of your building that may not be made a thing of beauty in itself as related to the whole.

The Closet Craze. Housewives erroneously gage convenience by the number and size of dark places in which to pack things out of sight and ventilation. The more closets you have the more you will have to have and as ordinarily used they are breeders of disease and poor housekeeping. Wardrobes, if you will, and light airy closets, but no dark pockets.

Simplicity. Do not think that simplicity means something like the side of a barn, but rather something with graceful sense of beauty in its utility from which discord and all that is meaningless has been eliminated. Do not imagine that repose means taking it easy for the sake of a rest, but rather taking it easily because perfectly adjusted in relation to the whole, in absolute poise, leaving nothing but a feeling of quiet satisfaction with its sense of completeness. These are the qualities that measure the true value of a work of art from the highest standpoint, and wonderfully fine qualities they are to live with from day to day. They are worth all the money man ever paid to get them. They creep into your building scheme as you work at harmonizing the elements of your home, the handling of the material, the construction of the windows, doors, walls, roof, with the various conditions and possibilities in proportion and combination. They are there only when *integrity* is there, when your work is *honest, true to itself,* in other words.

The day will come when the universal average of intelligence will be high enough to make it a thing of disrepute and a menace to the good morals of the community to build on any other basis.

Decoration. Decoration can tell your friends lots of things that you do not know and would not like if you did. It is of no use to you unless you do understand and appreciate it. It would not be sufficient justification for you to have it just because it looks rich or because somebody else had it.

1896: Architecture, Architect and Client

To the University Guild, Evanston, Ill.

Still fighting against the stagnant building ideas of the time, Wright was establishing himself as a factor to be reckoned with in that brilliant galaxy of Chicago architects at the turn of the century: Sullivan, Root, Adler, Burnham and the others.

Borrowed Finery. Most of our friends (some of ourselves) are, when it comes to architects, "art and decoration" masquerading in borrowed fineries—borrowed of another epoch—that cannot honestly fit them. The fashions and fads of our typical street grit the teeth of one so foolish as to take the matter seriously. Colonial and Renaissance, the château and the chalet. Anything that one can feel quite sure happened sometime, somewhere, and was not ridiculous; anything that is not our own, anything that is not American. Witness these ribald and inebriate freaks of fashion bedecked with painful deformities; the father of a respectable growing family would quite as soon paint his dress shirt front scarlet and stand in the middle of the road and yell as to own some of these if he knew what relation they bore to sound architectural conduct. And the ugly carpenter-built mansion with the mansard roof, an arrogant menace to the nature of all things holy, and (though somewhat better) this staring, wedding-cake artificiality of the Colonial pretense now measured by the mile; and as we handle them in the West, looking as though fashioned from cardboard with a pair of scissors and whitewashed for luck, or the borrowed affectation of simplicity which our imported English domestic architecture so heavily imposes. Simplicity cannot be borrowed. Murder will out!

Then the affected scene painting of your chateau, your "classic" villas.

And the classic? How the beauty-sophisticated Greek would shudder with impotent disgust if he could see the chaste proportions of his work mummified in your whitewashed imitations of his legitimately beautiful creations. The householder who longs for classic porticos or colonnades should be made to wear a tunic or a toga by ordinance.

Woodwork. Blame the market if you will, but words fail to express proper contempt for the meaningless average householder's "stuff"; from the gold chair, which is solid mahogany underneath, to the deadly piano machine; and the machine-carved overwrought state of things generally. The slick and shiny aspect of the supposed "beautiful" things, the glassy woodwork and floors. The "cold molasses" aspect of "piano-finished" furniture, truly horrible.

Honesty. To be honest commonly means to be undisguised, frankly showing purpose, free from deceit and hypocrisy. Every work of art that *amounted* to anything was all that first and whatever else it was afterward. To call the present state of things dishonesty is harsh, but if we were calling things by their right names, that is what we would call it.

When dishonesty is not intentional as such, we modify the term. But the harm is done nevertheless.

Paintings or Portfolios? No prints or pictures intrude upon attention here, but the walls so quiet in the perfection of their framing finish and mystery of color are backgrounds for the pictures living there. How much more important, significant, the living moving pictures become, emphasized and bettered by the gentle harmonious breadth round about.

Do not imagine that "pictorial" art is banished there. It is cherished and respected too highly to let it become inert or quarrelsome or common. A broad oak surface with shelf above and simple dark framed surface over, contains yet conceals choice things for rare entertainment, when mood requires their use. Impressions fresh and keen, suited to the mood this architectural portfolio holds, with an appropriate setting just above for any one of them or perhaps two of the best the world affords, in print or etching, paint or water color. As music is provided for—"built in"—so is painting built in.

Individuality. There should be as many types of house as there are types of people, and as many differentiations of the types as there are different people.

It is the architect's duty and his privilege to conserve these interests in the light of the individuality of the homemaker for whom he is chosen interpreter.

European Studies. We can at least be honest with ourselves as a preliminary to a better condition, and can discourage the folly of sending our young men abroad to grow up in artistic *hothouses* that they may wilt and shrivel uselessly when transplanted to the soil they should have grown in, indigenous, in order to bear good fruit. Let them go abroad to widen their horizon when strong enough to assimilate, not merely absorb.

1900: A Philosophy of Fine Art

TO THE ARCHITECTURAL LEAGUE, THE ART INSTITUTE, CHICAGO.

This is the first formal record of Wright addressing his profession. At this period he was still making drawings to show builders of his houses what to leave off! "No plinth. No astrigal," they read.

The Pure at Home. Personally, I have small respect for the mere human animal, and no enthusiasm for homilies upon the purity of the social state emanating from those whose personal belongings are nasty with ignorance, whose homes are a fashionable tangle of meaningless things and whose persons are freaks of fashion. The homes of America need the application of intelligent interest that is rare, if they are to have an artistic, and, therefore let it be said, in a *spiritual* sense, the "airing" that will make them fit for the souls to grow in.

The Vulgar Rich. A child born in the artificial environment of a city home has a small chance. The atmosphere he breathes there is bad because he is impressed from birth with fashion and sham, not ceremoniously alone, but *actually,* in the expression of almost everything he touches, and this is so because the expression of everything that touches *him* depends for its integrity upon the power of men to put into these artificial things the loveliness one finds in the woods and wild flowers, which is neither more or less than the truth and harmony of *nature,* and that power in this age is, to say the least, sickly. There are *spiritual needs* in human character building to be served, and the sort of beauty that satisfies their growth is as organic and clean a revelation of natural conditions as a dynamo, an engine, or a battleship. But these needs seem to go unsatisfied, if they do not die, and are unknown in the life of the average citizen today. As a rule, the more money spent in attaining this reflection of one's spirit, one's attitude of mind, in one's surroundings, the more painful the result, until the maximum is reached in the homes of the very rich; they are poisonous. The greater the material opportunity, the less true poetry, the less helpful significance results. It was my ill fortune to be shown through the palace of one of Chicago's great captains of industry a short time ago. His pride in his belongings was immense, and he submitted that nothing in Italy could hold a candle to the magnificence of it all; but he was simply paying a half million dollars to advertise to posterity the fact that he was neither scholar nor gentleman. There was no single beautiful touch to mitigate the horror of the "tout ensemble" (toot and scramble). This refreshing experience was repeated a short time ago in the home of a trust magnate who reveled in the sort of thing caricatured in the funny papers, and that I had always supposed overdrawn. But the funny papers were feeble and kind compared to the hopeless vulgarity of the reality. Such homes are the result of a lust for possession, not an expression of a sympathetic love for the beautiful, and this lust is as conspicuous in the homes of New York's 400 as in the homes of their more clumsy Chicago imitators. Such perversion is contaminating to a degree we dimly realize, and concerns us all.

Picturizing. If you see a picture in which perhaps a cow is looking out at you "real," so "lifelike," rather buy the cow, because the picture in all human probability is worthless. A picture should be more than an imitation of a real object and more than a pretended hole in the wall, through which you see a story about something, or the winter in summer or the summer in winter! There are many degrees of this and none are beautiful. "Breaking Home Ties" and its vast kith and kin are not *art!*

Program Notes. The programs are written to entertain the hopelessly objective mind, but they are an insult to the finer feelings of an intelligent audience. Theodore Thomas himself knew better. Be content to let the harmonies you hear color your moods and excite or soothe your imagination. Yield your temperament to your composer, but when you hear anything like the pattering of hoofs, the crowing of the cock, the firing of cannon, the twittering of birds, or the wailing of the damned, revolt!

"Why So Hot?" We marvel with a tinge of envy at the simple inevitableness with which the life principle in so slight a thing as a willow wand, for instance, will find fullness of expression as a willow tree (a glorious sort of completeness) with that absolute repose which is of destiny fulfilled. Inevitably, the secret of the acorn is the glory of the oak. The fretted cone arises as the stately pine, finding the fullness of a destined life in its untrammeled expression, simply, beautifully, naturally. And then we worship at the shrine of nature and go to her for inspiration: to learn why we have laid upon us an *artificiality* that blights and oftentimes conceals *ourselves* and in course of time and education deforms perhaps past recognition the fulfillment of the life principle implanted in us. We walk in

the cool, calm shade of the trees, and they say to us as they said to Emerson long ago, "Why so hot, my little man?" And we wonder why, indeed, so hot!

The Use of Art. Civilization means for us a conventionalizing of our original state of nature, and it is here that the work of the arts is inevitable unless the light of the race is to go out. For art is the great conservator of the finer sensibilities of a people. It is their only prophecy, the only light by which this conventionalizing process we call civilization is to make its institutions eventually harmonious with the conditions of our life.

Conventionalization. If Egypt had plucked the flower as it grew and had given us merely an imitation of it in stone, it would have died with the original. But in turning it to stone and fitting it to grace a column capital the Egyptian artist put it through a rare and difficult process, wherein its natural character was really revealed and intensified in terms of stone, gaining for it an imperishable significance, for the life principle of the flower is translated to terms of building stone to satisfy the ideal of a real "need" and this is conventionalization, and it is poetry.

A vital point of difference between a professional man and a man of business is that money making to the professional man, should, by virtue of his assumption, be incidental; to the businessman it is primary.

Money has its limitations; while it may buy quantity, there is something beyond it and that is *quality*.

When the practice of a profession touching the arts is assumed, certain obligations to the public concerning quality and beyond money making are also assumed and without their faithful discharge the professional man degenerates to the weakest type of social menial in the entire system; an industrial parasite.

An architect practices a fine art as a profession with the commercial and the scientific of his time as his technique. Men are his tools.

In this age of "quantity" there is a growing tendency on the part of the public to disregard the architect in favor of the plan-factory magnate or architectural broker, and there is consequent confusion in the mind of the young architect of today and of tomorrow as to the sound constitution of his ideal, if that ideal is to be consistent with the "success" every man of him hopes to achieve. This confusion exists and naturally enough because the topography of his field of action has changed. It has changed to such an extent that in the letter at least the antique professional standard he may not recognize if he would. But the spirit of practice in the old field is still sound to the core; the spirit that made of the professional man a champion of finer forces in the lives of his own people.

The influence chiefly responsible for this change and most easily recognized is that of science commercialized.

The tremendous forward march of scientific attainment with attendant new forces and resources; cultivation of the head at cost to the heart, of mind and matter at the expense of the emotions; has given to him new and masterful tools that demand of him their proper use and have taken from him temporarily his power so to use them.

Because he has failed to realize and grasp his situation in its new bearings, he is not quite like his brother the artist, "a thing afraid" of organization and its symbol the machine. But the architect, the master of creative effort whose province it was to make imperishable record of the noblest in the life of his race in his time, for the time being has been caught in commercial rush and whirl and hypnotized into trying to be the commercial himself.

He has degenerated to a faker. A faker who flatters thin business imbecility with "art architecture shop fronts" worn in the fashion of the old "dickey," or panders to silly women his little artistic sweets. His "art is upon the 'town' to be chucked beneath the chin by every passing gallant, coaxed within the drawing room of the period and there betrayed as a proof of culture and refinement."

Do you wonder at the prestige of the plan factory when architecture has become a commodity. A *thing* to be applied like a poultice or a porous plaster. Do you wonder that architecture becomes of less and less consequence to the public and that the architect has small standing except as he measures his success by the volume of business he transacts.

Divorced from fine art the architect is something yet to be classified, though he is tagged with a license in Illinois. So is the banana peddler and the chiropodist.

Do you wonder that "the people" demand that he be at least a good businessman, a good salesman, as something that they can understand and appreciate; when the commodity he is selling has been dead to them so long as to be unrecognizable, except by virtue of association with the dim past and therefore not quite respectable even yet to do without something of the sort.

That commodity is as dead to the salesman as to the buyer, and to the fact that the thing is more easily handled dead than alive, the salesman, captain of industry though he be, owes his existence.

In business it is in the stock pattern that fortunes are made.

So in architecture, it is in the ready-made article that the money lies, altered to fit by any popular "sartorial artist"; the less alteration the greater the profit; and the "architect."

The present generation of the successful architect has been submerged, overwhelmed by the commercialism of his time. He has yielded to the confusion and feverish demand of the moment and has become a high-grade salesman of a high-priced imported article. His duty to the public as professional man laid aside, if it was ever realized, and merely because the public was ignorant of its claim and willing to buy even if the paint came off and the features peeled.

What has been gained by his feverish haste to offer his art on the altar of commercial sacrifice has been quantity at expense to quality, a general depreciation of architectural values and a corruption of the birthright of the "buyers."

In consequence architecture today has not even commercial integrity, and the architect as he practices his profession is humiliated and craven.

Robbed by his own cowardice and mediocrity of his former commanding position in the arts he hesitates between stalking his victim outright or working wires (otherwise his friends) for the "job," as his opportunity is now styled.

He joins the club and poses, or hanging to the coat tails of his friends he teases for the "jobs" they may carry in their pockets, his mouth sticky and hands dirty, pulling and working for "more." Then he starves in the lower ranks of a doubtful aristocracy unless he comes by influence in other than architectural ways, by inheritance, by marriage, or by politics. Does a sale of property appear in a trade journal, immediately the owner is besieged by 10 "first-class architects" suing for the privilege of submitting "samples free of charge," assuring the owner meanwhile that he would be granting a personal favor in permitting them to do so, and if the samples were not what he wanted they would love each other none the less. Or his friend drops in shortly after the owner decides to build, and incidentally mentions so and so as a good fellow and a winning architect. His wife perhaps has had influence brought to bear before he gets home, and while against the principles of the architect to work for nothing, yet the combination is of such a friendly nature as to form a special case and "sketches," in this instance in place of "samples," are finally submitted to all intents and purposes as before, but a little higher in the social scale inasmuch as the method is less rude and abrupt.

The latest development is the hiring of a professional promoter by the year to drum up "trade"; mine and countermine the social system with pitfalls for the unwary to be ensnared for the practice of his principle. And talk to the best of him concerning "professional" advertising; making capital of himself in subtle, telling ways; poor devil; the naïveté of some of him would wring the tear of pity from commerce herself. How many architects would live (and they are just the number that *should* live) if they depended upon the work that came to them because of intelligent, critical appreciation of actual qualifications or work performed? There would be a good many, but probably about 7 percent of the profession. There is usually the maneuver, the pull, sometimes methods more open, but no more weak and shameful.

Because this matter of architecture itself has become of little moment to the average client, architecture as a fine art is really out of it, and for the present architecture as a commodity is a case of friendly favor and interference, or a matter of "fashion."

The fact that all this has become so generally accepted as good form, is proof of the architect's danger and the damnable weakness of his position.

Another feature of his present plight is that not wholly respecting himself, (how can he?) he is apt to be a hypersensitive individual, and like other unfortunates who depend upon preeminence of personality to get in the way of "the choosers" he is interested in pretty much everything as long as he counts one and at that No. 1; none of his bloom or luster is to be rubbed off by contact. So, concerted effort in matters touching the welfare of his profession, is rare among him.

Perhaps this is in the nature of the proposition.

There are intelligent architects who argue that only the selfish few give value to art, the high lights only give value to the pattern of the fabric; but I believe it is because of warp and woof, undertone and motive, that he has any value as a "high light," and that that type of individualism is one of the superstitions he must shed before he really comes to his own.

The architect, so-called today, is struggling in a general depression in the level of his art owing to the unknown character of the country patiently awaiting his exploration, prophesied by the past but of which no map may yet be made and of which no chart has been provided by the schools.

He is complacent inanity personified and counts not at all. Or blinded by the baser elements of commerce, choked by greed, goaded by ambition for "success" of the current type, the feverish unrest common to false ideals racks his bones and wastes his substance until he finally settles, dazed and empty, in his muddy tracks, which amounts, I suppose, to giving the people what they want.

For the generalization of the situation, then, the architect is rapidly becoming accepted as a middle man or broker, with the business instinct and ability, but who can have no business integrity because of the nature of his self-imposed occupation. He sells the public ready-made imported architecture that he himself buys in a "job lot" of unfortunates in a "home" which he establishes to protect them from a condition which he himself has developed and fostered. This architecture is applied to his client's condition as a poultice or porous plaster would be applied to his aching back, and is accepted with a clamor for "more" through lack of acquaintance with the real thing, lack of an ideal and of true educational force in the profession itself. Meanwhile the younger aspirant for better things is either assimilated by the winners, plucked and shoved behind the scenes with the unfortunate, or settles down to "give the people what they want," which simply means producing more of the type the plan factory fashions.

An example of a once noble profession prostituted by "commercial knight of untiring industry," abandoned to her fate by the "architect" in quotation marks, who shrugs his shoulders, looks aghast and contributes innocuous expectation of her ability "to pull out" (and pull him out, too) to the general blight.

And why this network of cross-purposes?

Is it because the architect is now confronted with a condition which "they say" demands a combination of two of him, and a corps of trained experts besides, where before the architect alone was absolute?

Is it because he is now in a position that demands that an intricate commercial machine be perfected to carry into effect an idea?

Or is it because architecture is a great thing in small hands, and ideals, noble theories, if you will, "the rails of the track on which the car of progress runs," have fallen to disrepute?

"Give me a great thought," cried the dying Herder, "that I may refresh myself with it."

He was of the stuff from which an *architect* is made.

The regeneration of architecture does not lie in the hands of classicist or fashion mongers of the East nor of the West.

Their work is almost written at its length, and no spark of life and but a shroud of artistic respectability will cling to it half a century hence.

It is but archaeological dry bones bleaching in the sun.

America will regard it as crude. Chicago even now regards her county courthouse as something weak and servile, an insult to the people who entrusted to chosen ones the fruit of honest toil and were betrayed to perpetuate the degenerate art of a degenerate people.

The American Nation has a heart and backbone and a pattern of its own and is rapidly forming a mind of its own. It has not yet been taught self-expression except in the matter of dollars and cents. Recently of war. Presently light, grace, and ethics, true to as virile an individuality as history has known, will come as naturally to her as the breath of life that is already hers; and then, "O ye stuffed prophets of plethoric success," will she look with pride upon the time when you bedizened her with borrowed finery; pierced her ears for borrowed ornaments; taught her to speak with a lisp and mince in her gait. No! Your very success was your undoing and her disgrace.

In her new code no one man will be entrusted with the amount of work that occasioned the "plan factory." As no Rockefeller may rise to a legitimate point of vantage that would justify the control of such a vast share of the earth's resources, *how unspeakably vulgar and illegitimate will it be for one man to undertake in the fine arts more than he can characterize in noble fashion as a work of art!*

The plan factory is the product of a raw commercial state, perhaps a necessary evil to be passed through as we pass through the dark before day.

Perhaps the epidemic of Renaissance, French, Dutch, and English that encumbers the land was a contagious malady such as little children bring from school; soonest over soonest mended.

It is argued that we are witnessing the same development in architecture that we see is legitimate enough as a means to an end in trade, as the department store and the trust.

But it is not in architecture a development but a *reflection* or reflex action that is passing but causing painful confusion. It is making of art a network of cross-purposes, but temporarily.

We are witnessing the inroads of trade upon ground it can never hold, for there is underlying, undying distinction between art and trade as there is between science and religion. Perfect harmony in reality exists between the principles of art and the principles of commerce as we are coming to see it in religion and science, the one strengthening and confirming the other. Yet the principles governing trade, although harmonious with art, may never govern her. This we know to be true, for the subjective will never be governed by the objective.

The one is of the principle of life, the other a matter of its fruit.

Art will reign as long as life and greater than ever her prestige when the harmony between commerce, science, and art is better understood.

It is this harmony, this commercialism that the younger architect should strive to understand and appreciate, for it is the measure of his technique in his new field. But he should strive to understand it as a *master,* not as a *huckster.* To poetize and deify it as an instrument in his hands.

He should help his lame, halt, and blind profession again to its place by respecting his art and respecting himself; by making the solution of problems that come fairly his way such as will compel the recognition that there is no commercial dignity without that kind of art; that will make the man of business see that a Greek temple made over to trade is an unhallowed joke, and that he is himself the butt when genuine dignity and beauty might be his for less money; that will make the householder realize that if he would live in a Louis XV environment he is but a step removed from the savage with a ring in his nose, and make it felt that architecture is not a matter of the scene painting of periods nor a mere matter of scene painting in any sense whatever.

Give back the slogan "a good copy is better than a poor original" to those whose desire for "success" outmeasured their capacity to perform and who framed it in self-defense.

"A poor thing but mine own" is better stuff for men when coupled with reverence and honesty, and carries the fundamental principle of harmonious independence graven over the gate of the new country promised of old.

The architect should help the people to feel that architecture is a destroyer of vulgarity, sham, and pretense, a benefactor of tired nerves and jaded souls, an educator in the higher ideals and better purposes of yesterday, today, and tomorrow.

Such an art only is characteristic of the better phase of commercialism itself and is true to American independence, America's hatred of cant, hypocrisy, and base imitation.

When once Americans are taught at their firesides in terms of building construction the principles so dear to them, the architect will have arrived!

But his own education is a matter of the greatest concern. We all catch a glimpse of the magnificent awaiting him, but how to prepare him is a more difficult matter.

It is for a higher law and more freedom in his architectural school that we plead, not anarchy; a deeper sense of the significance to his art of nature, manly independence; and vigorous imagination; a truer reverence for his precedent. He should learn method of attack; have cultivated in him the quality that gets at an architectural proposition from the inside outward, for and by itself. He should be a thinking quantity when he leaves school, standing on his own legs (such as they are) with ears and eyes wide open, receptive, eager, and enthusiastic; his faculties sharpened by metaphysical drill; his heart wide open to beauty whether of a specific brand or no; and a *worker* first, last, and all the time, a *worker;* his mind alive to opportunity knowing the direction in which it lies, gaging his own fitness in relation to it; farsighted enough to decline the opportunity that he was unfitted to undertake, if it should come to him (and many such do come to all architects); courageous enough to decline it and wait for one "his size." And when it came he would make it count without making his client pay too large for a share of his education in the field.

He would gain experience and strength and build up solidly if slowly and the respect and confidence would in time be his that would make his personality a power for the architectural good of his country.

His experience is to be gained only by solving problems for and by themselves.

Advice never built a character worth the name, though the advice be good.

So an architect may practice architecture extensively with book and precedent and die without experience, without a character.

The man who has worked out the salvation of a summer cottage on his merits, held the conditions in rational solution and expressed them in terms of wood and plaster with beauty germane to the proposition, has more valuable experience than he who builds a city with the pomp and circumstance of established forms.

A more intimate knowledge of conditions he is to be called upon to serve are what the student needs in his school. The classic is well as far as the elemental principles that make ancient architecture live as fine art are the burthen of study; the latter valuable only as extraneous phenomena by means of which these elements in their time were made manifest. But the problems of today, the problems of transportation, warehousing, city building are his problems. Elevated railway systems and freight stations, manufactories, grain elevators and office buildings, the housing of highly organized industries, monumental in power and significance stripped and trained to the bone for action. The housing of a people; nervous, intellectual, receptive, and progressive.

Architecture is essentially the art of organization, and her sons should be prophetic generals in this period of crystallizing social forces.

The architect may poetize and deify a more magnificent period of the world's progression than has yet been his opportunity. An opportunity that has caught the architect of the present generation in its rush and whirl and hypnotized him into trying to be the commercial himself, wherefore he has dragged his ancient monuments to the market place, tortured them with ribs of steel, twisted and unstrung them, set them up on pins and perforated them until he has left them not a rag.

And the stock has almost sold out.

Let the young student now come to the front.

I have no quack nostrum for the sudden cure of the educated architect's complacent inertia nor his commercial delirium, and know of no short cut for him as he is coming on.

The education of the architect should commence when he is 2 days old (3 days is too much), and continue until he passes beyond, leaving his experiments by the wayside to serve his profession as warning signs or guide posts.

The kindergarten circle of sympathetic discernment should be drawn about him when he is born and he should be brought into contact with nature by prophet and seer until abiding sympathy with her is his. He should be a true child of hers, in touch with her moods, discerning her principles and harmonies until his soul overflows with love of nature in the highest and his mind is stored with a technical knowledge of her forms and processes.

Braced and stayed by that he should move into the thick of civilization to study man and his methods in the things that are his and the ways thereof, taking his averages and unraveling seeming inconsistencies, shoulder to shoulder with his fellow men as one with them.

Meanwhile as his discipline he should acquire the technical skill of the mill, forge, and try pit of commerce in the light of science; study the beauty of the world as created by the hand of man, as his birthright and his advantage; finding his passion and delight in various initial steps of composition with the encouraging guidance of a catholic-minded nature-wise and loving master.

A master that would permit him to honor his precedent too much to sacrifice it to the stagnation or the perversion of his own opportunism; who would hold with him that to "copy" was to cultivate a weakness, to draw from the cast an abomination; that mere imitation, beginning or ending, is forever contemptible and in the fine arts impossible. A master who would unconsciously imbue him with the sense of honor that recognizes the same right of a man to the work of his brain as to the work of his hands that he might in turn hand it on himself to his public. Nor would there be confusion in his master's mind as to the fact that architecture is a creative art or nothing. And that to take his place at his best technical discipline of the highest order he must have, but his technique would never drive his art nor would he ever mistake its place for his own.

In short a master who would make plain the distinction between fine art and fine artisanship.

Now he is taught certain architectural phraseology of form and color dubbed "grammar" by his professors, and much foreign technique.

If teaching him that minutes and modules of the architraves and cornice of one type in certain measure make Greek and of another type in combination make Roman and when they corrode each other the result is "Renaissance," then he is taught "grammar."

I imagine it to be a more difficult matter to teach him the "grammar" of Goth and Moor, but architecture has no business primarily with this "grammar" which at its best, I suppose, might mean putting the architectural together correctly, but as taught means putting the architectural together as predetermined by those false fashions of previous races and conditions.

So the young student is eternally damned by the dogmas of Vignola and Vitruvius, provided with a fine repertoire of stock phrases as architectural capital and with technique enough to make them go, if he is let alone and conditions are favorable, which he never is and they never are.

He comes to think these fine phrases and this technique are architecture and sells both in judicious mixture to the "buyers" as such with the circumstance of the "scholar" and the pomp of the "classical." He would be shocked if told that he is a swindler.

He is sent out a callow, complacent fledgling, sure of his precedent, afraid of little but failure to succeed, puffed up with architectural "excelsior" and wadded with "deafening," to become soaked and sodden in the field, hopelessly out of shape.

The architect primarily should have something of his own to say or keep silence. There are more legitimate fields of action for him than the field of architecture.

If he has that something to say in noble form, gracious line and living color, each expression will have a "grammar" of its own, using the term in its best sense, and will speak the universal language of beauty in no circumscribed series of set architectural phrases used by other people in other times, although a language in harmony with elemental laws to be deduced from the beautiful of all peoples in all time.

This elemental law and order of the beautiful is as much more profound than the accepted grammatical of phrase in architecture as nature is deeper than fashion.

Let the young student add to his wisdom the strength and wisdom of past ages; that is his advantage. *But let him live his own life nor mistake for the spirit, the letter.*

I would see him relieved of the unnatural educational incubus that sowed the seed of the plan factory and nurtured the false ideals that enable it to still exist.

I would see him relieved of architectural lockjaw not by prying the set teeth of his art apart with a crowbar nor by cracking its jaws with a sledge hammer, but by a realization that life was given the architect that architecture might grow and expand naturally as a noble fine art and as becomes a free-hearted, vigorous people.

It may be that the very cosmopolitan nature of our Nation will prevent a narrow confirmation of any one type.

I hope that we are destined to greater variety in unity that has yet existed in the art of a great people.

The very strength of individuality developed in a free nation and the richness of our inheritance will find expression in more diverse and splendid ways than could be expected of a more narrowly nurtured race. Yet it will find expression in an art that is indigenous and characteristic as an architecture measured by the laws of fine art, the hardy grace of the wild flower perhaps rather than the cultivated richness of the rose, but a further contribution to the art of the world, no servile extraction!

The architect has a hard road to travel and far to go.

He should know what he is to encounter in the field and he should be trained to meet it by men who have faced it in all its ugly significance for architecture and life, with unconquerable soul and clear vision.

He should understand that to go into the field penniless with a family to support means the ultimate addition of one more craven to the ranks, unless some chance saves him, or his fortitude is of the stuff that will see his wife and children suffer for ideals that may seem ridiculous and are to the average mind incomprehensible.

If he goes single-handed he must be content to walk behind, to work and wait.

The work to be done by the young architect entering the lists would better be done by him whose board and lodging is assured for life and whose communication with his base of supplies is not apt to be cut off.

He is going into a country almost abandoned to the enemy.

Yet the hardy pioneer who takes his architectural life in hand and fares boldly forth in quest of his ideal, not scorning hardtack for food nor a plank for a bed:

> "Withal a soul like the bird,
> Who pausing in her flight,
> Awhile on boughs too slight,
> Feels them give way beneath her and yet sings,
> Knowing that she hath wings;"

is perhaps the stuff from which the missionary we need is to come; the spirit that conquered Western wilds and turned them to fallow fields transmuted to the realm of art; a boy with the heart of a king; the scent of the pinewoods deep in his nostrils, sweetness and light in his soul; the erudition of the world at his fingers' ends. If he is the stuff that architects are made of he is not to be discouraged by limitations.

The limitations within which an artist works do grind him and sometimes seem insurmountable. Yet without these very limitations there is no art. They are at once his problems and his best friends; his salvation in disguise.

In the arts every problem carries within itself its own solution and the only way yet discovered to reach it is a very painstaking way; to look sympathetically within the thing itself, to proceed to analyze and sift it, to extract its own consistent and essential beauty which means its *common sense truthfully idealized.*

There lies the heart of the poetry that lives in architecture.

That is what they should teach the young architect in the schools, beginning early. But the schools will have to be taught before they will ever teach him.

His scientific possibilities and demands have outrun his hand-made art as planned for him in the school curriculum. He is without lettered precedent as he stands today on the threshold of great development in the industrial direction of the world.

A highly organized, complex condition confronts him.

He will understand it, learn the secret of its correspondences and their harmonies and he will work with them, not against them. For his art is of life itself, it will endure.

Life is preparing the stuff to satisfy the coming demand, and the architect will know the capacities of modern methods, processes and machines and become their master. He will sense the significance to his art of the new materials that are his, of which steel is but one.

He will show in his work that he has been emancipated from the meager unit established by brick arch and stone lintel, and his imagination will transfigure to new beauty all primitive art.

He will realize that the narrow limitations of structure outlined in his precedents are too mean and small to be longer useful or binding, and that he is comparatively a free man to clothe new structural conditions in the living flesh of virile imagination.

He will write large in beautiful character the song of steel and steam:

> "Lord thou hast made this world below the shadow of a dream
> And taught by time I take it so, exceptin' always steam."

The architect will weld that strain and build that song in noble line and form.

He will write that record for all time.

He may not last to "judge her line or take her curve," but he may say that he, too, has lived and worked; whether he has done well or ill, he will have worked as a man and given a shoulder to his fellows climbing after.

1900: Japanese Prints

INTRODUCTION TO EXHIBITION CATALOG, THE ART INSTITUTE, CHICAGO, 1906.

Wright's introduction to Japanese prints came at the Columbian Exposition in 1893, where examples of Hokusai and Hiroshigi were shown. Here, in an exceptionally complicated medium, he saw a simplicity of effect which instantly appealed to him. "It was my own stuff," he later said. He began to collect prints on a large scale. The influence of this art on his draftsmanship is easily apparent, and the overtones of Japanese architecture which many have detected in his buildings probably derives more from Japanese prints than from any study of Japanese architecture.

Influence of Japanese Prints. Every dead wall in the land bears witness to its influence, for it has given us what we used to call "poster art." In England, as a patent instance, Aubrey Beardsley and his kith and kin happened because of it. And modern France, the first to discover its charm, has fallen under its spell completely. Paris fashions are more influenced by it every year. The German and Austrian secessionists owe it no small debt of gratitude and its influence is still young. The German mind has recently awakened to its significance and with characteristic thoroughness.

It has preached the gospel of simplification as no other means has ever preached it and taught that organic integrity within the work of art itself is fundamentally a law of beauty. Without it you may make your work a meretricious mask with literal suggestion or effects, but not true art. That quality in the work which is real escaped and the would-be artist remains where he belongs, outside. It has taught that no more than a sand bank and the sea, a foreground, a telegraph pole, and a weed in arrangement may yield a higher message of love and beauty, a surer proof of life, than Raphael's Madonnas or Angelo's magnificent pictorial sculpture. It has taught that sentiment has nothing in common with sentimentality or sensuous feeling with sensuality; that integrity of means to ends is in art indispensable to the poetry of results, and that the life of a work of art consists and inheres within the work itself; an integrity in fine as organic as anything that grows.

Owing to its ethnic eccentricity this art is a particularly safe means of cultivation for us because the individual initiative of the artist is not paralyzed with forms which he can use ready-made. It may become most useful on this account as a corrector of the temptation to imitation that besets our artists on every hand. For the architect, particularly, it is inspiring owing to its essentially structural character, and it is encouraging because it is a striking proof of the fact that any true artist's limitations are always his best friends.

Real and Ideal. A flower is beautiful, Why? Because in its geometry and qualities it is in rhythm of line and color, a form; an expression of that precious something in ourselves which we instinctively know to be life. "An eye looking upon us from out the great inner sea of beauty," a proof of harmony in the nature of the universe. We intuitively feel it, and "It is beautiful," we say. When we say, "It is beautiful," we mean that that quality in us which is life recognizes itself or at least its own; we vibrate a sympathetic chord struck by the flower.

As it is with the flower so it is with a work of art and to a greater degree; because the flower in question is a blossom of the human soul and therefore more intimate, for in it we find the lineaments of human thought and feeling; the human touch given in terms of the same qualities that made the flower beautiful. And this quality of absolute beauty in the result is the life of the work of art more truly than any literal import or significance it may possess whatsoever. It is the perception of this quality; the ability to perceive it, perhaps, in the work of art; that we woefully lack. Failing to perceive it we remain untouched by the true quickening power of the work, and remain outside in the realm of the literal (the objective), the realistic but not the real. That in art which is real escapes us.

The Lotus and Acanthus. To know a thing, what we can really call knowing, a man must first know the thing, sympathize with it. So Egypt knew the lotus and translated the flower to the dignified stone forms of their architecture. This was the lotus conventionalized.

Greece knew and idealized the acanthus in stone translation. This was the acanthus conventionalized.

If Egypt had plucked the lotus as it grew and given us a mere imitation of it in stone, the stone forms would have died with the original. But in translating its life's principle to terms of stone adapted to grace a column capital, the Egyptian artist put it through a rare and spiritual process whereby its natural character was really intensified and revealed in terms of stone fitted to its use. The lotus gained thus imperishable significance for the life principle in the flower it translated. This is conventionalization, it is reality, and it is poetry. As the Egyptian took the lotus, the Greek his acanthus, and the Japanese every natural thing on earth, as we may take any natural flower or thing, so civilization must take the natural man to fit him for his place in this great piece of architecture we call the social state. And today, as centuries ago, it is the prophetic artist eye that must reveal idealized, conventionalized, this natural state harmoniously with his life principle. It cannot be otherwise. All the sheer wisdom of science, the cunning of politics, and the prayers of religion can but stand and wait for the revelation; awaiting the artist's conventionalization of life principle that shall make our social living beautiful, organically true.

Behind all institutions or dogmatic schemes, whatever their worth may be or their antiquity, behind them all is something produced and preserved for its aesthetic worth; the song of the poet, some artist vision, the pattern seen on the mount.

1901: The Art and Craft of the Machine

LECTURE AT HULL HOUSE, CHICAGO.

This is the famous "Hull House Lecture," later reprinted in full in Modern Architecture, *Wright's Princeton lectures in 1930. It is the first decisive acceptance of the machine by an American architect, and was widely hailed at the time. It was re-written and delivered to the Western Society of Engineers in 1901, and printed in revised form in 1901 in the catalog of the 14th Annual Exhibition of the Chicago Architectural Club. Further revised it was delivered in 1904 to the convention of the Daughters of the American Revolution in Chicago.*

Democracy and Its Forms. I do not believe we will ever again have the uniformity of type which has characterized the so-called great "styles." Conditions have changed. Our ideal is democracy; the highest possible expression of the individual as a unit not inconsistent with a harmonious whole. The average human intelligence rises steadily, and as the individual unit grows more and more to be trusted we will have an architecture with richer variety in unity than has ever arisen before. But the forms must be born out of our changed conditions. They must be *true* forms; otherwise the best that tradition has to offer is only an inglorious masquerade, devoid of vital significance or true spiritual value.

Obstacles. The trials of the early days were many and at this distance, picturesque. Workmen seldom like to think, especially if there is financial risk entailed. At your peril do you disturb their established processes mental or technical. To do anything in an unusual, even if in a better and simpler way is to complicate the situation at once. Simple things at that time in any industrial field were nowhere at hand. A piece of wood without a molding was an anomaly; a plain wooden slat instead of a turned baluster, a joke; the omission of the merchantable "grille," a crime. Plain fabrics for hangings or floor covering were nowhere to be found in stock.

Casement Windows. Single-handed I waged a determined battle for casements swinging out, although it was necessary to have special hardware made for them as there was none to be had this side of England.

Use of the Machine. An artist's limitations are his best friends. The machine is here to stay. It is the forerunner of the democracy that is our dearest hope. There is no more important work before the architect now than to use this normal tool of civilization to the best advantage instead of prostituting it as he has hitherto done in reproducing with murderous ubiquity forms born of other times and other conditions and which it can only serve to destroy.

Dead Forms. The old structural forms which up to the present time have spelled "architecture" are decayed. Their life went from them long ago and new conditions industrially, steel and concrete and terra cotta in particular, are prophesying a more plastic art wherein as the flesh is to our bones so will the covering be to the structure, but more truly and beautifully expressive than ever.

Individualism. I believe that only when one individual forms the concept of the various projects and also determines the character of every detail in the sum total, even to the size and shape of the pieces of glass in the windows, the arrangement and profile of the most insignificant of the architectural members, will unity be secured which is the soul of the individual work of art.

1902: The Modern Home as a Work of Art

TO THE CHICAGO WOMEN'S CLUB.

This lecture followed the publication of two widely-discussed articles by Wright in the Ladies' Home Journal, *and reflects the authority with which he already spoke in these early years. At this period the Chicago Women's Club was an important factor in Chicago culture. In this year, too, the first exhibition of Wright's buildings was held. Wright was building widely in Chicago. More than half a dozen buildings a year were being erected, all bearing the imprint of the new style.*

"In 1902, the World Was New." I believe the time not so far distant when the "American home" will, generally, be owned by the man who paid for it; owned in this sense: it will belong to its site and to the country, as a matter of course. Naturally, in the light of a finer consideration for the modern opportunity, will grow a more *practicable* truth and beauty. An American home will be the product of our own time, spiritually, as well as physically. And it will be respected the world over, because of its integrity; its real worth as a great work of art.

Common Brick. Make the walls of brick that the fire touched to tawny gold or ruddy tan, the choicest of all earth's hues. They will not rise rudely above the sod as though shot from beneath by a catapult, but recognize the surface of the ground on which they stand, gently spreading there to a substantial base that makes the building seem to stand more firmly in its socket in the earth and carry with a profile of grace the protection of its sheltering eaves.

Fixtures. Consider everything in the nature of a hanging fixture a weakness, and naked radiators an abomination.

The Degradation of Art. "Art," in the now popular sense of that term, has a practical value only to the shopkeeper. It is a word to conjure with in connection with trash; a commercial parasite; a social sham. Granting that familiarity can still breed contempt in this commercial age, then art has indeed struck the bottom of the pit.

Science, the Emancipator. Science, with no intention on her part, for she does not love him, has emancipated the artist by providing him with a magnificent physical resource and technique on a scale that is for the moment confusing and appalling to him. When he learns to use this new equipment in light, yet too strong for him, we will have buildings beside which the old orders will seem fragmentary, stupid, and crude.

True Ownership. Many wealthy people are little more than the janitors of their possessions.

1904: The Art and Craft of the Machine

To the Chicago Chapter, Daughters of the American Revolution.

This revision of the earlier Hull House lecture restates the same thesis but with heightened significance and with more emphasis on the vision of the future artist in command of the new forces unleashed by the machine.

Challenge of the Machine. In this day and generation we must recognize that this transforming force whose outward sign and symbol is the thing of brass and steel we call a machine, is now grown to the point that the artist must take it up, no longer to protest. Genius must dominate the work of the contrivance it has created. This plain duty is relentlessly marked out for the artist in this, the Machine Age. He cannot set it aside, although there is involved an adjustment to cherished gods, perplexing and painful in the extreme, and though the fires of long-honored ideals shall go down to ashes. They will reappear, phoenix-like, with new life and purposes.

The Machine and the City. Upon this faith in art as the organic heart of the scientific frame of things, I base a belief that we must look to the artist brain of all brains to grasp the significance to society of this thing we call the machine, which is no more or less than the principle of organic growth working irresistibly the will of life through the medium of man. We are drawn helplessly into its mesh as we tread our daily round. It has become commonplace background of modern existence and in too many lives the foreground, middle distance, and the future. At best we are some co-operative part in a vast machinery, seemingly controlled by some great crystallizing principle in nature. If you would see how interwoven it is in the warp and woof of civilization, if indeed it is not the very framework, go at night-fall to the top of one of the down-town steel giants and you may see how in the image of material man, at once his glory and his menace, is this thing we call a city. There beneath you is the monster, stretching acre upon acre into the far distance. High over head hangs the stagnant pall of its fetid breath, reddened with light from myriad eyes endlessly, everywhere blinking.

Thousands of acres of cellular tissue, the city's flesh outspreads, layer upon layer, enmeshed by an intricate network of veins and arteries radiating into the gloom, and in them, with muffled, persistent roar, circulating as the blood circulates in your veins, is the almost ceaseless beat of the activity to whose necessities it all conforms.

The poisonous waste is drawn from the system of this gigantic creature by infinitely ramifying, thread-like ducts, gathering at their sensitive terminals matter destructive to its life, hurrying it to millions of small intestines to be collected in turn by larger, flowing to the great sewers, on to the drainage canal, and finally to the ocean.

This wondrous flesh is again knit and interknit with a nervous system effective and complete, delicate filaments of hearing, knowing, and almost feeling the pulse of its organism, acting intelligently upon ligaments and tendons for motive impulse, and in all is flowing the impelling fluid of man's own life.

Its muscles are the Corliss tandems, whirling their hundred-ton fly-wheels, fed by gigantic rows of water tube boilers burning oil, a solitary man slowly pacing here and there regulating the little valves controlling the deafening roar of the flaming gas, while the incessant clicking and shifting of the governor gear controlling these modern Goliaths seems a visible brain in action, as it registers infallibly in the enormous magnets, purring in the giant embrace of great induction coils, generating the vital current meeting on the instant in the rolling cars on elevated tracks ten miles away.

More quietly, whispering down the long low rooms of factory buildings buried in the gloom beyond, range on range of stanch, beautifully perfected automatons murmur contentedly, automatons that would have the American manufacturing industry of five years ago by the throat to-day; manipulating steel as delicately as a mystical shuttle of the modern loom manipulates a silk thread in the shimmering pattern of a dainty gown. Night and day these nervous minions of the machine obediently serve the master mind with sensitive capacities as various as those of man himself. Here reflected in steam, steel, and electrical energy is a creature grown in response to man's needs, and in his image, daily becoming more sensitive and complete.

And the labored breathing, the murmur, the clangor, and the roar!—how the voice of this greatest of machines, a great city, rises to proclaim the marvel of its structure; the ghastly warning boom from the deep throats of vessels heavily seeking inlet to the waterway below, answered by the echoing clangor of the bridge bells, growing nearer and more ominous.

warning the living current from the swinging bridge as the vessel cuts for a moment the flow of the nearer artery, and now closing upon its stately passage just in time to receive, in a rush of steam as a streak of light, the avalanche of blood and metal hurled across it and gone roaring into the night on its glittering bands of steel, faithfully encircled in its flight by slender magic lines tick-tapping its protection.

Nearer, in the building ablaze with midnight activity, a wide, white band streams into the marvel of the multiple press, receiving unerringly the indelible impression of the human hopes, joys, and fears throbbing in the pulse of the modern activity and as infallibly as the gray matter of the human brain receives the impression of the senses, coming forth as millions of neatly folded, perfected news-sheets, teeming with vivid appeals, good and evil passions; weaving a web of inter-communication so far-reaching that distance becomes as nothing, the thought of one man in one corner of the earth one day visible to all men the next day; the doings of all the world reflected as in a glass—so marvelously sensitive this simple band streaming endlessly from day to day becomes in the grasp of the multiple press.

If the pulse of this great activity to which the tremor of the mammoth skeleton beneath your feet is but an awe-inspiring response, is thrilling, what of this prolific silent obedience? Remain to contemplate this wonder until the twinkling lights perish in groups, followed one by one, leaving others to smother in the gloom; until the fires are banked, the tumult slowly dies to an echo here and there. Then the darkened pall is lifted and moonlight outlines the sullen, shadowy masses of structure deeply cut here and there by half-luminous channels; huge patches of shadow, shade, and darkness intermingle mysteriously in block-like plan and sky-line; the broad surface of the lake beside, placid and resplendent with a silver gleam. And there reflect that the texture of the tissue of this great machine, this forerunner of the democracy we hope for, has been deposited, particle by particle, in blind obedience to law—the organic law to which the great solar universe is but an obedient machine, and marvel that this masterful force is as yet untouched by art or artist. A magnificent truth with no guise of beauty disguised by tattered garments long outgrown; the outward sign of an inner plan wherein combinations of capital and great industrial tendencies are but symptoms, government's imperfect manifestations, whereof wear and friction are social injustice and waste is war.

1908-1918: In the Cause of Architecture

1908: In the Cause of Architecture, I

FROM THE *Architectural Record*, MARCH, 1908.

This was the first of two papers addressed to the architectural profession in which Wright summarized his views on architecture and the experience of 15 years of independent practice. The second paper, which follows out of its chronological sequence, answered some objections which were raised against the first and disowned the swarm of Wright imitators in the movement then known as "the Prairie Style."

Radical though it be, the work here illustrated is dedicated to a cause conservative in the best sense of the word. At no point does it involve denial of the elemental law and order inherent in all great architecture; rather, is it a declaration of love for the spirit of that law and order, and a reverential recognition of the elements that made its ancient letter in its time vital and beautiful.

Primarily, nature furnished the materials for architectural motifs out of which the architectural forms as we know them today have been developed, and, although our practice for centuries has been for the most part to turn from her, seeking inspiration in books and adhering slavishly to dead formulae, her wealth of suggestion is inexhaustible; her riches greater than any man's desire. I know with what suspicion the man is regarded who refers matters of fine art back to nature. I know that it is usually an ill-advised return that is attempted, for nature in external, obvious aspect is the usually accepted sense of the term and the nature that is reached. But given inherent vision there is no source so fertile, so suggestive, so helpful aesthetically for the architect as a comprehension of natural law. As nature is never right for a picture so is she never right for the architect; that is, not ready-made. Nevertheless, she has a practical school beneath her more obvious forms in which a sense of proportion may be cultivated, when Vignola and Vitruvius fail as they must always fail. It is there that he may develop that sense of reality that translated to his own field in terms of his own work will lift him far above the realistic in his art; there he will be inspired by sentiment that will never degenerate to sentimentality and he will learn to draw with a surer hand the ever-perplexing and difficult line between the curious and the beautiful.

A sense of the organic is indispensable to an architect; where can he develop it so surely as in this school? A knowledge of the relations of form and function lies at the root of his practice; where else can he find the pertinent object lessons nature so readily furnishes?

Where can he study the differentiations of form that go to determine character as he can study them in the trees? Where can that sense of inevitableness characteristic of a work of art be quickened as it may be by intercourse with nature in this sense?

Japanese art knows this school more intimately than that of any people. In common use in their language there are many words like the word "edaburi," which, translated as near as may be, means the formative arrangement of the branches of a tree. We have no such word in English, we are not yet sufficiently civilized to think in such terms; but the architect must not only learn to think in such terms but he must learn in this school to fashion his vocabulary for himself and furnish it in a comprehensive way with useful words as significant as this one.

For 7 years it was my good fortune to be the understudy of a great teacher and a great architect, to my mind the greatest of his time: Mr. Louis H. Sullivan.

Principles are not invented, they are not evolved by one man or one age; but Mr. Sullivan's perception and practice of them amounted to a revelation at a time when they were commercially inexpedient and all but lost to sight in current practice. The fine art sense of the profession was at that time practically dead; only glimmerings were perceptible in the work of Richardson and of Root.

Adler and Sullivan had little time to design residences. The few that were unavoidable fell to my lot outside of office hours. So, largely, it remained for me to carry into the field of domestic architecture the battle they had begun in commercial building. During the early years of my own practice I found this lonesome work. Sympathizers of any kind were then few and they were not found among the architects. I well remember how "the message" burned within me, how I longed for comradeship until I began to know the younger men and how welcome was Robert Spencer, and then Myron Hunt, and Dwight Perkins, Arthur Heun, George Dean, and Hugh Garden. Inspiring days they were, I am sure, for us all. Of late we have been too busy to see one another often, but the "new school of the Middle West" is beginning to be talked about and perhaps some day it is to be. For why not the same "life" and blood in architecture that is the essence of all true art?

In 1894, with this text from Carlyle at the top of the page, "The ideal is within thyself, thy condition is but the stuff thou art to shape that same ideal out of," I formulated the following "propositions." I set them down here much as they were written then, although in the light of experience they might be stated more completely and succinctly.

I. Simplicity and repose are qualities that measure the true value of any work of art.

But simplicity is not in itself an end nor is it a matter of the side of a barn but rather an entity with a graceful beauty in its integrity from which discord, and all that is meaningless, has been eliminated. A wild flower is truly simple. Therefore:

1. A building should contain as few rooms as will meet the conditions which give it rise and under which we live, and which the architect should strive continually to simplify; then the ensemble of the rooms should be carefully considered that comfort and utility may go hand in hand with beauty. Beside the entry and necessary workrooms there need be but three rooms on the ground floor of any house, living room, dining room, and kitchen, with the possible addition of a "social office"; really there need be but one room, the living room with requirements otherwise sequestered from it or screened within it by means of architectural contrivances.

2. Openings should occur as integral features of the structure and form, if possible, its natural ornamentation.

3. An excessive love of detail has ruined more fine things from the standpoint of fine art or fine living than any one human shortcoming; it is hopelessly vulgar. Too many houses, when they are not little stage settings or scene paintings, are mere notion stores, bazaars or junk shops. Decoration is dangerous unless you understand it thoroughly and are satisfied that it means something good in the scheme as a whole, for the present you are usually better off without it. Merely that it "looks rich" is no justification for the use of ornament.

4. Appliances or fixtures as such are undesirable. Assimilate them together with all appurtenances into the design of the structure.

5. Pictures deface walls oftener than they decorate them. Pictures should be decorative and incorporated in the general scheme as decoration.

6. The most truly satisfactory apartments are those in which most or all of the furniture is built in as a part of the original scheme. The whole must always be considered as an integral unit.

II. There should be as many kinds (styles) of houses as there are kinds (styles) of people and as many differentiations as there are different individuals. A man who has individuality (and what man lacks it?) has a right to its expression in his own environment.

III. A building should appear to grow easily from its site and be shaped to harmonize with its surroundings if nature is manifest there, and if not try to make it as quiet, substantial, and organic as she would have been were the opportunity hers.

We of the Middle West are living on the prairie. The prairie has a beauty of its own and we should recognize and accentuate this natural beauty, its quiet level. Hence, gently sloping roofs, low proportions, quiet sky lines, suppressed heavy-set chimneys, and sheltering overhangs, low terraces and out-reaching walls sequestering private gardens.

IV. Colors require the same conventionalizing process to make them fit to live with that natural forms do; so go to the woods and fields for color schemes. Use the soft, warm, optimistic tones of earths and autumn leaves in preference to the pessimistic blues, purples or cold greens and grays of the ribbon counter; they are more wholesome and better adapted in most cases to good decoration.

V. Bring out the nature of the materials, let their nature intimately into your scheme. Strip the wood of varnish and let it alone; stain it. Develop the natural texture of the plastering and stain it. Reveal the nature of the wood, plaster, brick or stone in your designs; they are all by nature friendly and beautiful. No architectural treatment can be really a matter of fine art when these truly natural characteristics are, or their essential nature is, outraged or neglected.

VI. A house that has character stands a good chance of growing more valuable as it grows older while a house in the prevailing mode, whatever that mode may be, is soon out of fashion, stale, and unprofitable.

Buildings like people must first be sincere, must be true and then withal as gracious and lovable as may be.

Above all, integrity. The machine is the normal tool of our civilization; give it work that it can do well; nothing is of greater importance. To do this will be to formulate new industrial ideals, sadly needed.

These propositions are chiefly interesting because for some strange reason they were novel when formulated in the face of conditions hostile to them and because the ideals they phrase have been practically embodied in the buildings that were built to live up to them. The buildings of recent years have not only been true to them, but are in many cases a further development of the simple propositions so positively stated then.

Happily, these ideals are more commonplace now. Then the sky lines of our domestic architecture were fantastic abortions, tortured by features that disrupted the distorted roof surfaces from which attenuated chimneys like lean fingers threatened the sky; the invariably tall interiors were cut up into box-like compartments, the more boxes the finer the house; and "architecture" chiefly consisted in healing over the edges of the curious collection of holes that had to be cut in the walls for light and air and to permit the occupant to get in or out. These interiors were always slaughtered with the butt and slash of the old plinth and corner block trim, of dubious origin, and finally smothered with horrible millinery by way of "decoration."

That individuality in a building was possible for each homemaker, or desirable, seemed at that time to rise to the dignity of an idea. Even cultured men and women care so little for the spiritual integrity of their environment; except in rare cases they are not touched, they simply do not care for the matter so long as their dwellings are fashionable or as good as those of their neighbors and keep them dry and warm. A structure has no more meaning to them aesthetically than has the stable to the horse. And this came to me in the early years as a definite discouragement. There are exceptions, and I found them chiefly among American men of business with unspoiled instincts and untainted ideals. A man of this type usually has the faculty of judging for himself. He has rather liked the "idea" and much of the encouragement this work receives comes straight from him because the "common sense" of the thing appeals to him. While the "cultured" are still content with their small châteaux, Colonial wedding cakes, English affectations or French millinery, he prefers a poor thing but his own. He errs on the side of character, at least, and when the lest of time has tried his country's development architecturally, he will have contributed his quota, small enough in the final outcome though it be; he will be regarded as a true conservator.

In the hope that some day America may live her own life in her own buildings in her own way, that is, that we may make the best of what we have for what it honestly is or may become, I have endeavored in this work to establish a harmonious relationship between ground plan and elevation of these buildings, considering the one as a solution and the other an expression of the conditions of a problem of which the whole is a project. I have tried to establish an organic integrity to begin with, forming the basis for the subsequent working out of a significant grammatical expression and making the whole, as nearly as I could, consistent.

What quality of style the buildings may possess is due to the artistry with which the conventionalization as a solution and an artistic expression of a specific problem within these limitations has been handled. The types are largely a matter of personal taste and may have much or little to do with the American architecture for which we hope.

From the beginning of my practice the question uppermost in my mind has been not "what style," but "What is style?" and it is my belief that the chief value of the work illustrated here will be found in the fact that if in the face of our present day conditions any given type may be treated independently and imbued with the quality of style, then a truly noble architecture is a definite possibility, so soon as Americans really demand it of the architects of the rising generation.

I do not believe we will ever again have the uniformity of type which has characterized the so-called great "styles." Conditions have changed; our ideal is democracy, the highest possible expression of the individual as a unit not inconsistent with a harmonious whole. The average of human intelligence rises steadily, and as the individual unit grows more and more to be trusted we will have an architecture with richer variety in unity than has ever arisen before; but the forms must be born out of our changed conditions, they must be *true* forms, otherwise the best that tradition has to offer is only an inglorious masquerade, devoid of vital significance or true spiritual value.

The trials of the early days were many and at this distance picturesque. Workmen seldom like to think, especially if there is financial risk entailed; at your peril do you disturb their established processes mental or technical. To do anything in an unusual, even if in a better and simpler way, is to complicate the situation at once. Simple things at that time in any industrial field were nowhere at hand. A piece of wood without a molding was an anomaly; a plain wooden slat instead of a turned baluster a joke; the omission of the merchantable "grille" a crime; plain fabrics for hangings or floor covering were nowhere to be found in stock.

To become the recognized enemy of the established industrial order was no light matter, for soon whenever a set of my drawings was presented to a Chicago millman for figures he would willingly enough unroll it, read the architect's name, shake his head and return it with the remark that he was "not hunting for trouble"; sagacious owners and general contractors tried cutting out the name, but in vain, his perspicacity was ratlike, he had come to know "the look of the thing." So, in addition to the special preparation in any case necessary for every little matter of construction and finishing, special detail drawings were necessary merely to show the things to be left off or not done, and not only studied designs for every part had to be made but quantity surveys and schedules of millwork furnished the contractors beside. This, in a year or two, brought the architect face to face with the fact that the fee for his service "established" by the American Institute of Architects was intended for something stock and shop, for it would not even pay for the bare drawings necessary for conscientious work.

The relation of the architect to the economic and industrial movement of his time, in any fine art sense, is still an affair so sadly out of joint that no one may easily reconcile it. All agree that something has gone wrong and except the architect be a plan-factory magnate, who has reduced his art to a philosophy of old clothes and sells misfit or made-over, ready-to-wear garments with commercial aplomb and social distinction, he cannot succeed on the present basis established by common practice. So, in addition to a situation already complicated for them, a necessarily increased fee stared in the face the clients who dared. But some did dare, as the illustrations prove.

The struggle then was and still is to make "good architecture," "good business." It is perhaps significant that in the beginning it was very difficult to secure a building loan on any terms upon one of these houses, now it is easy to secure a better loan than ordinary; but how far success has attended this ambition the owners of these buildings alone can testify. Their trials have been many, but each, I think, feels that he has as much house for his money as any of his neighbors with something in the home intrinsically valuable besides, which will not be out of fashion in one lifetime, and which contributes steadily to his dignity and his pleasure as an individual. . . .

Photographs do not adequately present these subjects. A building has a presence as has a person that defies the photographer, and the color so necessary to the complete expression of the form is necessarily lacking, but it will be noticed that all the structures stand upon their foundations to the eye as well as physically. There is good, substantial preparation at the ground for all the buildings and it is the first grammatical expression of all the types. This preparation, or water table, is to these buildings what the stylobate was to the ancient Greek temple. To gain it, it was necessary to reverse the established practice of setting the supports of the building to the outside of the wall and to set them to the inside, so as to leave the necessary support for the outer base. This was natural enough and good enough construction but many an owner was disturbed by private information from the practical contractor to the effect that he would have his whole house in the cellar if he submitted to it. This was at the time a marked innovation, though the most natural thing in the world, and to me, to this day, indispensable.

With this innovation established, one horizontal stripe of raw material, the foundation wall above ground, was eliminated and the complete grammar of type one made possible. A simple, unbroken wall surface from foot to level of second story sill was thus secured, a change of material occurring at that point to form the simple frieze that characterizes the earlier buildings. Even this was frequently omitted as in the Francis Apartments and many other buildings and the wall was let alone from base to cornice or eaves.

"Dress reform houses" they were called, I remember, by the charitably disposed. What others called them will hardly bear repetition.

As the wall surfaces were thus simplified and emphasized the matter of fenestration became exceedingly difficult and more than ever important, and often I used to gloat over the beautiful buildings I could build if only it were unnecessary to cut holes in them; but the holes were managed at first frankly as in the Winslow house and later as elementary constituents of the structure grouped in rhythmical fashion, so that all the light and air and prospect the most rabid client could wish would not be too much from an artistic standpoint; and of this achievement I am proud. The groups are managed, too, whenever required, so that overhanging eaves do not shade them, although the walls are still protected from the weather. Soon the poetry-crushing characteristics of the guillotine window, which was then firmly rooted, became apparent, and single-handed I waged a determined battle for casements swinging out, although it was necessary to have special hardware made for them as there was none to be had this side of England. Clients would come ready to accept any innovation but "those swinging windows," and when told that they were in the nature of the proposition and that they must take them or leave the rest, they frequently employed "the other fellow" to give them something "near," with the "practical" windows dear to their hearts.

With the grammar so far established came an expression pure and simple, even classic in atmosphere, using that much-abused word in its best sense; implying, that is, a certain sweet reasonableness of form and outline naturally dignified.

I have observed that nature usually perfects her forms; the individuality of the attribute is seldom sacrificed; that is, deformed or mutilated by cooperative parts. She rarely says a thing and tries to take it back at the same time. She would not sanction the "classic" proceeding of, say, establishing an "order," a colonnade, then building walls between the columns of the order reducing them to pilasters, thereafter cutting holes in the wall and pasting on cornices with more pilasters around them, with the result that every form is outraged, the whole an abominable mutilation, as is most of the architecture of the Renaissance wherein style corrodes style and all the forms are stultified.

In laying out the ground plans for even the more insignificant of these buildings a simple axial law and order and the ordered spacing upon a system of certain structural units definitely established for each structure in accord with its scheme of practical construction and aesthetic proportion, is practiced as an expedient to simplify the technical difficulties of execution, and although the symmetry may not be obvious always the balance is usually maintained. The plans are as a rule much more articulate than is the school product of the Beaux-Arts. The individuality of the various functions of the various features is more highly developed; all the forms are complete in themselves and frequently do duty at the same time from within and without as decorative attributes of the whole. This tendency to greater individuality of the parts emphasized by more and more complete articulation will be seen in the plans for Unity Church, the cottage for Elizabeth Stone at Glencoe and the Avery Coonley house in process of construction at Riverside, Ill. Moreover, these ground plans are merely the actual projection of a carefully considered whole. The "architecture" is not "thrown up" as an artistic exercise, a matter of elevation from a preconceived ground plan. The schemes are conceived in three dimensions as organic entities, let the picturesque perspective fall how it will. While a sense of the incidental perspectives the design will develop is always present, I have great faith that if the thing is rightly put together in true organic sense with proportions actually right the picturesque will take care of itself. No man ever built a building worthy the name of architecture who fashioned it in perspective sketch to his taste and then fudged the plan to suit. Such methods produce mere scene painting. A perspective may be a proof but it is no nurture.

As to the mass values of the buildings the aesthetic principles outlined in proposition III will account in a measure for their character.

In the matter of decoration the tendency has been to indulge it less and less, in many cases merely providing certain architectural preparation for natural foliage or flowers, as it is managed in, say, the entrance to the Lawrence house at Springfield. This use of natural foliage and flowers for decoration is carried to quite an extent in all the designs and, although the buildings are complete without this efflorescence, they may be said to blossom with the season. What architectural decoration the buildings carry is not only conventionalized to the point where it is quiet and stays as a sure foil for the nature forms from which it is derived and with which it must intimately associate, but it is always *of* the surface, never *on* it.

The windows usually are provided with characteristic straight line patterns absolutely in the flat and usually severe. The nature of the glass is taken into account in these designs as is also the metal bar used in their construction, and most of them are treated as metal "grilles" with glass inserted forming a simple rhythmic arrangement of straight lines and squares made as cunning as possible so long as the result is quiet. The aim is that the designs shall make the best of the technical contrivances that produce them.

In the main the ornamentation is wrought in the warp and woof of the structure. It is constitutional in the best sense and is felt in the conception of the ground plan. To elucidate this element in composition would mean a long story and perhaps a tedious one, though to me it is the most fascinating phase of the work, involving the true poetry of conception.

The differentiation of a single, certain simple form characterizes the expression of one building. Quite a different form may serve for another, but from one basic idea all the formal elements of design are in each case derived and held well together in scale and character. The form chosen may flare outward, opening flowerlike to the sky as in the Thomas house; another, droop to accentuate artistically the weight of the masses; another be noncommittal or abruptly emphatic, or its grammar may be deduced from some plant form that has appealed to me, as certain properties in line and form of the sumac were used in the Lawrence house at Springfield; but in every case the motif is adhered to throughout so that it is not too much to say that each building aesthetically is cut from one piece of goods and consistently hangs together with an integrity impossible otherwise.

In a fine art sense these designs have grown as natural plants grow, the individuality of each is integral and as complete as skill, time, strength, and circumstances would permit.

The method in itself does not of necessity produce a beautiful building, but it does provide a framework as a basis which has an organic integrity, susceptible to the architects' imagination and at once opening to him nature's wealth of artistic suggestion, ensuring him a guiding principle within which he can never be wholly false, out of tune, or lacking in rational motif. The subtleties, the shifting blending harmonies, the cadences, the nuances are a matter of his own nature, his own susceptibilities and faculties.

But self-denial is imposed upon the architect to a far greater extent than upon any other member of the fine art family. The temptation to sweeten work, to make each detail in itself lovable and expressive, is always great; but that the whole may be truly eloquent of its ultimate function restraint is imperative. To let individual elements arise and shine at the expense of final repose is for the architect a betrayal of trust, for buildings are the background or framework for the human life within their walls and a foil for the nature efflorescence without. So architecture is the most complete of conventionalizations and of all the arts the most subjective except music.

Music may be for the architect ever and always a sympathetic friend whose counsels, precepts, and patterns ever are available to him and from which he need not fear to draw. But the arts are today all cursed by literature; artists attempt to make literature even of music, usually of painting and sculpture and doubtless would of architecture also, were the art not moribund; but whenever it is done the soul of the thing dies and we have not art but something far less for which the true artist can have neither affection nor respect.

Contrary to the usual supposition this manner of working out a theme is more flexible than any working out in a fixed, historic style can ever be, and the individuality of those concerned may receive more adequate treatment within legitimate limitations. This matter of individuality puzzles many; they suspect that the individuality of the owner and occupant of a building is sacrificed to that of the architect who imposes his own upon Jones, Brown, and Smith alike. An architect worthy of the name has an individuality, it is true; his work will and should reflect it, and his buildings will all bear a family resemblance one to another. The individuality of an owner is first manifest in his choice of his architect, the individual to whom he entrusts his characterization. He sympathizes with his work; its expression suits him and this furnishes the common ground upon which client and architect may come together. Then, if the architect is what he ought to be, with his ready technique he conscientiously works for the client, idealizes his client's character and his client's tastes and makes him feel that the building is his, as it really is to such an extent that he can truly say that he would rather have his own house than any other he has ever seen. Is a portrait, say, by Sargent any less a revelation of the character of the subject because it bears his stamp and is easily recognized by anyone as a Sargent. Does one lose his individuality when it is interpreted sympathetically by one of his own race and time who can know him and his needs intimately and idealize them; or does he gain it only by having adopted or adapted to his condition a ready-made historic style which is the fruit of a seedtime other than his, whatever that style may be.

The present industrial condition is constantly studied in the practical application of these architectural ideals and the treatment simplified and arranged to fit modern processes and to utilize to the best advantage the work of the machine. The furniture takes the clean cut, straight-line forms that the machine can render far better than would be possible by hand. Certain facilities, too, of the machine, which it would be interesting to enlarge upon, are taken advantage of; and the nature of the materials is usually revealed in the process.

Nor is the atmosphere of the result in its completeness new and hard. In most of the interiors there will be found a quiet, a simple dignity that we imagine is only to be found in the "old" and it is due to the underlying organic harmony, to the each in all and the all in each throughout. This is the modern opportunity, to make of a building, together with its equipment, appurtenances, and environment, an entity which shall constitute a complete work of art; and a work of art more valuable to society as a whole than has before existed because discordant conditions, endured for centuries, are smoothed away; everyday life here finds an expression germane to its daily existence; an idealization of the common need sure to be uplifting and helpful in the same sense that pure air to breathe is better than air poisoned with noxious gases.

An artist's limitations are his best friends. The machine is here to stay. It is the forerunner of the democracy that is our dearest hope. There is no more important work before the architect now than to use this normal tool of civilization to the best advantage instead of prostituting it as he has hitherto done in reproducing with murderous ubiquity forms born of other times and other conditions and which it can only serve to destroy.

The exteriors of these structures will receive less ready recognition perhaps than the interiors and because they are the result of a radically different conception as to what should constitute a building. We have formed a habit of mind concerning architecture to which the expression of most of these exteriors must be a shock, at first more or less disagreeable, and the more so as the habit of mind is more narrowly fixed by so-called classic training. Simplicity is not in itself an end; it is a means to an end. Our aesthetics are dyspeptic from incontinent indulgence in "Frenchite" pastry. We crave ornament for the sake of ornament; cover up our faults of design with ornamental sensualities that were a long time ago sensuous ornament. We will do well to distrust this unwholesome and unholy craving and look to the simple line, to the clean though living form and quiet color for a time until the true significance of these things has dawned for us once more.

The old structural forms, which up to the present time have spelled "architecture," are decayed. Their life went from them long ago and new conditions industrially, steel and concrete and terra cotta in particular, are prophesying a more plastic art wherein as the flesh is to our bones so will the covering be to the structure; but more truly and beautifully expressive than ever. But that is a long story. This reticence in the matter of ornamentation is characteristic of these structures and for at least two reasons: first, they are the expression of an idea that the ornamentation of a building should be constitutional, a matter of the nature of the structure beginning with the ground plan. In the buildings themselves, in the sense of the whole, there is lacking neither richness nor incident but their qualities are secured not by applied decoration, they are found in the fashioning of the whole, in which color, too, plays as significant a part as it does in an old Japanese wood block print. Second, because as before stated, buildings perform their highest function in relation to human life within and the natural efflorescence without; and to develop and maintain the harmony of a true chord between them making of the building in this sense a sure foil for life, broad simple surfaces and highly conventionalized forms are inevitable. These ideals take the buildings out of school and marry them to the ground; make them intimate expressions or revelations of the exteriors; individualize them regardless of preconceived notions of style. I have tried to make their grammar perfect in its way and to give their forms and proportions an integrity that will bear study, although few of them can be intelligently studied apart from their environment. So, what might be termed the democratic character of the exteriors is their first undefined offense: the lack, wholly, of what the professional critic would deem architecture; in fact, most of the critic's architecture has been left out.

There is always a synthetic basis for the features of the various structures, and consequently a constantly accumulating residue of formula, which becomes more and more useful; but I do not pretend to say that the perception or conception of them was not at first intuitive, or that those that lie yet beyond will not be grasped in the same intuitive way; but, after all, architecture is a scientific art, and the thinking basis will ever be for the architect his surety, the final court in which his imagination sifts his feelings.

The few draftsmen so far associated with this work have been taken into the drafting room, in every case almost wholly unformed, many of them with no particular previous training, and patiently nursed for years in the atmosphere of the work itself, until, saturated by intimate association, at an impressionable age, with its motifs and phases, they have become helpful.

To develop the sympathetic grasp of detail that is necessary before this point is reached has proved usually a matter of years, with little advantage on the side of the college-trained understudy. These young people have found their way to me through natural sympathy with the work, and have become loyal assistants. The members, so far, all told here and elsewhere, of our little university of 14 years' standing are: Marion Mahony, a capable assistant for 11 years; William Drummond, for 7 years; Francis Byrne, 5 years; Isabel Roberts, 5 years; George Willis, 4 years; Walter Griffin, 4 years; Andrew Willatzen, 3 years; Harry Robinson, 2 years; Charles E. White, Jr., 1 year; Erwin Barglebaugh and Robert Hardin, each 1 year; Albert McArthur, entering.

Others have been attracted by what seemed to them to be the novelty of the work, staying only long enough to acquire a smattering of form, then departing to sell a superficial proficiency elsewhere. Still others shortly develop a mastery of the subject, discovering that it is all just as they would have done it, anyway, and, chafing at the unkind fate that forestalled them in its practice, resolve to blaze a trail for themselves without further loss of time. It is urged against the more loyal that they are sacrificing their individuality to that which has dominated this work; but it is too soon to impeach a single understudy on this basis, for, although they will inevitably repeat for years the methods, forms, and habit of thought, even the mannerisms of the present work, if there is virtue in the principles behind it that virtue will stay with them through the preliminary stages of their own practice until their own individualities truly develop independently. I have noticed that those who have made the most fuss about their "individuality" in early stages, those who took themselves most seriously in that regard, were inevitably those who had least.

Many elements of Mr. Sullivan's personality in his art (what might be called his mannerisms) naturally enough clung to my work in the early years, and may be readily traced by the casual observer; but for me one real proof of the virtue inherent in this work will lie in the fact that some of the young men and women who have given themselves up to me so faithfully these past years will some day contribute rounded individualities of their own, and forms of their own devising to the new school.

This year I assign to each a project that has been carefully conceived in my own mind, which he accepts as a specific work. He follows its subsequent development through all its phases in drawing room and field, meeting with the client himself on occasion, gaining an all-round development impossible otherwise, and insuring an enthusiasm and a grasp of detail decidedly to the best interest of the client. These privileges in the hands of selfishly ambitious or overconfident assistants would soon wreck such a system; but I can say that among my own boys it has already proved a moderate success, with every prospect of being continued as a settled policy in future.

Nevertheless, I believe that only when one individual forms the concept of the various projects and also determines the character of every detail in the sum total, even to the size and shape of the pieces of glass in the windows, the arrangement and profile of the most insignificant of the architectural members, will that unity be secured which is the soul of the individual work of art. This means that fewer buildings should be entrusted to one architect. His output will of necessity be relatively small; small, that is, as compared to the volume of work turned out in any one of fifty "successful offices" in America. I believe there is no middle course worth considering in the light of the best future of American architecture. With no more propriety can an architect leave the details touching the form of his concept to assistants, no matter how sympathetic and capable they may be, than can a painter entrust the painting in of the details of his picture to a pupil; for an architect who would do individual work must have a technique well developed and peculiar to himself, which, if he is fertile, is still growing with his growth. To keep everything "in place" requires constant care and study in matters that the old-school practitioner would scorn to touch.

As for the future, the work shall grow more truly simple; more expressive with fewer lines; fewer forms; more articulate with less labor; more plastic; more fluent, although more coherent; more organic. It shall grow not only to fit more perfectly the methods and processes that are called upon to produce it, but shall further find whatever is lovely or of good repute in method or process, and idealize it with the cleanest, most virile stroke I can imagine. As understanding and appreciation of life matures and deepens, this work shall prophesy and idealize the character of the individual it is fashioned to serve more intimately, no matter how inexpensive the result must finally be. It shall become in its atmosphere as pure and elevating in its humble way as the trees and flowers are in their perfectly appointed way, for only so can architecture be worthy of its high rank as a fine art, or the architect discharge the obligation he assumes to the public, imposed upon him by the nature of his own profession.

1914: In the Cause of Architecture, II

FROM THE *Architectural Record*, MAY, 1914.

"Style, therefore, will be the man. It is his. Let his forms alone."

"Nature has made creatures only; art has made men." Nevertheless, or perhaps for that very reason, every struggle for truth in the arts and for the freedom that should go with the truth has always had its own peculiar load of disciples, neophytes, and quacks. The young work in architecture here in the Middle West, owing to a measure of premature success, has for some time past been daily rediscovered, heralded and drowned in noise by this new characteristic feature of its struggle. The so-called "movement" threatens to explode soon in foolish exploitation of unripe performances or topple over in pretentious attempts to "speak the language." The broker, too, has made his appearance to deal in its slender stock in trade, not a wholly new form of artistic activity certainly, but one serving to indicate how profitable this intensive rush for a place in the "new school" has become.

Just at this time it may be well to remember that "every form of artistic activity is not art."

Obviously this stage of development was to be expected and has its humorous side. It has also unexpected and dangerous effects, astonishingly in line with certain prophetic letters written by honest "conservatives" upon the publication of the former paper of 1908.

Although an utterance from me of a critical nature is painful, because it must be a personal matter, perhaps a seeming retraction on my part, still all that ever really happens is "personal matter" and the time has come when forbearance ceases to be either virtue or convenience. A promising garden seems to be rapidly overgrown with weeds, notwithstanding the fact that "all may raise the flowers now, for all have got the seed." But the seed has not been planted; transplanting is preferred, but no amount of transplanting can raise the needed flowers.

To stultify or corrupt our architectural possibilities is to corrupt our aesthetic life at the fountain head. Her architecture is the most precious of the susceptibilities of a young, constructive country in this constructive stage of development; and maintaining its integrity in this respect, therefore, distinctly a cause.

When, 21 years ago, I took my stand, alone in my field, the cause was unprofitable, seemingly impossible, almost unknown, or, if known, was, as a rule, unhonored and ridiculed; Montgomery Schuyler was the one notable exception to the rule. So swiftly do things "come on" in this vigorous and invigorating age that although the cause itself has had little or no recognition, the work has more than its share of attention and has attracted to itself abuses seldom described (never openly attacked) but which a perspective of the past 6 years will enable me to describe, as I feel they must render the finer values in this work abortive for the time being, if they do not wholly defeat its aim. Many a similar work in the past has gone prematurely to ruin owing to similar abuses; to rise again, it is true; but retarded generations in time.

I still believe that the ideal of an organic architecture forms the origin and source, the strength and, fundamentally, the significance of everything ever worthy the name of architecture.

And I know that the sense of an organic architecture, once grasped, carries with it in its very nature the discipline of an ideal at whatever cost to self-interest or the established order.

It is itself a standard and an ideal and I maintain that only earnest artist integrity, both of instinct and of intelligence, can make any forward movement of this nature in architecture of lasting value.

The ideal of an organic architecture for America is no mere license for doing the thing that you please to do as you please to do it in order to hold up the strange thing when done with the "see what I have made" of childish pride. Nor is it achieved by speaking the fancied language of "form and function"; cant terms learned by rote; or prating foolishly of "progress before precedent"; that unthinking, unthinkable thing! In fact, it is precisely the total absence of any conception of this ideal standard that is made conspicuous by this folly and the practices that go with it. To reiterate the statement made in 1908: this ideal of an organic architecture for America was touched by Richardson and Root, and perhaps other men; but was developing consciously 28 years ago in the practice of Adler and Sullivan when I went to work in their office. This ideal combination of Adler and Sullivan was then working to produce what no other combination of architects nor any individual architect at that time dared even preach: a sentient, rational building that would owe its "style" to the integrity with which it was individually fashioned to serve its particular purpose; a "thinking" as well as "feeling" process, requiring the independent work of true artist imagination; an ideal that is dynamite, cap and fuse, in selfish, insensible hands; personal ambition, the lighted match.

At the expiration of a 6-year apprenticeship, during which time Louis Sullivan was my master and inspiration, 21 years ago I entered a field he had not, in any new spirit, touched, the field of domestic architecture, and began to break ground and make the forms I needed, alone, absolutely alone.

These forms were the result of a conscientious study of materials and of the machine which is the real tool, whether we like it or not, that we must use to give shape to our ideals; a tool which at that time had received no such artistic consideration from artist or architect. And that my work now has individuality, the strength to stand by itself, honors Mr. Sullivan the more. The principles, however, underlying the fundamental ideal of an organic architecture, common to his work and to mine, are common to all work that ever rang true in the architecture of the world, and free as air to any pair of honest young lungs that will breathe deeply enough. But I have occasion to refer only to that element in this so-called "new movement" which I have characterized by my own work and which should and, in a more advanced stage of culture, would be responsible to me for use or abuse of the forms and privileges of that work. Specifically, I speak only to that element within this element, now beyond private reach or control, ruthlessly characterizing and publicly exploiting the cause it does not comprehend or else that it cannot serve.

Someone for the sake of that cause must have some conscience in the matter and tell the truth. Since disciples, neophytes, and brokers will not, critics do not, and the public cannot, I will. I will be suspected of the unbecoming motives usually ascribed to any man who comes to the front in behalf of an ideal, or his own; nevertheless, somehow, this incipient movement, which it has been my life work to help outfit and launch, must be protected or directed in its course. An enlightened public opinion would take care of this, but there is no such opinion. In time there will be; meantime good work is being wasted, opportunities destroyed or, worse, architectural mortgages on future generations forged wholesale; and in architecture they must be paid with usurious interest.

The sins of the architect are permanent sins.

To promote good work it is necessary to characterize bad work as bad.

Half-baked, imitative designs (fictitious semblances) pretentiously put forward in the name of a movement or a cause, particularly while novelty is the chief popular standard, endanger the cause, weaken the efficiency of genuine work, for the time being at least; lower the standard of artistic integrity permanently; demoralize all values artistically;

until utter prostitution results. This prostitution has resulted in the new work partly, I have now to confess, as a byproduct of an intimate, personal touch with the work, hitherto untried in the office of an American architect; and partly, too, perhaps, as one result of an ideal of individuality in architecture, administered in doses too strong, too soon, for architectural babes and sucklings; but chiefly, I believe, owing to almost total lack of any standard of artist integrity among architects, as a class, in this region at least. Of ethics we hear something occasionally; but only in regard to the relation of architects to each other when a client is in question; never in relation to sources of inspiration, the finer material the architect uses in shaping the thing he gives to his client. Ethics that promote integrity in this respect are as yet unformed and the young man in architecture is adrift in the most vitally important of his experiences; he cannot know where he stands in the absence of any well-defined principles on the part of his confreres or his elders. Such principles must now be established.

If I had a right to project myself in the direction of an organic architecture 21 years ago, it entailed the right to my work and, so far as I am able, a right to defend my aim. Also, yet not so clearly, I am bound to do what I can to save the public from untoward effects that follow in the wake of my own break with traditions. I deliberately chose to break with traditions in order to be more true to tradition than current conventions and ideals in architecture would permit. The more vital course is usually the rougher one and lies through conventions oftentimes settled into laws that must be broken, with consequent liberation of other forces that cannot stand freedom. So a break of this nature is a thing dangerous, nevertheless indispensable, to society. Society recognizes the danger and makes the break usually fatal to the man who makes it. It should not be made without reckoning the danger and sacrifice, without ability to stand severe punishment, nor without sincere faith that the end will justify the means; nor do I believe it can be effectively made without all these. But who can reckon with the folly bred by temporal success in a country that has as yet no artistic standards, no other god so potent as that same success? For every thousand men nature enables to stand adversity, she, perhaps, makes one man capable of surviving success. An unenlightened public is at its mercy always; the "success" of the one thousand as well as of the one in a thousand; were it not for the resistance of honest enmity, society, nature herself even would soon cycle madly to disaster. So reaction is essential to progress, and enemies as valuable an asset in any forward movement as friends, provided only they be honest; if intelligent as well as honest, they are invaluable. Some time ago this work reached the stage where it sorely needed honest enemies if it were to survive. It has had some honest enemies whose honest fears were expressed in the prophetic letters I have mentioned.

But the enemies of this work, with an exception or two, have not served it well. They have been either unintelligent or careless of the gist of the whole matter. In fact, its avowed enemies have generally been of the same superficial, time-serving spirit as many of its present load of disciples and neophytes. Nowhere even now; save in Europe, with some few notable exceptions in this country; has the organic character of the work been fairly recognized and valued; the character that is perhaps the only feature of lasting vital consequence.

As for its peculiarities; if my own share in this work has a distinguished trait, it has individuality undefiled. It has gone forward unswerving from the beginning, unchanging, yet developing, in this quality of individuality, and stands, as it has stood for 19 years at least, an individual entity, clearly defined. Such as it is, its "individuality" is as irrevocably mine as the work of any painter, sculptor, or poet who ever lived was irrevocably his. The form of a work that has this quality of individuality is never the product of a composite. An artist knows this; but the general public, near artist and perhaps "critic," too, may have to be reminded or informed. To grant a work this quality is to absolve it without further argument from anything like composite origin, and to fix its limitations.

There are enough types and forms in my work to characterize the work of an architect, but certainly not enough to characterize an architecture. Nothing to my mind could be worse imposition than to have some individual, even temporarily, deliberately fix the outward forms of his concept of beauty upon the future of a free people or even of a growing city. A tentative, advantageous forecast of probable future utilitarian development goes far enough in this direction. Any individual willing to undertake more would thereby only prove his unfitness for the task, assuming the task possible or desirable. A socialist might shut out the sunlight from a free and developing people with his own shadow, in this way. An artist is too true an individualist to suffer such an imposition, much less perpetrate it; his problems are quite other. The manner of any work (and all work of any quality has its manner) may be for the time being a strength, but finally it is a weakness; and as the returns come in, it seems as though not only the manner of this work or its "clothes," but also its strength in this very quality of individuality, which is a matter of its soul as well as of its forms, would soon prove its undoing, to be worn to shreds and tatters by foolish, conscienceless imitation. As for the vital principle of the work (the quality of an organic architecture) that has been lost to sight, even by pupils. But I still believe as firmly as ever that without artist integrity and this consequent individuality manifesting itself in multifarious forms, there can be no great architecture, no great artists, no great civilization, no worthy life. Is, then, the very strength of such a work as this is its weakness? Is it so because of a false democratic system naturally inimical to art? Or is it so because the commercialism of art leaves no noble standards? Is it because architects have less personal honor than sculptors, painters, or poets? Or is it because fine buildings are less important now than fine pictures and good books?

In any case, judging from what is exploited as such, most of what is beginning to be called the "New School of the Middle West" is not only far from the ideal of an organic architecture, but getting farther away from it everyday.

A study of similar situations in the past will show that any departure from beaten paths must stand and grow in organic character or soon fall, leaving permanent waste and desolation in final ruin; it dare not trade long on mere forms, no matter how inevitable they seem. Trading in the letter has cursed art for centuries past, but in architecture it has usually been rather an impersonal letter of those decently cold in their graves for sometime.

One may submit to the flattery of imitation or to caricature personally; everyone who marches or strays from beaten paths must submit to one or to both, but never will one submit tamely to caricature of that which one loves. Personally, I too am heartily sick of being commercialized and traded in and upon; but most of all I dread to see the types I have worked with so long and patiently drifting toward speculative builders, cheapened or befooled by senseless changes, robbed of quality and distinction, dead forms or grinning originalities for the sake of originality, an endless string of hacked carcasses, to encumber democratic front yards for five decades or more. This, however, is only the personal side of the matter and to be endured in silence were there any profit in it to come to the future architecture of the "melting pot."

The more serious side and the occasion for this second paper is the fact that emboldened or befooled by its measure of "success," the new work has been showing weaknesses instead of the character it might have shown some years hence were it more enlightened and discreet, more sincere and modest, prepared to wait, to wait to prepare.

The average American man or women who wants to build a house wants something different, "something different" is what they say they want, and most of them want it in a hurry. That this is the fertile soil upon which an undisciplined "language-speaking" neophyte may grow his crop to the top of his ambition is deplorable in one sense but none the less hopeful in another and more vital sense. The average man of business in America has truer intuition, and so a more nearly just estimate of artistic values, when he has a chance to judge between good and bad, than a man of similar class in any other country. But he is prone to take that "something different" anyhow; if not good then bad. He is rapidly outgrowing the provincialism that needs a foreign-made label upon "art," and so, at the present moment, not only is he in danger of being swindled, but likely to find something peculiarly his own, in time, and valuable to him, if he can last. I hope and believe he can last. At any rate, there is no way of preventing him from getting either swindled or something merely "different"; nor do I believe it would be desirable if he could be, until the inorganic thing he usually gets in the form of this "something different" is put forward and publicly advertised as of that character of the young work for which I must feel myself responsible.

I do not admit that my disciples or pupils, be they artists, neophytes, or brokers, are responsible for worse buildings than nine-tenths of the work done by average architects who are "good school"; in fact, I think the worst of them do better; although they sometimes justify themselves in equivocal positions by reference to this fact. Were no more to come of my work than is evident at present, the architecture of the country would have received an impetus that will finally resolve itself into good. But to me the exasperating fact is that it might aid vitally the great things we all desire, if it were treated on its merits, used and not abused. Selling even good versions of an original at second hand is in the circumstances not good enough. It is cheap and bad, demoralizing in every sense. But, unhappily, I have to confess that the situation seems worse where originality, as such, has thus far been attempted, because it seems to have been attempted chiefly *for its own sake,* and the results bear about the same resemblance to an organic architecture as might be shown were one to take a classic column and, breaking it, let the upper half lie carelessly at the foot of the lower, then setting the capital picturesquely askew against the half thus prostrate, one were to settle the whole arrangement as some structural feature of street or garden.

For worker or broker to exhibit such "designs" as efforts of creative architects, before the ink is yet dry on either work or worker, is easily done under present standards with "success," but the exploit finally reflects a poor sort of credit upon the exploited architect and the cause. As for the cause, any growth that comes to it in a "spread" of this kind is unwholesome. I insist that this sort of thing is not "new school," nor this the way to develop one. This is piracy, lunacy, plunder, imitation, adulation, or what you will; it is not a developing architecture when worked in this fashion, nor will it ever become one until purged of this spirit; least of all is it an organic architecture. Its practices belie any such character.

"Disciples" aside, some 15 young people, all entirely inexperienced and unformed—but few had even college educations—attracted by the character of my work, sought me as their employer. I am no teacher; I am a worker; but I gave to all, impartially, the freedom of my workroom, my work, and myself, to imbue them with the spirit of the performances for their own sakes; and with the letter for my sake; so that they might become useful to me; because the nature of my endeavor was such that I had to train my own help and pay current wages while I trained them.

The nature of the profession these young people were to make when they assumed to practice architecture entails much more careful preparation than that of the "good school" architect; theirs is a far more difficult thing to do technically and artistically, if they would do something of their own. To my chagrin, too many are content to take it "ready-made," and with no further preparation hasten to compete for clients of their own. Now 15 good, bad, and indifferent are practicing architecture in the Middle West, South, and Far West and with considerable "success." In common with the work of numerous disciples (judging from such work as has been put forward publicly), there is a restless jockeying with members, one left off here, another added there, with varying intent; in some a vain endeavor to reindividualize the old types; in others an attempt to conceal their origin, but always—ad nauseam—the inevitable reiteration of the features that gave the original work its style and individuality. To find fault with this were unfair. It is not unexpected nor unpromising except in those unbearable cases where badly modified *inorganic* results seem to satisfy their authors' conception of originality; and banalities of form and proportion are accordingly advertised in haste as work of creative architects of a "new school." That some uniformity in performance should have obtained for some years is natural; it could not be otherwise, unless unaware I had harbored marked geniuses. But when the genius arrives nobody will take his work for mine; least of all will he mistake my work for his own creation.

"The letter killeth." In this young work at this time, still it is the letter that killeth, and emulation of the "letter" that gives the illusion or delusion of "movement." There is no doubt, however, but that the sentiment is awakened which will mean progressive movement in time. And there are many working quietly who, I am sure, will give a good account of themselves.

Meanwhile, the spirit in which this use of the letter has its rise is important to any noble future still left to the cause. If the practices that disgrace and demoralize the soul of the young man in architecture could be made plain to him; if he could be shown that inevitably equivocation dwarfs and eventually destroys what creative faculty he may possess; that designing lies, in design to deceive himself or others, shuts him out absolutely from realizing upon his own gifts; no matter how flattering his opportunities may be; if he could realize that the artist heart is one uncompromising core of truth in seeking, in giving, or in taking; a precious service could be rendered him. The young architect who is artist enough to know where he stands and man enough to use honestly his parent forms as such, conservatively, until he feels his own strength within him, is only exercising an artistic birthright in the interest of a good cause; he has the character at least from which great things may come. But the boy who steals his forms; "steals" them because he sells them as his own for the moment of superficial distinction he gains by trading on the results; is no artist, has not the sense of the first principles of the ideal that he poses and the forms that he abuses. He denies his birthright, an act characteristic and unimportant; but for a mess of pottage, he endangers the chances of a genuine forward movement, insults both cause and precedent with an astounding insolence quite peculiar to these matters in the United States, ruthlessly sucks what blood may be left in the tortured and abused forms he caricatures and exploits, like the parasite he is.

Another condition as far removed from creative work is the state of mind of those who, having in the course of their day's labor put some stitches into the "clothes" of the work, assume, therefore, that style and pattern are rightfully theirs and wear them defiantly unregenerate. The gist of the whole matter artistically has entirely eluded them. This may be the so-called "democratic" point of view; at any rate it is the immemorial error of the rabble. No great artist nor work of art ever proceeded from that conception, nor ever will.

Then there is the soiled and soiling fringe of all creative effort, a type common to all work everywhere that meets with any degree of success, although it may be more virulent here because of low standards; those who benefit by the use of another's work and to justify themselves depreciate both the work and worker they took it from; the type that will declare, "In the first place, I never had your shovel; in the second place, I never broke your shovel; and in the third place, it was broken when I got it, anyway;" the type that with more crafty intelligence develops into the "coffin worm." One of Whistler's "coffin worms" has just wriggled in and out.

But underneath all, I am constrained to believe, lies the feverish ambition to get fame or fortune "quick," characteristic of the rush of commercial standards that rule in place of artist standards, and consequent unwillingness to wait to prepare thoroughly.

"Art to one is high as a heavenly goddess; to another only the thrifty cow that gives him his butter," said Schiller; and who will deny that our profession is prostitute to the cow, meager in ideals, cheap in performance, commercial in spirit: demoralized by ignoble ambition? A foolish optimism regarding this only serves to perpetuate it. Foolish optimism and the vanity of fear of ridicule or "failure" are both friends of ignorance.

In no country in the world do disciples, neophytes, or brokers pass artist counterfeit so easily as in these United States. Art is commercialized here rather more than anything else, although the arts should be as free from this taint as religion. But has religion escaped?

So the standard of criticism is not only low; it is often dishonest or faked somewhere between the two, largely manufactured to order for profit or bias. Criticism is worked as an advertising game, traders' instincts subject to the prevailing commercial taint. Therein lies a radically evil imposition that harms the public; that also further distorts, confuses and injures values and promotes bad work; that tends to render the integrity of artist and commerce alike a stale and unprofitable joke, and to make honest enemies even harder to find than honest friends. The spirit of fair play, the endeavor to preserve the integrity of values, intelligently, on a high plane in order to help in raising the level of the standard of achievement in the country, and to refrain from throwing the senseless weight of the mediocre and bad upon it; all this is unhappily too rare among editors. The average editor has a "constituency," not a standard. This constituency is largely the average architect who has bought the "artistic" in his architecture as one of its dubious and minor aspects, or the sophisticated neophyte, the broker, and the quack, to whom printers' ink is ego-balm and fortune.

So until the standard is raised any plea for artist integrity is like a cry for water in the Painted Desert. As for competent criticism, the honest work of illuminating insight, where is it? Nothing is more precious or essential to progress. Where is the editor or critic not narrow or provincial? Or loose and ignorant? Or cleverly or superficially or cowardly commercial? Let him raise this standard! Friend or foe, there is still a demand for him even here; but if he did, he would fail, gloriously fail, of "success."

Is architecture, then, no longer to be practiced as an art? Has its practice permanently descended to a form of mere "artistic activity"?

The art of architecture has fallen from a high estate, lower steadily since the men of Florence patched together fragments of the art of Greece and Rome and in vain endeavor to reestablish its eminence manufactured the Renaissance. It has fallen from the heavenly "Goddess of Antiquity" and the Middle Ages to the thrifty cow of the present day. To touch upon these matters in this country is doubly unkind, for it is to touch upon the question of "bread and butter" chiefly. Aside from the consciencеless ambition of the near artist (more sordid than any greed of gold) and beneath this thin pretense of the ideal that veneers the curious compound of broker and neophyte there lurks, I know, for any young architect an ever present dread of the kind of "failure" that is the obverse of the kind of "success" that commercialized standards demand of him if he is to survive. Whosoever would worship his heavenly goddess has small choice; he must keep his eye on the thrifty cow or give up his dream of "success"; and the power of discrimination possessed by the cow promises ill for the future integrity of an organic architecture. The net result of present standards is likely to be a poor wretch, a coward who aspires pretentiously or theoretically, advertises cleverly and milks surreptitiously. There is no real connection between aspiration and practice except a tissue of lies and deceit; there never can be. The young architect before he ventures to practice architecture with an ideal, today, should first be sure of his goddess and then, somehow, be connected with a base of supplies from which he cannot be cut off, or else fall in with the rank and file of the "good school" of the hour. Anyone who has tried it knows this; that is, if he is honest and is going to use his own material as soon as he is able. So the ever present economic question underlies this question of artist integrity, at this stage of our development, like quicksand beneath the footing of a needed foundation, and the structure itself seems doomed to shreds and cracks and shores and patches, the deadening compromises and pitiful makeshifts of the struggle to "succeed"! Even the cry for this integrity will bind the legion together, as one man, against the crier and the cry.

This is art, then, in a sentimental democracy, which seems to be only another form of selfsame hypocrisy? Show me a man who prates of such "democracy" as a basis for artist endeavor, and I will show you an inordinately foolish egotist or a quack. The "democracy" of the man in the American street is no more than the gospel of mediocrity. When it is understood that a great democracy is the highest form of aristocracy conceivable, not of birth or place or wealth, but of those qualities that give distinction to the man as a man, and that as a social state it must be characterized by the honesty and responsibility of the absolute individualist as the unit of its structure, then only can we have an art worthy the name. The rule of mankind by mankind is one thing; but false "democracy," the hypocritical sentimentality politically practiced and preached here, usually the sheep's clothing of the proverbial wolf, or the egotistic dream of self-constituted patron saints is quite another thing. "The letter killeth," yes; but more deadly still is the undertow of false democracy that poses the man as a creative artist and starves him to death unless he fakes his goddess or persuades himself, with "language," that the cow is really she. Is the lack of an artist conscience, then, simply the helpless surrender of the would-be artist to this wherewithal democracy with which a nation soothes itself into subjection? Is the integrity for which I plead here no part of this time and place? And is no young aspirant or hardened sinner to blame for lacking it? It may be so. If it is, we can at least be honest about that, too. But what aspiring artist could knowingly face such a condition? He would choose to dig in the ditch and trace his dreams by lamplight, on scrap paper, for the good of his own soul; a sweet and honorable, if commercially futile, occupation.

It has been my hope to have inspired among my pupils a personality or two to contribute to this work, some day, forms of their own devising, with an artistic integrity that will help to establish upon a firmer basis the efforts that have gone before them and enable them in more propitious times to carry on their practice with a personal gentleness, wisdom, and reverence denied to the pioneers who broke rough ground for them, with a wistful eye to better conditions for their future.

And I believe that, cleared of the superficial pose and push that is the inevitable abuse of its opportunity and its nature, and against which I ungraciously urge myself here, there will be found good work in a cause that deserves honest friends and honest enemies among the better architects of the country. Let us have done with "language" and unfair use of borrowed forms; understand that such practices or products are not of the character of this young work. This work is a sincere endeavor to establish the ideal of an organic architecture in a new country; a type of endeavor that alone can give lasting value to any architecture and that is in line with the spirit of every great and noble precedent in the world of forms that has come to us as the heritage of the great life that has been lived, and in the spirit of which all great life to be will still be lived.

And this thing that eludes the disciple, remains in hiding from the neophyte, and in the name of which the broker seduces his client, What is it? This mystery requiring the catch phrases of a new language to abate the agonies of the convert and in the name of which ubiquitous atrocities have been and will continue to be committed, with the deadly enthusiasm of the ego-mania that is its plague. First, a study of the nature of materials you elect to use and the tools you must use with them, searching to find the characteristic qualities in both that are suited to your purpose. Second, with an ideal of organic nature as a guide, so to unite these qualities to serve that purpose, that the fashion of what you do has integrity or is *natively fit,* regardless of preconceived notions of style. *Style* is a byproduct of the process and comes of the man or the mind in the process. The style of the thing, therefore, will be the man; it is his. *Let his forms alone.*

To adopt a "style" as a motive is to put the cart before the horse and get nowhere beyond the "styles"; never to reach *style.*

It is obvious that this is neither ideal nor work for fakers or tyros; for unless this process is finally so imbued, informed, with a feeling for the beautiful that grace and proportion are inevitable, the result cannot get beyond good engineering.

A light matter this, altogether? And yet an organic architecture must take this course and belie nothing, shirk nothing. Discipline! The architect who undertakes his work seriously on these lines is emancipated and imprisoned at the same time. His work may be severe; it cannot be foolish. It may lack grace; it cannot lack fitness altogether. It may seem ugly; it will not be false. No wonder, however, that the practice of architecture in this sense is the height of ambition and the depth of poverty!

Nothing is more difficult to achieve than the integral simplicity of organic nature, amid the tangled confusions of the innumerable relics of form that encumber life for us. To achieve it in any degree means a serious devotion to the "underneath" in an attempt to grasp the *nature* of building a beautiful building beautifully, as organically true in itself, to itself and to its purpose, as any tree or flower.

That is the need, and the need is demoralized, not served, by the same superficial emulation of the letter in the new work that has heretofore characterized the performances of those who start out to practice architecture by selecting and electing to work in a ready-made "style."

1910: Studies and Executed Buildings

FROM *Ausgeführte Bauten und Entwürfe,* BERLIN, 1910.

This celebrated monograph, luxuriously printed by Wasmuth, and later pirated in cheap editions in Japan and Germany, was the principal vehicle for the Wright influence on architectural design in Europe.

FLORENCE, ITALY, *June 1910.*

Since a previous article, written in an endeavor to state the nature of the faith and practice fashioning this work, I have had the privilege of studying the work of that splendid group of Florentine sculptors and painters and architects, and the sculptor-painters and painter-sculptors, who were also architects: Giotto, Masaccio, Mantegna, Arnolfo, Pisano, Brunelleschi, Bramante, Sansovino, and Angelo.

No line was drawn between the arts and their epoch. Some of the sculpture is good painting; most of the painting is good sculpture; and in both lie the patterns of architecture. Where this confusion is not a blending of these arts, it is as amazing as it is unfortunate. To attempt to classify the works severely as pure painting, pure sculpture or pure architecture would be quite impossible, if it were desirable for educational purposes. But be this as it may, what these men of Florence absorbed from their Greek, Byzantine, and Roman forbears, they bequeathed to Europe as the kernel of the Renaissance; and this, if we deduct the Gothic influence of the Middle Ages, has constituted the soul of the academic fine arts on the Continent.

From these Italian flames were lighted myriads of French, German, and English lights that flourished, flickered feebly for a time, and soon smoldered in the sensuality and extravagance of later periods, until they were extinguished in banal architecture like the Rococo, or in nondescript structures such as the Louvre.

This applies to those buildings which were more or less "professional" embodiments of a striving for the beautiful, those buildings which were "good school" performances, which sought consciously to be beautiful. Nevertheless, here as elsewhere, the true basis for any serious study of the art of architecture is in those indigenous structures, the more humble buildings everywhere, which are to architecture what folklore is to literature or folk songs are to music, and with which architects were seldom concerned. In the aggregate of these lie the traits that make them characteristically German or Italian, French, Dutch, English, or Spanish in nature, as the case may be. The traits of these structures are national, of the soil; and, though often slight, their virtue is intimately interrelated with environment and with the habits of life of the people. Their functions are truthfully conceived, and rendered directly with natural feeling. They are always instructive and often beautiful. So, underlying the ambitious and self-conscious blossoms of the human soul, the expressions of "Mariolatry," or adoration of divinity, or cringing to temporal power; there is the love of life which quietly and inevitably finds the right way; and in lovely color, gracious line, and harmonious arrangement imparts it untroubled by any burden; as little concerned with literature or indebted to it as the flower by the wayside that turns its petals upward to the sun is concerned with the farmer who passes in the road or is indebted to him for the geometry of its petals or the mathematics of its structure.

Of this joy in living, there is greater proof in Italy than elsewhere. Buildings, pictures, and sculpture seem to be born, like the flowers by the roadside, to sing themselves into being. Approached in the spirit of their conception, they inspire us with the very music of life.

No really Italian building seems ill at ease in Italy. All are happily content with what ornament and color they carry, as naturally as the rocks and trees and garden slopes which are one with them. Wherever the cypress rises, like the touch of a magician's wand, it resolves all into a composition harmonious and complete.

The secret of this ineffable charm would be sought in vain in the rarefied air of scholasticism or pedantic fine art. It lies close to the earth. Like a handful of the moist, sweet earth itself it is so simple that, to modern minds, trained in intellectual gymnastics, it would seem unrelated to great purposes. It is so close that almost universally it is overlooked by the pedant.

Along the wayside some blossom, with unusually glowing color or prettiness of form, attracts us; held by it, we accept gratefully its perfect loveliness; but, seeking to discover the secret of its charm, we find the blossom, whose more obvious claim first arrests our attention, intimately related to the texture and shape of its foliage; we discover a strange sympathy between the form of the flower and the system upon which the leaves are arranged about the stalk. From this we are led to observe a characteristic habit of growth, and resultant nature of structure, having its first direction and form in the roots hidden in the warm earth, kept moist by the conservative covering of leaf mold. This structure proceeds from the general to the particular in a most inevitable way, arriving at the blossom to proclaim in its lines and form the nature of the structure that bore it. It is an organic thing. Law and order are the basis of its finished grace and beauty; its beauty is the expression of fundamental conditions in line, form and color, true to them, and existing to fulfill them according to design.

We can in no wise prove beauty to be the result of these harmonious internal conditions. That which through the ages appeals to us as beautiful does not ignore in its fiber the elements of law and order. Nor does it take long to establish the fact that no lasting beauty ignores these elements ever present as conditions of its existence. It will appear, from study of the forms or styles which mankind has considered beautiful, that those which live longest are those which in greatest measure fulfill these conditions. That a thing grows is no concern of ours, because the quality of life is beyond us and we are not necessarily concerned with it. Beauty, in its essence, is for us as mysterious as life. All attempts to say what it is, are as foolish as cutting out the head of a drum to find whence comes the sound. But we may study with profit these truths of form and structure, facts of form as related to function, material traits of line determining character, laws of structure inherent in all natural growth. We ourselves are only a product of natural law. These truths, therefore, are in harmony with the essence of our own being, and are perceived by us to be good. We instinctively feel the good, true, and beautiful to be essentially one in the last analysis. Within us there is a divine principle of growth to some end; accordingly we select as good whatever is in harmony with this law.

We reach for the light spiritually, as the plant does physically, if we are sound of heart and not sophisticated by our education.

When we perceive a thing to be beautiful, it is because we instinctively recognize the rightness of the thing. This means that we have revealed to us a glimpse of something essentially of the fiber of our own nature. The artist makes this revelation to us through his deeper insight. His power to visualize his conceptions being greater than our own, a flash of truth stimulates us, and we have a vision of harmonies not understood today, though perhaps to be tomorrow.

This being so, whence came corrupt styles like the Renaissance? From false education, from confusion of the curious with the beautiful. Confounding the sensations awakened by the beautiful with those evoked by things merely curious is a fatal tendency which increases as civilization moves away from nature and founds conventions in ignorance of or defiance of natural law.

The appreciation of beauty on the part of primitive peoples, Mongolian, Indian, Arab, Egyptian, Greek, and Goth, was unerring. Because of this their work is coming home to us today in another and truer Renaissance, to open our eyes that we may cut away the dead wood and brush aside the accumulated rubbish of centuries of false education. This Renaissance means a return to simple conventions in harmony with nature. Primarily it is a simplifying process. Then, having learned the spiritual lesson that the East has power to teach the West, we may build upon this basis the more highly developed forms our more highly developed life will need.

Nature sought in this way can alone save us from the hopeless confusion of ideas that has resulted in the view that beauty is a matter of caprice, that it is merely a freak of imagination; to one man divine; to another hideous; to another meaningless. We are familiar with the assertion that, should a man put eleven stovepipe hats on top of the cornice of his building and find them beautiful, why then they are beautiful. Yes, perhaps to him; but the only possible conclusion is, that, like the 11 hats on the cornice, he is not beautiful, because beauty to him is utter violation of all the harmonies of any sequence or consequence of his own nature. To find inorganic things of no truth of relation beautiful is but to demonstrate the lack of beauty in oneself and one's unfitness for any office in administering the beautiful, and to provide another example of the stultification that comes from the confusion of the curious with the beautiful.

Education seems to leave modern man less able than the savage to draw the line between these qualities.

A knowledge of cause and effect in line, color and form, as found in organic nature, furnishes guide lines within which an artist may sift materials, test motives, and direct aims, thus roughly blocking out, at least, the rational basis of his ideas and ideals. Great artists do this by instinct. The thing is felt or divined, by inspiration perhaps, as synthetic analysis of their works will show. The poetry which is prophecy is not a matter to be demonstrated. But what is of great value to the artist in research of this nature is knowledge of those facts of relation, those qualities of line, form and color which are themselves a language of sentiment, and characterize the pine as a pine as distinguished from those determining the willow as a willow; those characteristic traits which the Japanese seize graphically and unerringly reduce to simple geometry; the graphic soul of the thing, as seen in the geometrical analyses of Hokusai. Korin was the conscious master of the essential in whatever he rendered, and his work stands as a convincing revelation of the soul of the thing he portrayed. So it will be found with all great work, with the paintings of Velasquez and Frans Hals; with Gothic architecture: organic character in all.

By knowledge of nature in this sense alone are these guiding principles to be established. Ideals gained within these limitations are never lost, and an artist may defy his "education." If he is really for nature in this sense, he may be "a rebel against his time and its laws. but never lawless."

The debased periods of the world's art are far removed from any conception of these principles. The Renaissance, Baroque, Rococo, the styles of the Louis, are not developed from within. There is little or nothing organic in their nature; they are put on from without. The freedom from the yoke of authority which the Renaissance gave to men was seemingly a great gain; but it served only to bind them senselessly to tradition, and to mar the art of the Middle Ages past repair. One cannot go into the beautiful edifices of this great period without hatred of the Renaissance growing in his soul. It proves itself a most wantonly destructive thing in its hideous perversity. In every land where the Gothic or Byzantine, or the Romanesque, that was close to Byzantine, grew, it is a soulless blight, a warning, a veritable damnation of the beautiful. What lovely things remain, it left to us in spite of its nature or when it was least itself. It was not a development; it was a disease.

This is why buildings growing in response to actual needs, fitted into environment by people who knew no better than to fit them to it with native feeling (buildings that grew as folklore and folk song grew), are better worth study than highly self-conscious academic attempts at the beautiful; academic attempts which the nations seem to possess in common as a gift from Italy, after acknowledging her source of inspiration.

All architecture worthy the name is a growth in accord with natural feeling and industrial means to serve actual needs. It cannot be put on from without. There is little beyond sympathy with the spirit creating it and an understanding of the ideals that shaped it that can legitimately be utilized. Any attempt to use forms borrowed from other times and conditions must end as the Renaissance ends, with total loss of inherent relation to the soul life of the people. It can give us only an extraneous thing in the hands of professors that means little more than a mask for circumstance or a mark of temporal power to those whose lives are burdened, not expressed, by it; the result is a terrible loss to life for which literature can never compensate. Buildings will always remain the most valuable asset in a people's environment, the one most capable of cultural reaction. But until the people have the joy again in architecture as a living art that one sees recorded in buildings of all the truly great periods, so long will architecture remain a dead thing. It will not live again until we break away entirely from adherence to the false ideals of the Renaissance. In that whole movement art was reduced to the level of an expedient. What people has a future content with that? Only that of parasites, feeding on past greatness, and on the road to extinction by some barbarian race with ideals and hungering for their realization in noble concrete form.

In America we are more betrayed by this condition than the people of older countries, for we have no traditional forms except the accumulated ones of all peoples that do not without sacrifice fit new conditions, and there is in consequence no true reverence for tradition. As some sort of architecture is a necessity, American architects take their pick from the world's stock of "ready-made" architecture, and are most successful when transplanting form for form, line for line, enlarging details by means of lantern slides from photographs of the originals.

This works well. The people are architecturally clothed and sheltered. The modern comforts are smuggled in cleverly, we must admit. But is this architecture? Is it thus tradition molded great styles? In this polyglot tangle of borrowed forms, is there a great spirit that will bring order out of chaos? vitality, unity, and greatness out of emptiness and discord?

The ideals of the Renaissance will not, for the Renaissance was inorganic.

A conception of what constitutes an organic architecture will lead to better things once it is planted in the hearts and minds of men whose resource and skill, whose real power, are unquestioned, and who are not obsessed by expedients and forms, the nature and origin of which they have not studied in relation to the spirit that produced them. The nature of these forms is not taught in any vital sense in any of the schools in which architects are trained.

A revival of the Gothic spirit is needed in the art and architecture of modern life; an interpretation of the best traditions we have in the world made with our own methods, not a stupid attempt to fasten their forms upon a life that has outgrown them. Reviving the Gothic spirit does not mean using the forms of Gothic architecture handed down from the Middle Ages. It necessarily means something quite different. The conditions and ideals that fixed the forms of the twelfth are not the conditions and ideals that can truthfully fix the forms of the twentieth century. The spirit that fixed those forms is not the spirit that will fix the new forms. Classicists and schools will deny the new forms, and find no "Gothic" in them. It will not much matter. They will be living, doing their work quietly and effectively, until the borrowed garments, cut over to fit by the academies, are cast off, having served only to hide the nakedness of a moment when art became detached, academic, alien to the lives of the people.

America, more than any other nation, presents a new architectural proposition. Her ideal is democracy, and in democratic spirit her institutions are professedly conceived. This means that she places a life premium upon individuality, the highest possible development of the individual consistent with a harmonious whole, believing that a whole benefited by sacrifice of that quality in the individual rightly considered his "individuality" is undeveloped; believing that the whole, to be worthy as a whole, must consist of individual units, great and strong in themselves, not yoked from without in bondage, but united within, with the right to move in unity, each in its own sphere, yet preserving this right to the highest possible degree for all. This means greater individual life and more privacy in life, concerns which are peculiarly one's own. It means lives lived in greater independence and seclusion, with all toward which an English nobleman aspires, but with absolute unwillingness to pay the price in paternalism and patronage asked of him for the privilege. This dream of freedom, as voiced by the Declaration of Independence, is dear to the heart of every man who has caught the spirit of American institutions; therefore the ideal of every man American in feeling and spirit. Individuality is a national ideal. Where this degenerates into petty individualism, it is but a manifestation of weakness in the human nature, and not a fatal flaw in the ideal.

In America each man has a peculiar, inalienable right to live in his own house in his own way. He is a pioneer in every right sense of the word. His home environment may face forward, may portray his character, tastes, and ideas, if he has any, and every man here has some somewhere about him.

This is a condition at which Englishmen or Europeans, facing toward traditional forms which they are in duty bound to preserve, may well stand aghast. An American is in duty bound to establish traditions in harmony with his ideals, his still unspoiled sites, his industrial opportunities, and industrially he is more completely committed to the machine than any living man. It has given him the things which mean mastery over an uncivilized land, comfort and resources.

His machine, the tool in which his opportunity lies, can only murder the traditional forms of other peoples and earlier times. He must find new forms, new industrial ideals, or stultify both opportunity and forms. But underneath forms in all ages were certain conditions which determined them. In them all was a human spirit in accord with which they came to be; and where the forms were true forms, they will be found to be organic forms, an outgrowth, in other words, of conditions of life and work they arose to express. They are beautiful and significant, studied in this relation. They are dead to us, borrowed as they stand.

I have called this feeling for the organic character of form and treatment the Gothic spirit, for it was more completely realized in the forms of that architecture, perhaps, than any other. At least the infinitely varied forms of that architecture are more obviously and literally organic than any other, and the spirit in which they were conceived and wrought was one of absolute integrity of means to ends. In this spirit America will find the forms best suited to her opportunities, her aims and her life.

All the great styles, approached from within, are spiritual treasure houses to architects. Transplanted as forms, they are tombs of a life that has been lived.

This ideal of individuality has already ruthlessly worked its way with the lifeless carcasses of the foreign forms it has hawked and flung about in reckless revel that in East, as well as West, amounts to positive riot.

Brown calls loudly for Renaissance, Smith for a French chateau, Jones for an English manor house, McCarthy for an Italian villa, Robinson for Hanseatic, and Hammerstein for Rococo, while the sedately conservative families cling to "old colonial" wedding cakes with demurely conscious superiority. In all this is found the last word of the *inorganic*. The Renaissance ended in this, a thing absolutely removed from time, place or people; borrowed finery put on hastily, with no more conception of its meaning or character that Titania had of the donkey she caressed. "All a matter of taste," like the hats on the cornice.

A reaction was inevitable.

It is of this reaction that I feel qualified to speak; for the work illustrated in this volume, with the exception of the work of Louis Sullivan, is the first consistent protest in bricks and mortar against this pitiful waste. It is a serious attempt to formulate some industrial and aesthetic ideals that in a quiet, rational way will help to make a lovely thing of an American's home environment, produced without abuse by his own tools, and dedicated in spirit and letter to him.

The ideals of Ruskin and Morris and the teaching of the Beaux-Arts have hitherto prevailed in America, steadily confusing, as well as in some respects revealing to us our opportunities. The American, too, of some old-world culture, disgusted by this state of affairs, and having the beautiful harmony in the architecture of an English village, European rural community, or the grandiloquent planning of Paris in view, has been easily persuaded that the best thing we could do was to adopt some style least foreign to us, stick to it and plant it continually; a parasitic proceeding, and in any case futile. New York is a tribute to the Beaux-Arts so far as surface decoration goes, and underneath a tribute to the American engineer.

Other cities have followed her lead.

Our better-class residences are chiefly tributes to English architecture, cut open inside and embellished to suit; porches and "conveniences" added: the result in most cases a pitiful mongrel. Painfully conscious of their lack of traditions, our get-rich-quick citizens attempt to buy tradition ready made, and are dragged forward, facing backwards, in attitudes most absurd to those they would emulate, characteristic examples of conspicuous waste.

The point in all this is the fact that revival of the ideals of an organic architecture will have to contend with this rapidly increasing sweep of imported folly. Even the American with some little culture, going contrary to his usual course in other matters, is becoming painfully aware of his inferiority in matters of dress and architecture, and goes abroad for both, to be sure they are correct. Thus assured, he is no longer concerned, and forgets both. That is more characteristic of the eastern than the western man. The real American spirit, capable of judging an issue for itself upon its merits, lies in the West and Middle West, where breadth of view, independent thought and a tendency to take common sense into the realm of art, as in life, are more characteristic. It is alone in an atmosphere of this nature that the Gothic spirit in building can be revived. In this atmosphere, among clients of this type, I have lived and worked.

Taking common sense into the holy realm of art is a shocking thing and most unpopular in academic circles. It is a species of vulgarity; but some of these questions have become so perplexed, so encrusted, by the savants and academies, with layer upon layer of "good school," that their very nature is hidden; approached with common sense, they become childishly simple.

I believe that every matter of artistic import which concerns a building may be put to the common sense of a businessman on the right side every time, and thus given a chance at it, he rarely gives a wrong decision. The difficulty found with this man by the Renaissance, when he tries to get inside; that is, if he does more than merely give the order to "go ahead"; arises from the fact that the thing has no organic basis to give; there is no good reason for doing anything any particular way rather than another way which can be grasped by him or anybody else; it is all largely a matter of taste. In an organic scheme there are excellent reasons why the thing is as it is, what it is there for, and where it is going. If not, it ought not to go, and as a general thing it doesn't. The people themselves are part and parcel and helpful in producing the organic thing. They can comprehend it and make it theirs, and it is thus the only form of art expression to be considered for a democracy, and, I will go so far as to say, the truest of all forms.

So I submit that the buildings here illustrated have for the greatest part been conceived and worked in their conclusion in the Gothic spirit in this respect as well as in respect to the tools that produced them, the methods of work behind them, and, finally, in their organic nature considered in themselves. These are limitations, unattractive limitations; but there is no project in the fine arts that is not a problem.

With this idea as a basis comes another conception of what constitutes a building.

The question then arises as to what is style. The problem no longer remains a matter of working in a prescribed style with what variation it may bear without absurdity if the owner happens to be a restless individualist: so this question is not easily answered.

What is style? Every flower has it; every animal has it; every individual worthy the name has it in some degree, no matter how much sandpaper may have done for him. It is a free product, a byproduct, the result of an organic working out of a project in character and in one state of feeling.

An harmonious entity of whatever sort in its entirety cannot fail of style in the best sense.

In matters of art the individual feeling of the creative artist can but give the color of his own likes and dislikes, his own soul to the thing he shapes. He gives his individuality, but will not prevent the building from being characteristic of those it was built to serve, because it necessarily is a solution of conditions they make, and it is made to serve their ends in their own way. Insofar as these conditions are peculiar in themselves, or sympathy exists between the clients and the architect, the building will be their building. It will be theirs much more truly than though in ignorant selfhood they had stupidly sought to use means they had not conquered to an end imperfectly foreseen. The architect, then, is their means, their technique and interpreter; the building, an interpretation if he is a true architect in Gothic sense. If he is chiefly concerned in some marvelous result that shall stand as architecture in good form to his credit, the client be damned, why, that is a misfortune which is only another species of the unwisdom of his client. This architect is a dangerous man, and there are lots of his kind outside, and some temptations to him inside, the ranks of the Gothic architects. But the man who loves the beautiful, with ideals of organic natures if an artist, is too keenly sensible of the nature of his client as a fundamental condition in his problem to cast him off, although he may give him something to grow to, something in which he may be a little ill at ease at the outset.

In this lies temptation to abuses. Where ignorance of the nature of the thing exists or where there is a particular character or preference, it is to a certain extent the duty of an architect to give his client something dated ahead; for he is entrusted by his client with his interests in matters in which, more frequently than not, the client is ignorant. A commission therefore becomes a trust to the architect. Any architect is bound to educate his client to the extent of his true skill and capacity in what he as a professional adviser believes to be fundamentally right. In this there is plenty of leeway for abuse of the client; temptations to sacrifice him in the interest of personal idiosyncrasies, to work along lines instinctively his preference, and therefore easy to him. But in any trust there is chance of failure. This educational relationship between client and architect is more or less to be expected, and of value artistically for the reason that, while the architect is educating the client, the client is educating him. And a certain determining factor in this quality of style is this matter growing out of this relation of architect and client to the work in hand, as well as the more definite elements of construction. This quality of style is a subtle thing, and should remain so. Style is not to be defined in itself so much as to be regarded as a natural result of *artistic integrity.*

Style, then, if the conditions are consistently and artistically cared for little by little will care for itself. As for working in a nominated style beyond a natural predilection for certain forms, it is unthinkable by the author of any true creative effort.

Given similar conditions, similar tools, similar people, I believe that architects will, with a proper regard for the organic nature of the thing produced, arrive at various results sufficiently harmonious with each other and with great individuality. One might swoop all the Gothic architecture of the world together in a single nation; and mingle it with buildings treated horizontally as they were treated vertically or treated diagonally, buildings and towers with flat roofs, long, low buildings with square openings, mingled with tall buildings with pointed ones, in the bewildering variety of that marvelous architectural manifestation; and harmony in the general ensemble inevitably result; the common chord in all being sufficient to bring them unconsciously into harmonious relation.

It is this ideal of an organic architecture working out with normal means to a consistent end that is the salvation of the architect entrusted with liberty. He is really more severely disciplined by this high ideal than his brothers of the styles, and consequently he is less likely to falsify his issue.

So to the schools looking askance at the mixed material entrusted to their charge, thinking to save the nation a terrible infliction of the wayward dreams of mere idiosyncrasies by teaching "the safe course of a good copy," we owe thanks for a conservative attitude, but censure for failure to give to material needed by the nation, constructive ideals that would from *within* discipline sufficiently, at the same time leaving a chance to work out a real thing in touch with reality with such souls as they have. In other words, they are to be blamed for not inculcating in students the conception of architecture as an organic expression of the nature of a problem, for not teaching them to look to this nature for the elements of its working out in accordance with principles found in natural organisms. Study of the great architecture of the world solely in regard to the spirit that found expression in the forms should go with this. But before all should come the study of the nature of materials, the *nature* of the tools and processes at command, and the *nature* of the thing they are to be called upon to do.

A training of this sort was accorded the great artists of Japan. Although it was not intellectually self-conscious, I have no doubt the apprenticeship of the Middle Ages wrought like results.

German and Austrian art schools are getting back to these ideas. Until the student is taught to approach the beautiful from within, there will be no great living buildings which in the aggregate show the spirit of true architecture.

An architect, then, in this revived sense, is a man disciplined from within by a conception of the organic nature of his task, knowing his tools and his opportunity, working out his problems with what sense of beauty the gods gave him.

He, disciplined by the very nature of his undertakings, is the only safe man.

To work with him is to find him master of means to a certain end. He acquires a technique in the use of his tools and materials which may be as complete and in every sense as remarkable as a musician's mastery of the resources of his instrument. In no other spirit is this to be acquired in any vital sense; and without it, well, a good copy is the safest thing. If one cannot live an independent life, one may at least become a modest parasite.

It is with the courage that a conviction of the truth of this point of view has given that the problems in this work have been attempted. In that spirit they have been worked out, with what degree of failure or success no one can know better than I. To be of value to the student they must be approached from within, and not from the viewpoint of the man looking largely at the matter from the depths of the Renaissance. Insofar as they are grasped as organic solutions of conditions they exist but to serve, with respect for the limitations imposed by our industrial conditions, and having in themselves a harmony of idea in form and treatment that makes something fairly beautiful of them in relation to life, they will be helpful. Approached from the point of view that seeks characteristic beauty of form and feature as great as that of the Greeks, the Goths or the Japanese, they will be disappointing; and I can only add, it is a little too soon yet to look for such attainment. But the quality of style, in the indefinable sense that it is possessed by any organic thing, that they have. Repose and quiet attitudes they have. Unity of idea, resourceful adaptation of means, will not be found wanting, nor that simplicity of rendering which the machine makes not only imperative but opportune. Although complete, highly developed in detail they are not.

Self-imposed limitations are in part responsible for this lack of intricate enrichment, and partly the imperfectly developed resources of our industrial system. I believe, too, that much ornament in the old sense is not for us yet; we have lost its significance, and I do not believe in adding enrichment merely for the sake of enrichment. Unless it adds clearness to the enunciation of the theme, it is undesirable, for it is very little understood.

I wish to say, also, what is more to the point, that in a structure conceived in the organic sense, the ornamentation is conceived in the very ground plan, and is of the very constitution of the structure. What ornamentation may be found added purely as such in this structure is thus a makeshift or a confession of weakness or failure.

Where the warp and woof of the fabric do not yield sufficient incident or variety, it is seldom patched on. Tenderness has often to be sacrificed to integrity.

It is fair to explain the point, also, which seems to be missed in studies of the work, that in the conception of these structures they are regarded as severe conventions whose chief office is a background or frame for the life within them and about them. They are considered as foils for the foliage and bloom which they are arranged to carry, as well as a distinct chord or contrast, in their severely conventionalized nature, to the profusion of trees and foliage with which their sites abound.

So the forms and the supervisions and refinements of the forms are, perhaps, more elemental in character than has hitherto been the case in highly developed architecture. To be lived with, the ornamental forms of one's environment should be designed to wear well, which means they must have absolute repose and make no especial claim upon attention; to be removed as far from realistic tendencies as a sense of reality can take them. Good colors, soft textures, living materials, the beauty of the materials revealed and utilized in the scheme, these are the means of decoration considered purely as such.

And it is quite impossible to consider the building one thing and its furnishings another, its setting and environment still another. In the spirit in which these buildings are conceived, these are all one thing, to be foreseen and provided for in the nature of the structure. They are all mere structural details of its character and completeness. Heating apparatus, lighting fixtures, the very chairs and tables, cabinets and musical instruments, where practicable, are of the building itself. Nothing of appliances or fixtures is admitted purely as such where circumstances permit the full development of the building scheme.

Floor coverings and hangings are as much a part of the house as the plaster on the walls or the tiles on the roof. This feature of development has given most trouble, and so far is the least satisfactory to myself, because of difficulties inherent in the completeness of conception and execution necessary. To make these elements sufficiently light and graceful and flexible features of an informal use of an abode requires much more time and thought and money than are usually forthcoming. But it is approached by some later structures more nearly, and in time it will be accomplished. It is still in a comparatively primitive stage of development; yet radiators have disappeared, lighting fixtures are incorporated, floor coverings and hangings are easily made to conform. But chairs and tables and informal articles of use are still at large in most cases, even though designed in feeling with the building.

There are no decorations, nor is there place for them as such. The easel picture has no place on the walls. It is regarded as music might be, suited to a mood, and provided for in a recess of the wall if desired, where a door like the cover of a portfolio might be dropped and the particular thing desired studied for a time; left exposed for days, perhaps, to give place to another, or entirely put away by simply closing the wooden portfolio. Great pictures should have their gallery. Oratorio is not performed in a drawing room. The piano, where possible, should and does disappear in the structure, its keyboard or openwork or tracery necessary for sound its only visible feature. The dining table and chairs are easily managed in the architecture of the building. So far this development has progressed.

Alternate extremes of heat and cold, of sun and storm, have also to be considered. The frost goes 4 feet into the ground in winter; the sun beats fiercely on the roof with almost tropical heat in summer: an umbrageous architecture is almost a necessity, both to shade the building from the sun and protect the walls from freezing and thawing moisture, the most rapidly destructive to buildings of all natural causes. The overhanging eaves, however, leave the house in winter without necessary sun, and this is overcome by the way in which the window groups in certain rooms and exposures are pushed out to the gutter line. The gently sloping roofs grateful to the prairie do not leave large air spaces above the rooms; and so the chimney has grown in dimensions and importance, and in hot weather ventilates at the high parts the circulating-air spaces beneath the roofs, fresh air entering beneath the eaves through openings easily closed in winter.

Conductor pipes, disfiguring downspouts, particularly where eaves overhang, in this climate freeze and become useless in winter, or burst with results disastrous to the walls; so concrete rain basins are built in the ground beneath the angles of the eaves, and the water drops through open spouts into their concave surfaces, to be conducted to the cistern by underground drain tiles.

Another modern opportunity is afforded by our effective system of hot water heating. By this means the forms of buildings may be more completely articulated, with light and air on several sides. By keeping the ceilings low, the walls may be opened with series of windows to the outer air, the flowers and trees, the prospects, and one may live as comfortably as formerly, less shut in. Many of the structures carry this principle of articulation of various building arts to the point where each has its own individuality completely recognized in the plan.

The dining room and kitchen and sleeping rooms thus become in themselves small buildings, and are grouped together as a whole, as in the Coonley house. It is also possible to spread the buildings, which once in our climate of extremes were a compact box cut into compartments, into a more organic expression, making a house in a garden or in the country the delightful thing in relation to either or both that imagination would have it.

The horizontal line is the line of domesticity.

The virtue of the horizontal lines is respectfully invoked in these buildings. The inches in height gain tremendous force compared with any practicable spread upon the ground.

To Europeans these buildings on paper seem uninhabitable; but they derive height and air by quite other means and respect an ancient tradition, the only one here worthy of respect, the prairie.

In considering the forms and types of these structures, the fact that they are nearly buildings for the prairie should be borne in mind; the gently rolling or level prairies of the Middle West; the great levels where every detail of elevation becomes exaggerated; every tree a tower above the great calm plains of its flowered surfaces as they lie serene beneath a wonderful sweep of sky. The natural tendency of every ill-considered thing is to detach itself and stick out like a sore thumb in surroundings by nature perfectly quiet. All unnecessary heights have for that reason and for other reasons economic been eliminated, and more intimate relation with out-door environment sought to compensate for loss of height.

The differentiation of a single, certain simple form characterizes the expression of one building. Quite a different form may serve for another; but from one basic idea all the formal elements of design are in each case derived and held together in scale and character. The form chosen may flare outward, opening flowerlike to the sky, as in the Thomas house; another, droop to accentuate artistically the weight of the masses; another be noncommittal or abruptly emphatic, or its grammar may be deduced from some plant form that has appealed to me, as certain properties in line and form of the sumac were used in the Lawrence house at Springfield; but in every case the motif is adhered to throughout.

In the buildings themselves, in the sense of the whole, there is lacking neither richness nor incident; but these qualities are secured not by applied decoration, they are found in the fashioning of the whole, in which color, too, plays as significant a part as it does in an old Japanese wood block print.

These ideals take the buildings out of school and marry them to the ground; make them intimate expressions or revelations of the interiors; individualize them, regardless of preconceived notions of style. I have tried to make their grammar perfect in its way, and to give their forms and proportions an integrity that will bear study, although few of them can be intelligently studied apart from their environment.

A study of the drawings will show that the buildings presented fall readily into three groups having a family resemblance; the low-pitched hip roofs, heaped together in pyramidal fashion, or presenting quiet, unbroken sky lines; the low roofs with simple pediments countering on long ridges; and those topped with a simple slab. Of the first type, the Winslow, Henderson, Willits, Thomas, Heurtley, Heath, Cheney, Martin, Little, Gridley, Millard, Tomek, Coonley, and Westcott houses, the Hillside Home School and the Pettit Memorial Chapel are typical. Of the second type, the Bradley, Hickox, Davenport, and Dana houses are typical. Of the third, atelier for Richard Bock, Unity Church, the concrete house of the *Ladies' Home Journal,* and other designs in process of execution. The Larkin Building is a simple, dignified utterance of a plain, utilitarian type, with sheer brick walls and simple stone copings. The studio is merely an early experiment in "articulation."

A type of structure especially suited to the prairie will be found in the Coonley, Thomas, Heurtley, Tomek, and Robie houses, which are virtually one floor arrangements, raised a low story height above the level of the ground. Sleeping rooms are added where necessary in another story.

There is no excavation for this type except for heating purposes. The ground floor provides all necessary room of this nature, and billiard rooms, or playrooms for the children. This plan raises the living rooms well off the ground, which is often damp, avoids the ordinary damp basement, which, if made a feature of the house, sets it so high above the surface, if it is to be made dry, that, in proportion to the ordinary building operation, it rises like a menace to the peace of the prairie.

It is of course necessary that mural decoration and sculpture in these structures should again take their places as architectural developments conceived to conform to their fabric.

To thus make of a dwelling place a complete work of art; in itself as expressive and beautiful and more intimately related to life than anything of detached sculpture or painting; lending itself freely and suitably to the individual needs of the dwellers; a harmonious entity; fitting in color, pattern, and nature the utilities; and in itself really an expression of them in character; this is the modern American opportunity. Once founded, this will become a tradition, a vast step in advance of the day when a dwelling was an arrangement of separate rooms, mere chambers to contain aggregations of furniture, the utility comforts not present. An organic entity this, as contrasted with that aggregation; surely a higher ideal of unity; a higher and more intimate working out of the expression of one's life in one's environment. One thing instead of many things; a great thing instead of a collection of smaller ones.

The drawings, by means of which these buildings are presented here, have been made expressly for this work from colored drawings which were made from time to time as the projects were presented for solution. They merely aim to render the composition in outline and form, and suggest the sentiment of the environment. They are in no sense attempts to treat the subject pictorially, and in some cases fail to convey the idea of the actual building. A certain quality of familiar homelikeness is thus sacrificed in these presentments to a graceful decorative rendering of an idea of an arrangement suggesting, in the originals, a color scheme. Their debt to Japanese ideals, these renderings themselves sufficiently acknowledge.

1917: Antique Color Prints

PREFACE TO CATALOGUE OF THE ARTS CLUB, CHICAGO.

This exhibition was chosen from Wright's extensive collection of Japanese prints which, before their virtual liquidation in 1927, formed one of the most important collections of their kind in the world. As indicated in the text, Wright chose the prints to be exhibited, and prepared the installation.

Shibaraku: It is the Japanese word for "wait a moment"—a dramatic moment made famous by the great actor Danjuro in the role of that name as he came forward in the splendid red, flowing robes patterned with the gigantic white crests that were the mark of his distinguished house. To all who would "look" this is the "wait and listen" moment to let it be said that in ancient Tokio an art was born nearer "democratic" than any ever seen.

The people loved and possessed it. It was made for them, except as the humble artists made it for themselves with that joy in the making that alone lives in art.

You are to see a few rare, perishable leaves from a prolific, wondrous volume, and richly voluminous and beautifully embroidered it was in that time. Since then what has escaped destruction has been scattered by the winds of chance to the far corners of earth. For Tokio civilization was as frail as it was exquisite. Its framework and utensils were of beautifully treated wood and silken paper. Its sword was keen and of steel. Were it not for reverential Japanese care for things beautiful all these exciting traces of the image-seeking mind would have perished because they were then regarded no more seriously than we now regard printed souvenirs of our holidays and seasons or photographs of favorite actors and actresses. And since the time of Harunobu all Tokio has been shaken or burned to the ground at least five times. The remarkable preservation of such fragile art objects under these conditions is evidence of true devotion.

Country people returning from visits to the new capital—Tokio—stowed them away in the devices of their domesticity and forgot them or pasted them on screens or hung them upon pillars of their houses as decoration, and so were the unwitting means of saving most of "our" collections.

From remote country districts, from Ise to Sendai, little by little, as prices have soared pieces have come fluttering back to Tokio to be seized and gloated over by the epicurean collector with his strange combination of love and self-interest—love for the beautiful and sordid calculation.

But thanks to his acquisitive instinct!

He, too, has been the means of handing over to us in great variety the precious record of a glory that was Old Japan; a civilization wherein art was not divorced from nature, when Eternity was Now.

It is a record, rich with the motifs that made that civilization what it was to the eye.

And it was primarily a festival for eyes.

The figure pieces of this great period from 1740 to 1820 reveal the incomparable instinct for harmonious elegance that characterized the time and its traditions. The range of discovered subjects is already wide—as wide as it is likely to be, although a few new pieces still come to light each year.

It ranges from the monumental simplicity of the primitives of the Kwaigetsudo, printed in black, and the painted Urushiye, to the fully developed color prints in the sweet refinement of Harunobu and the bewildering gamut of Shunsho. Then on by way of masterly Kiyonaga with his regal compositions and swinging calligraphic stroke to the dissolute, sentient grace of the consummate Utamaro, the idol of the "artist absolute." Then downward to the decline and confusion of all noble qualities in Yeisen, Yeizan and Kunisada.

The landscapes (a later development) are the most complete and poetic interpretation of the nature of a natural domain ever recorded by native sons.

Fascinating as each subject is in itself it is in the aggregate that the salient native charm and full integrity of means to ends of this art and craft become so convincing and entrancing. Then it lives as a vivified revelation of that unity in variety that is the soul of the whole visible world of form—and that does not pass. It is of the inward sea, treasure of the profound depths of the soul. These garnered leaves from a perished volume are stamped with an intrinsic art.

So long as art lives they will remain the basis of a world-wide clearing away of the rubbish a vain "realism" has unloaded upon a too human world. Imbued with a point of view inevitable to them, our vision, too, seeks essentials of form, line and color and the rhythms peculiar to each. Scenes familiar enough to us all about us live again with significance renewed and refreshed, not only as landscape or as Japanese prints, but a simplifying light, spiritual in quality, has come through them to unburden the Western mind sagging with its sordid load.

Our land is richer in every sense than their land.

They were richer in what life is than we are.

These iridian sheets of tender, lustrous fiber, stamped with colored carvings, teach us lessons we have good reason to receive with gratitude.

The slender stock the whole world holds of these perishable documents ought to be cherished and guarded by custodians not too selfish—and yet sensible, too, of the priceless character of the record held in trust as an original force, a light for those who can see in all future culture.

The Japanese were awakened too late to the precious character of this inheritance peculiar to them.

The aristocracy despised it as vulgar. The old type of aristocracy despised anything held in common. The new aristocracy had not yet arisen. It is still slow in coming.

The subject matter of the figure pieces is still offensive to Japanese polite society. Not so the landscapes of Hiroshige and Hokusai; and as the art and institutions of Old Japan give way to uglier Western models the Japanese gentleman of leisure now sees the most valuable poetic record of a beauty fast passing away forever from him and from his land, filched from his children before his eyes—and for a sum paltry enough. With characteristic prodigality where works of art are concerned he now vies with others in paying "the highest price." But the value of works of art in Japan seems, along with the other modern improvements, to be augmented by the importance of him who once owned it or the size of the sum paid for it. No Japanese cares to make and hold a collection if foredoomed to remain inferior in it, and our Western collections (my own included) have gained much in recent years by this trait of his.

Hiroshige "outcasts" of a few years ago, are now bought by the Japanese themselves at prices that make the hardened avidity of even the American collector hesitate.

Hiroshige is the latest arrival in the sacred places of upper printdom. His fertility of resource and his industry are alike amazing. Yet, among the thousand or more subjects signed by him none lacks true artistic distinction seen properly printed. For it must be borne in mind that this produce was stamped in a mutable medium upon a mutable substance by a means that could never be twice alike except by strange coincidence. After it was stamped the fabric of the whole underwent transmutation by time and was modified as light had its way with colors that etherealize as they wane. So the fabric as a whole is one of delightful differences and heart breaking or ravishing surprises. Frequently I have got together five or six Hiroshige—all prints of the same subject, so differently printed that they were in effect as many different designs.

No subject which there is good reason to believe a composition by Hiroshige is negligible in art. But art and craftsmanship are inseparable in the print. The bane of any attempt to form an idea of the splendid flight and range of his genius is found when the craftsmanship failed in the disreputable remnant of cheap, badly printed editions carelessly struck from worn-out blocks, to be had for a dollar or two in curio shops. These inferior prints have cursed and confused their superiors which are alone representative, and especially so as Hiroshige prints of superior editions are as rare as primitives.

Hiroshige is coming into his own largely through the conservation in the past ten years of really fine examples of his work in the great collections by the discerning amateur. The Spaulding collection of Boston is an astonishing revelation of Hiroshige's extent and the grasp and sweep of his genius. It is almost unbelievable that so much good work could be done within the lifetime of a single artist. But Hiroshige loved much, so was tireless and doubtless inspired many to take his designs and work with him upon them "in character" in details that might safely be entrusted to them by the master. But why attempt to explain?

It is certain that the mass of work signed by his name is all of a piece and in the same feeling, except certain instances in later work.

While the style swings easily from the delicate, expressive tenderness and grace of the early horizontal compositions to the sure strength and splendid breadth of the uprights in the "Hundred Views," yet it is the same character, the same hand, the same soul in all.

As always about artistic phenomena, literature has gathered about the print since the initial brochures of the DeGoncourt. Primarily it was French. France, the discoverer, discovered the print. In English we have been treated to much perfunctory misinformation. Germany later took up the subject with more weight than light. Japan at last is contributing with authority.

America, meantime, has taken to prints as she takes to everything, reckless of cost and determined to win—whatever that may mean. But we have genuine amateurs among us who understand, and in the hands of several such are the greatest collections in the world, save, possibly, one, and that one is French. Minor collections of great importance are many and in good hands. America, too, has the best of the literature, for not only can she say it: she can sing it better than anyone ever said it. There is no dearth of writing, nor ever will be.

There are not enough exhibitions.

So a fascinating world within a world has grown rapidly among us these past twenty years, increasing steadily in extent and significance as collections have grown richer and as appreciation deepens, and the collections become shrines for the artist pilgrims in need of worship or in search of light.

But still the precious original is all too sacred to the few who, chosen by it, are enslaved by it. Because it is no secret that the prints choose whom they love and there is then no salvation but surrender.

In arranging the exhibition I have chosen prints in varied "conditions."

They are composed on the walls—toned and bright together—like an autumnal forest wherein the trees, once all verdant, have asserted themselves in those glowing changes which have their counterpart in the antique print.

It has always seemed to me a stupid crime to use the white mat as a uniform standard for a collection of prints. It naturally crucifies all but "bright" prints. Those richly endowed by time are ignorantly neglected or ruthlessly sacrificed by the average connoisseur. The time will soon come when collections made in that way will be referred to as all "very bright clean stuff," but the most glorious print and eventually the most sought for will be that masterpiece time has mellowed and honored with the development of its inner nature —an element precious in old pottery. Qualities indescribably rich and tender develop in and from the print as verdigris comes to bronze—qualities that as legitimately enhance its value.

This will be true of the print that still lives in color, because only then is it enriched by its honorable age. Lifeless brown prints, or prints merely faded, will never be desirable.

The upstanding bright print has, owing to the white-mat standard, commanded enormous premiums, relatively absurd. Premiums should go the other way.

Abuse, or wear and tear, are never beautiful, but age should, and will always be, a richer qualification, not a disqualifiication, in all that really lives, and especially so of the freshness of youth.

But beautifully mellowed prints will always be rare. More of them go down to ruin with use and the trials of exposure to smoke and light. There will always be one hundred "bright" prints to every one developed beautifully by age.

1918-1928: The Nature of Materials

1918: Chicago Culture

To the Chicago Women's Aid, 1918.

Here is the Chicago of the Literary Times *era as seen by one of its most cultivated citizens. There is some plain speaking in this lecture, as in the observation on the Chicago Auditorium, and a depth of appreciation that may seem surprising.*

Ten years ago, at a dinner given a visiting artist (Ashbee of London, who had criticized us rather freely) one of our magnates got up and boasted that "Chicago wasn't much on culture now, maybe, but when she did get after culture she'd make culture hum." Chicago brag, but true! Chicago got after culture. Chicago has made culture hum. The kind of culture Chicago "got after" likes it and hums loud. No one interested in the subject can ignore it. But I want to say more about the men and the culture that are getting after the culture that Chicago "got after."

No one thinks of this city as the art center of the Western World. It is famous for so much else and otherwise. And yet the broad free spirit of Chicago has given great things in art to the light here, that if conceived elsewhere would have died still-born. This is due to Chicago's superior discernment. I do not pretend that it is due simply to the nature of the thing.

Chicago is the national capital of the essentially American spirit. Chicago in spite of the culture she "got after" is a very real place. To know Chicago is an experience in first principles; a despair and a great hope. A despair, not so much because Chicago is cruel and crude as because "culture" has been stuck upon its surface as a businessman's expedient or thoughtlessly bought by the rich as luxury. Bought in blissful ignorance of the more vital, less fashionable contribution Chicago has to make to life.

Is anything uglier than just dirt, unless it is noise? We have both in abundance. Someone defines dirt as matter out of place, and in this sense Chicago's culture is dirt; matter out of place in all its ugliness. Hundreds of thousands of houses that are little stage settings in various periods where "pa" and "ma" don't belong, and where it would be immoral, shocking, or absurd for them to be and seen in which they seldom fail to be ridiculous. See the assortment on the drive or any favored section of the city! See our "beastly rich" in their store clothes at the opera; our badly overdressed business women in their tall white shoes or their equivalent in our offices. A type of little girl badly overdone has made her appearance on our streets, pseudo Parisian probably. Our hotels, one and all, parade an air of magnificence and expense as a substitute for privacy, modesty, and comfort, offering the outward show of the continental hotel without real service, without politeness, without individuality.

Yes, life is on too easy or too hard terms here in Chicago if without money, and with it, still empty of the warmth, cordiality, and individuality that make life in Europe enjoyable almost everywhere.

The pernicious papier-mache elegance of our theaters is, in architectural spirit, level with the morals of the Folies Bergères. The city's public buildings are foolish lies. The Art Institute itself is a stupid building with no countenance and elaborate flanks; the Public Library, two buildings one on top of the other in disgraceful quarrel; the Post Office, a boyish atelier project regardless of its purpose; the City Hall, a big bluff in vain "classic" costing the city many thousands a month for huge columns, themselves a troublesome and expensive load instead of carrying the load as columns used to do. A certain careless prosperous dishonesty characterizes the cultural fabric of the city of Chicago as it does of America.

One of Chicago's influential, admirable architects, and one who has built some good houses and fine industrial buildings, told me not long ago of a wealthy widow from some town down in the Middle West who came to ask him to build a monument to her husband, a local politician some months dead. She wanted to buy an exact replica of the Greek monument to Lysicrates, to be set up on their lot in the home-town cemetery. To her, a beautiful thought for her dead husband.

Hoping to dissuade her Mr. Shaw told her of the great cost of such an undertaking. But happening to go East about that time he met some of the influential architects of New York, Boston, and Philadelphia. At dinner he told the story and to his surprise they said, "By all means go back and build it for her; a beautiful thing like that couldn't fail to be educational." There it is. The costly fallacy behind all this stark, staring, naked. The shameless irrelevant use of a beautiful thing, its abuse, therefore, justified as educational! With such advocates on top, what chance has the eternal fitness of things underneath?

Abuse, you see, is "academic" now.

Another traveled rich woman adored the Petit Trianon. She must have it for a house, only it was a story too low. So Mr. Shaw put another story on the Trianon for her. If he had not done it someone else would have and probably would have done it worse. Mr. Shaw said so.

I sneered and he turned and showed me a Gothic building he had just finished as a home for some Chicago businessman and asked if I liked it any better. It was chaste, severe, very well done like a little stage setting of a twelfth century play, of course, with modern improvements. I utterly failed to imagine anyone entering it otherwise than in costume. And yet this hard-headed Chicago businessman elected to buy Gothic. That was his cultural expedient. Really, are we too, in Chicago, plundering the old world of all its finery and dressing ourselves up in it regardless as a kind of masquerade. I can see it as great fun (very expensive fun), but how can it be seen as culture when the essence of all true culture is a *development* of self-expression.

No, not *culture*. It is a cheap *substitute* for culture hired and paid for by the hour. Accumulation, not realization. Purchase, not production.

A despair.

Nevertheless, set against this fashionable folly with its fatuous inelegance there is something vital, indigenous to Chicago, the seeds of a genuine culture, the great hope of America quietly working here eventually to come up through this imposition, to show it for what it is and refute it.

Even our pretended culture is not yet vicious. It is thoughtless always; boorish, often; sometimes low; always wasteful; usually absurd; but Chicago takes this sham culture as "the thing" with no real thought about it at all nor any real taste for it. Therefore, it is potential vulgarity when not inane. Only when we do accept it with "that little knowledge which is a dangerous thing" does it become hopeless.

The big impulse of great unspoiled power has its oversoul in Chicago in significant movements in architecture, music, literature, the theater, education, and recreation; culture that means a true new life worthy of a great new Nation. These movements and the men who made them are at home in Chicago. And they ought not to be wasted.

Time was when, if Chicago had a boy who shied at business, seemed good-for-nothing, therefore, she would send him down to the Art Institute to have an "artist" made of him. She thought maybe *that* was what was the matter with him. Even now it is a popular superstition that aesthetic people have long, slim hands, a graceful habit in beatitudes, jar easily from them, and shudder slightly when jarred.

Perhaps the aesthetic "consumer" is like that.

The aesthetic "producer" certainly is not.

Homer, Michelangelo, Bramante, Rodin, Carlyle, Goethe, Shelley, William Blake, and Beethoven were more like the ideal of the creative artist reared by Romain Rolland in Jean-Christophe.

The artist's needs are as other men's, intensified. He is broad, strong, resourceful, typified by a love of life that survives great trials and comes through with a song in his heart, resilient, however his spirit be outraged or his body broken.

Zarathustra's prayer is his, "This do I ask of Thee, O Lord; speak and make me to know the truth."

It is where life is fundamental and free that men develop the vision needed to reveal the human soul in the blossoms it puts forth; blossoms we choose to call "works of art," and we sometimes neglect to call the worker artist, but subsequent generations never do. In a great workshop like Chicago this creative power germinates, even though the brutality and selfish preoccupation of the place drive it elsewhere for bread.

Men of this type have loved Chicago, have worked for her, and believed in her. The hardest thing they have to bear is her shame. These men could live and work here when to live and work in New York would stifle their genius and fill their purse. As a New York preacher put it, "New York is a good place in which to sell fish, but there are no trout in her streams." The art of the talented men who have gone to New York has gradually succumbed to the fashionable squalor and ceaseless gyration of the place, as their bodies might to a mortal sickness. New York still believes that art should be imported; brought over in ships; and is a quite contented market place.

So while New York has reproduced much and produced nothing, Chicago's achievements in architecture have gained world-wide recognition as a distinctively American architecture.

Louis Sullivan gave America the skyscraper as an organic modern work of art. While America's architects were stumbling at its height, piling one thing on top of another, foolishly denying it, Louis Sullivan seized its height as its characteristic feature and made it sing; a new thing under the sun!

One of the world's greatest architects, he gave us again the ideal of a great architecture that informed all the great architectures of the world.

Chicago's Auditorium, an early work of his, together with his great-souled executive partner. Dankmar Adler, is one of the city's first civic triumphs famous throughout the world as an architect's masterpiece. Some of its delicate golden traceries have been obliterated and the quiet balance of the big beautiful room destroyed by a petticoat of red paint below its waist line, applied by a Chicago society amateur. Perhaps Chicago is the only city in the world that would permit an affront of the kind to one of its greatest men to pass unrebuked. It is because this "culture" we have on top is necessarily pseudo Venetian or pseudo something; it can be nothing else. But the Auditorium still stands, a noble achievement.

Men who give great impulse to the city's character; men who are the life of its ideas, are never official or a part of its social machinery.

In John Root, too, Chicago had a man of genius. He outlined the Columbian Fair that astonished and delighted the world. Daniel Burnham, his partner, seized it in his powerful executive grasp and it was realized. The same grasp has left the city a plan for a greater Chicago, essentially good. It will be realized, too, but in its execution, entrusted as it is to Beaux-Arts graduates, it will finally resemble anything but an individual expression of the great Chicago smokestack that is more truly a work of art than the gray ghosts of a dubious past now haunting the lake-front part at the foot of Monroe Street.

Looking north you may see them, smokestacks and pylons together. It is the pretentious pylons that suffer by contrast.

In domestic architecture we have what some are calling the "new school of the Middle West." This great Chicago prairie has a quiet beauty all its own. But these dwellings referred to recognize circumstance and fact with quiet masses, fashioned in new spirit with sure, sweeping lines. They are rational, individual, and organic. The world outside America, France, Germany, Austria, England, Holland, and Japan, have found these buildings beautiful.

Chicago industrial buildings, too, have set a new standard of excellence for the whole world. Many of them are works of art, perhaps, because that is where we really live.

The Queen of Holland's Architect, Berlage, said, after coming here in quest of American culture, that the two things that impressed him most were Niagara Falls and the Larkin Building.

All this is a Chicago contribution to an art academically declared to be moribund!

In Jens Jensen, the landscape architect, Chicago has a native nature poet who has made the West Park system a delight to the country. He is a true interpreter of the peculiar charm of our prairie landscape. Jens Jensen should be interpreter in chief for Chicago for our wonderful park system; a system that together with our small playgrounds is one of the finest civic-urban features of the world; a recreation ground beyond compare. No small-hearted city, no city except Chicago could have established it or would have made the sacrifices necessary to maintain it. It is not least among the things to this city's everlasting credit.

After these fundamental aspects of the city's individual growth comes music.

Chicago has established good music in its midst. Theodore Thomas stayed here and found support. Chicago built a permanent home for his orchestra; a home that broke Theodore Thomas' heart because it was unfit for its purpose. The only place in it where music can be heard to advantage is just beneath the ceiling. But Chicago is not to blame for that. This love of music was an early sign that Chicago had a soul. Now a music-loving Chicago public understands and insists upon good music. Soon we will require chamber music, and quartettes like the Kneisels and Flonzaleys will belong to us. We have a composer or two attracting the attention of the music-loving world, less exotic than most, John Carpenter and Felix Borowsky. Harriet Monroe founded here the only American magazine of poetry, and it is a well-deserved success with its Vachel Lindsay, Carl Sandburg, and a host of young writers whose mark is made on the literary life of their country.

Margaret Anderson's *Little Review* made its passionate young bow here in the cause of literary freedom. It has fled to New York, no place for a freedom-loving thing in the arts; it will return or die.

Chicago, too, is the "big town" of those distinctively American forces in letters. Booth Tarkington, John McCutcheon, and George Ade, lively interpreters of the American thing; Booth Tarkington's work is a delight.

The literary list is, of course, a long one and likely to make my catalog tedious, but Chicago is the home of Gene Field, Hamlin Garland, Will Moody, Ernest Poole, Henry Webster, Robert Merrick, the Browns of *The Dial,* I. E. Friedman, Chatfield-Taylor, our own B.L.T., Ring Lardner, and Jack Lait. And there is Edgar Lee Masters and Thorstein Veblen with his theory of the leisure class, George Foster and Clarence Darrow, all a very moving and characteristic world in itself. Literature is the ubiquitous art of this age. Everybody writes something. Everywhere literature flourishes like the dragon's teeth sown ages ago. They must have been "type." Even the newspaper editorial is becoming a factor in modern life, thanks to the initiative (giving the devil his due) of the publisher, William Randolph Hearst.

We can escape literature nowhere and its entire fabric is drenched with sex. Newspapers recklessly smear sex everywhere. Every magazine everywhere has its nauseating ritual of the "girl" cover. The "he-and-she" novel is omnipresent, and the play is not more than a play of sex, while the concoctions for the tired businessman grow faster and more furious year by year. We are emerging from the darkness, in which sex's fundamental characteristics have been kept, to exposure gratuitous to say the least.

The very extravagance in all this is the hopeful sign of impending reaction.

Chicago's sky pilots rank with any, anywhere. David Swing, Jenkin Lloyd Jones, Bishop Cheney, Rabbi Hirsch, and Doctor Gunsaulus.

Jane Addams is a Chicago institution all by herself of world-wide fame and influence. What a fine possession she has been for Chicago.

In education John Dewey and Francis Parker are to our credit.

The "Little Theater," growing out of the new theater movement and Donald Robertson, took root here first in Maurice Brown's unostentatious "Little Theater" in the Fine Arts Building. It is a "movement" now and scattered over the country with headquarters in New York. New York doesn't believe anything really is until she has seized it and it "arrives" in New York. That is the way she seems to have of originating things. But she frankly prefers to import European models. They are more in keeping.

We have painters and sculptors, too—too many of them. Winners of salon prizes; men and women of undoubted talent like Lawton Parker, Jerome Blum, Pauline Palmer, William Henderson, Zukalsky, McNeil, and Lorado Taft.

But unfortunately we have less than nothing for them to paint or carve except the likenesses of well-to-do society folk. The fundamental condition of the painter's and sculptor's existence has been neglected by the very institution that devoted itself to forwarding them. But they seem to go right on trying to make an art of painting and sculpture for its own sake, and the easel picture has become our favorite vice comparable to pie, porches, and ice water.

Existing, really, for the painter and sculptor we have the Art Institute of Chicago, the best located, largest, and most successful in point of attendance of any institution of art in America. Happily, Chicago people are beginning to love it. Like the cathedral of the Middle Ages it is the one place in the city that should never be closed to the people at any time, even if it took three shifts to keep it open. A "gift" that would make that possible would have real democratic style and would need no bronze tablet to impress it upon the gratitude of the people or the character of our future.

The Arts Club of Chicago has extended the work of the Art Institute by profiting by "institute" mistakes. The Arts Club may prove valuable to Chicago.

One of the most valuable assets of "the Institute," Emma Church, broke away from it some time ago and has established and maintained a school of her own, doing work that has won significant recognition. Until recently the Art Institute had a monopoly of the professed "artistic" side of our culture.

For 25 years past the destiny of this important organ of our coming culture has been in the hand of a small group of public-spirited men who have loved works of art with more heat than light, and have collected much and given it all to Chicago. These men together with Lorado Taft, Ralph Clarkson, and Charles Francis Browne (sculptor and painters) have served the Art Institute of Chicago faithfully and well. Is it ungrateful to say that they, collectors, sculptor, and painters, are all that is the matter with it now?

The Art Institute has the greatest opportunity to aid and comfort the real culture that is getting after Chicago and to correct and mold or mitigate the horror of the culture she got after, were the Institute free. At least free to reject what passes for conservative when it is only stupid, or passes for right-mindedness when it is only prejudice. Free, that is, to get down beneath traditions of sculpture and painting to the real fundamentals of *culture*. It probably will become more free and vital. But academic centers have never been the life of art in any creative individual, city, or a nation. Original impulses live outside, hostile to established orders. Institutions are in their very nature hostile to these impulses. That hostility is the only way they have of remaining "institutions."

Academic recognition of good work is safe only when it may honor the *institution,* not the individual who has won what they covet and consent to honor themselves by accepting.

Centers like the Art Institute of Chicago should be reservoirs, conserving the sap of these "hostile" activities, making it available to young, inquiring or rebellious minds.

Never should these forces be so edited and emasculated as to be useless to the future.

Abuse of *institutional* privileges in a democracy must cease or we will always take the name for the thing. This is especially true in art. If democracy means anything at all in a fine art sense it means easier, surer recognition of the qualities of the individual; greater respect for the *nature* of individuality: not the usual premium put upon mediocrity in the interest of so-called public safety just because there are pretenders and shame in the world. Every noble forward movement will have its sordid, soiled fringe. It is better for democracy that any number of talents be given opportunity to prove unworthy than that one possible genius be denied.

Democracy can live by genius only. Its very soul is individuality.

An art institute should be no editor of genius in the spirit of connoisseur or collector. It should be an opportunity, a staff in the hand, a cloak for genius in the bitter wind that assails genius and criminal alike.

Were you to see the exhibition of the work of pupils covering the period of the life of this institution given here last month you would find painting worthy high praise. Sculpture, much of it, but only a little worthy a second look.

In architecture and allied arts and crafts, nothing. Oh! so much less than nothing!

This as culture is like an overhanging cornice, top side down upon the ground where the foundation ought to be. A wasteful pitiful perversion!

A sense of the altogether, that is, the eternal fitness of each to each and the each in all to the all in all, is the fundamental essential to culture, in individuals, citizens, or a country. And the crying need of this time and this place. The "altogether" in this sense always has been as it will always be more important than thrilling paintings or marble statues but without in the least lessening their desirability. They will take their places as the heightened expressions, perhaps, of its qualities, after these qualities have been established. Connoisseurs, critics, collectors increase, yet commonplace elegance is here, there and everywhere.

Harmonious elegance is desperately rare.

Fashion exists for commercial purposes only.

The fashionable thing is valueless to culture.

In art, democracy means that some thought of your own, some feeling you have about the thing yourself, should enter into everything you have or do, so that everything you have may be your own and everything you do be sincerely yourself. Democracy in this true sense is really the highest form of aristocracy the world has ever known. The aristocracy of qualities, not of birth or circumstances. Now, this should be as true of the art institute as it is of art. Slaves of fashion, human sheep, are the curse of this ideal; relics of an aristocracy that was an imposition and now is passing in anguish.

But civilization with us is simmering down to a case of too much "Marshall Field" to be culture. One is tempted to remark upon the amount of "Marshall Field" each fashionable woman carries about upon her person or drags after her by the hand, if she has children. It is alone an occupation; a feverish, uphappy, competitive quest; a blight; an undemocratic folly.

One beautiful dress, really individual and becoming, one hat that suits the face and both together sympathetic to the wearer, are worth all the fashionable changes in the shops; even if one had to wear just that hat and just that dress for life because they cost so much. Of course such things would cost more in time and study on your part and on the part of the artists who will be employed then and who will deserve to be well paid.

The same thing applies to your house and your furnishings and to your works of art.

If only we could get the significant outlines of democracy fixed within our vision we would have arrived, at least, at the beginning.

This is the spirit that must characterize Chicago.

Out of it, in time, will come something better worth living for than the senseless jam of ill-considered things that clutter the persons, the homes, and the thought of our Chicago women, rob their men of anything worthwhile to show for their ceaseless grinding efforts and their children of their finest hope for the future.

Nevertheless, Chicago is the only great city that is America-conscious, that has a sense of destiny; American. The case for American originality is at stake here. Chicago must find culture from *within* or all America is reduced to a colony of Europe; we of Chicago are her only hope.

When I think of the vast growth that is Chicago, realize that it all happened within the past 50 years, it seems one of the marvels of history that it is no worse than it is.

But we can now see what may easily be, if instead of the expedients of the businessmen drugged by commercialism we would cling to the practical and to principle for a time.

Chicago would establish then the great hope; democracy in its great fine art sense.

Chicago's location is little more than an accident.

It was virtually born in a swamp.

It has been the chief butcher shop of the world.

No wonder Chicago bought and borrowed her culture ready-made, and wears it as a cook wears her "picture hat," very much on one side, or well down over her eyes, stuck it on anyhow as best she can. She had to have the picture hat, along with the best of them, and have it quick. Any thinking about it had to be done afterward. If only Chicago would only devote herself to thinking about it now and would discard the damned thing.

Not so much mischief has yet been done as has already been done to Tokio by borrowed garments, exotic "culture." Tokio is the most awful of modern instances, although within 50 years New York's cultured expression, her "picture hat," will seem as odious and old-fashioned as General Grant Gothic does now. It will seem as enlightened as the brownstone fronts on Dearborn Avenue, as beautiful as the sacred old Pullman Building, our first sky-scraper. The same thing as this in principle is what New York has done. It is better done, that is all, and so, more dangerous.

The practices behind even our best efforts are foreign. They belong to "the Renaissance"; the setting sun of art all Europe mistook for dawn. The more enlightened artists of Europe know it. But we proceed with our expedient renascence of the Renaissance.

This supposed pretended democracy of ours is being rapidly buried beneath a rubbish heap, best and worst of all the world torn from its moorings, dumped in upon us by precept, by education, by "business is business" and by capricious, irresponsible wealth.

Mongrel taste with its derelict sentimentality is flinging it all into this welter of dangerous ambitions whence it emerges fit only for the morgue, a mangled style.

This soulless thing, the Renaissance, has had the upper hand of art, has betrayed the artist; and he in turn has betrayed his people long enough. Let us have done with it forever.

Protected by academic authority is this cowardly imitation of an imitation in the hands of men themselves no less an imitation, yet who, somehow, are accepted as artists on their own or each other's say-so. They would strangle the hope of integral beauty in a growing people, in a great Nation, in its infancy; yes, and in Chicago in its cradle. Because, for commercial and society reasons, we have had to have the semblance of culture for our great sudden city, put up quick, like a painted signboard above a shop; it has all been too easy for such men as advised Howard Shaw to go back and build the Choragic Monument to Lysicrates for the Illinois politician's widow; men who would sell us anything we would take, sell our birthright or mortgage our future to the past beyond redemption, barter it for a mess of pottage or for public recognition for an hour.

Our so-called culture, today, is a costly imposition upon our life in Chicago. No skill can make it right. Only revolt can save the city for culture that is for all time and develop the integrity of means to ends that is the fountain of youth in art.

A great artist looking from the windows of this building toward those gray ghosts, the pylons haunting the lake front opposite Monroe Street was asked by a friend who saw him thus regarding them, what he thought about them. He said, "If that is what the American people stand for now, from this time dates the downfall of the republic."

Some symbol, some proof of real culture, is needed of the city's genius in one preeminent self-expression. One thing Chicago must do as a symbol of her life: she must take her great heritage, the lake front, and shape it to her own liking. She must do something with it the like of which the world has not yet seen and that belongs in spirit to her.

The independence of Chicago, her integrity, her destiny as the capital of the American spirit is at stake.

The life of the soul of Chicago depends upon the rescue of this treasure of our people from fashionable degradation.

The artist is of his people and his time, and for them, whether accepted by them or not. He is uncoverer; discoverer of truth in new guise.

The creative artist is engaged in unwrapping the winding sheet that holds the world in bondage. He alone can set the world free.

He is no damnable excrescence on the face of things. He is never the parasite nor the traitor.

But, he must state his inspiration in terms of the character and need of his own time, of his own people; and his work is no less universal on that account.

Egyptian art was stated in terms of Egypt.

Just as a human being has his race stamped upon his features, great art will have the conditions of its existence indelibly fixed in its expression or as one of the fundamental laws of its very being. The art in a thing is the *understanding* in it, the *life* in it, the *love* in it. There is no substitute for art in this business of culture. Culture comes through being, not buying. Culture has never been bought. In all the life of all the ages opulence has eventually destroyed it. Culture is not something that you "take on" like polish. It is "the nature of the thing" developed to its highest qualities of usefulness and beauty.

Chicago has *everything* but culture!

1923: Experimenting with Human Lives

THE FINE ARTS SOCIETY, HOLLYWOOD, CALIF.

This little known pamphlet did more than state the case for non-rigid construction in earthquake areas: it opened the argument against centralization and the skyscraper, and paved the way for the creation of Broadacre City. Distributed principally in California, its plea for a revision of building practice did little to increase the author's popularity.

Tremblor and Skyscraper. The rim of the Pacific basin is no place to experiment with human lives in the interest of an architectural expedient. Los Angeles, San Francisco, Tokio, all on the rim of this great basin, are infested by that expedient. That expedient is the tall steel frame building we call the skyscraper, and it has no better scientific, aesthetic or moral basis for existence as a bid for human sacrifice than the greed of the speculative landlord, the unworthy ambition of commercialized architects, or false civic pride that encourages and protects both. This great basin of the Pacific is overloaded—overloaded with gigantic waters. Occasionally, as faults and fissures occur in its floor owing to the strains of this overload, water rushes down with enormous pressure to internal fires—creating steam and gases of incalculable power, seeking escape through other internal crevices leading to the upper air and convulse and alter the conformation of the earth-crust in doing so. If this, as a theory of seismic convulsion, is too simple to be scientific, there are many more complex to choose from—but the fact remains that the red line of seismic convulsion clings to the rim of the basin. The region ought to be considered in the light of its record.

Tokio and Yokohama again raise the question, "Why the skyscraper?"—a question from time to time successfully evaded by landlord and commercialized architect—and by false civic pride.

Chicago and New York, owing to naturally congested areas, had a real problem to meet and met it—perhaps wisely at that time—by the invention of the skyscraper. If confined to similar areas and circumstances it might be justified.

But with changed conditions the skyscraper, never more than a commercial expedient, is become a threat, a menace to the welfare of human beings. It is dangerous to construct, dangerous to maintain, dangerous to operate, and inevitably, as buildings ought to live, short-lived, destined to end finally in horrible disaster, even if not attacked from beneath. In any case the skyscraper is become an immoral expedient, one that demoralizes its neighbors, when it does not rob them, compelling them to compete in kind or perish.

No adjustment of the equities it destroys has yet been made. There is now no escape from it and no redress.

Its whole case is economic—but economic only as a pet temporary expedient of American get-rich-quick enterprise. Soon or late all steel framing will perish even where conditions are most favorable to its existence.

In Tokio conditions were naturally unfavorable. All steel perishes there with fearful rapidity owing to extraordinary humidity and a salt-sea atmosphere, machinery under Tokio sheds becoming useless from rust within the year. Steel pipe in Tokio buildings goes out of commission in from five to fifteen years.

In the light of advices now coming from Japan, all steel frame buildings were death-traps to some serious degree, their "architecture" shaken from the skeletons in the upper stories and in some cases, even of the lower stories, shattered and fell in the street. The Nagai building collapsed completely, burying hundreds in its ruin. The Kaijo building likewise.

In seismic disturbance, the perpetual wrenching or jolting of the semi-rigid frame weakens, cracks or breaks off its concrete shell, exposing the steel to flames which always accompany heavy tremblors, and steel, exposed to flame, soon bends its riveted knees and comes to the ground. Even when the skeletons themselves stand they are practically useless for rebuilding. What fool-hardy courage to reclothe inappropriate, hazardous skeletons that human souls may come again in droves to inhabit them just because the day of reckoning is out of sight, though surely lurking ahead or perhaps just around the corner. Shocks come suddenly. Elevators jamb when frames are twisted. It is impossible to empty the buildings quickly. Fright and panic take their toll though the building may stand.

The compensations offered by the skyscraper are all to the realty owners and to the sort of pride typified by the canyons of lower New York. The congestion induced by the exaggerated repetition of floor area creates great real estate values but tends eventually to destroy those values as may now be seen in Los Angeles. In that city this congestion turns to the disadvantage of the city proper by raising various contiguous business centers at the very gates of the city itself, creating a competitive confusion having some benefits but far greater waste.

In Chicago and New York the tax upon the service of the streets demanded by the multiplication of skyscrapers, is so great in congestion and cost, that it is now seriously proposed to assess the land value in multiples for each six stories imposed upon the land and tax it accordingly. This is proposed in justice to the city which pays the cost of the service, and in justice to the adjoining owners of lower buildings who are deprived of the use of the streets. Mrs. Hetty Green foresaw this and leased her land subject to taxes to be paid by the tenants. She refused to build skyscrapers.

Earthquake-proof Construction. Tenuous flexibility is the chance for life of any sound construction in an earthquake: flexibility of foundation, flexibility of superstructure secured by continuous, lateral, binding integuments from side to side in the floor planes of the structure, and balancing of all loads well over vertical supporting members by means of the cantilever.

Cobbett's "Wen." Our cities grow more and more a concession to the herd instinct and less and less places for the development and emphasis of the quality of individuality, and they become more and more unfit places for human beings, who value that quality of individuality as the most precious asset of human kind, as the supreme entertainment of life. Who sleeps, who lives in New York and Chicago's canyons if he can get away?

1925: In the Cause of Architecture

Wright frequently wrote under this title as a catch-all for his ideas on architecture. Many of these essays are roughly drafted or incomplete. He considered certain series of these essays—"In the Nature of Materials," for example—as logical groupings of related matter.

Internal Logic. There is a clearly defined style growing out of conditions. One may not like it, but, if one has studied architecture as an *art,* not merely accepted it as a recipe for cooking, then, I say, the harmonious organic nature of the whole will thrill and please and edify.

1927: A Plan for the Erection of a Modern Building

Bankers and Brokers. It needs no argument to convince anyone that new and constructive ideas in art and life cannot take place by appealing to the banker or broker. The banker is a banker because he hangs to the old order and is doomed to hang with it.

Wind and Water. In the field of architecture the old system of building was wasteful and none too useful. The old system by which the building was financed was a makeshift and so wasteful that the wind and water in most "financed" buildings has left the investors with no buildings and the bankers do not know what to do with the buildings on their hands by way of foreclosure.

1927: The Pictures We Make

"The American Way." Nationality is a craze with us. But why this term "America" became representative as the name of these United States at home and abroad is past recall. Samuel Butler fitted us with a good name. He called us Usonians, and our Nation of combined States, Usonia. Why not use the name?

It expresses well our character and is a noble word. That I presume is why no one uses it. It is truly significant. Therefore objectionable if not painful.

Significances. I am an artist interested in significances only where they may be useful expressions of this life as buildings, costumes, the theater, decoration, the art and craft of the age, those "things," therefore, that are the use and proof of our culture in our age.

Bureaucracy. This officialism of officers in millions of offices that officiate as the polyglot human mass moves and has its being. It perhaps takes a good one-fifth of society to keep the other four-fifths of society in order. "Society" is approximately one-fifth policeman it appears.

The petty official, ubiquitous in a democracy becomes the skeleton of the body politic, a self-conscious class apart. I have often wondered what would happen were the policeman to vanish and all officials take a long holiday.

The Archeological Test. Unless it is made natively fit, not again artificially artificial, what we call "culture" is going toward the complexity of dark and death, not toward the simplicity of light and life. The buttons and stuffs and dictums and wheels and things will eventually smother the essential life they were made to serve, and our civilization in turn will find its way to a scrap heap into which no subsequent race will paw for proofs of our quality with much success.

3000 A.D. Suppose in 10 centuries historians or antiquarians, if they happen to survive, seek significance of what *we* were in the veins of us, in the veins that remained, what would they find? That we were a jackdaw people with a monkey psychology given ever to the vice of devices, looking to devices for salvation.

Just the same, they *would* find bits of every civilization that ever had a place in the sun in all sorts of irrelevant places. They would find traces of Greek sarcophagi for banking houses, twelfth-century cathedrals for meeting houses; relics of dwellings in 57 varieties, none genuine in character and all mixed. They would find the toilet appurtenances of former ages parlor ornaments in ours. They would find plumbing, wiring, and a wilderness of wheels and complex devices of curious ingenuity. They might get traces of devices that enabled men to take to the air like birds or take to the water as fishes or both together, and they could get relics of our competent schemes of transportation, or remarkable voice transmission. But I think most characteristic of all would be our plumbing, our cast iron baths, water closets and washbowls, white tiles and piping. Next would be the vast confusion of riveted steel work in various states of disintegration where it was imbedded in concrete. Where it was not, all would be gone except here and there where whole machines might be entombed and so preserved to arouse speculation and curiosity. Or amusement, as they might be taken as relics of faith in devices, a faith that failed.

Certain fragments of stone buildings would remain to puzzle the savant, for they would be Greek or Roman or Medieval, Gothic or Egyptian, or Byzantine, or a psuedo Renaissance that was something that never told anyone anything and could tell them nothing. Only our industrial buildings could tell them anything about us at all. And but few of them would survive that long. Only those where steel was buried in concrete. The glass would be found but the frames would be gone. They would have no skyscraper to gage us. Not one would be there.

How and where, then, would our great progressive modern democratization take its place in the procession of those past civilizations that rose and fell in their appointed times and places? What is the nature of our contribution to the life and wisdom or the beauty of the ages? Going forward to look back upon it, what would we see were this tentative attempt to be suddenly interrupted and finished as it stands.

The New Within the Old: In this fusing of races to produce another race and a more human cause, a more *plastic* sense of life, a more liberal expression of manhood and womanhood, a common denominator will be found and made significant above the confusion, demoralization, and uproar of change. The new significances to be established from that will be plastic instead of the structuralities and imprisoning abstractions that were drastic and dying now because they were so drastic.

There is new freedom growing in all this cruel waste. A freedom already impatient of pseudo-classic falsifying, that will sweep our borrowed finery and the pictures we make in it to the museums.

Architecture as Entertainment. We could not live crowded into great cities unless we were "entertained." What entertains us is therefore invariably successful. So far as what you have, or what you are, entertains us, makes easy our lot, adds to its "picturesqueness," we want it.

This great city is the great market; the great place in which to sell anything, especially a place in which to sell yourself.

1928-1935: The International Style

1928: The Use of Metal Plates in the Art of Building

This unpublished paper contained ideas old and new. While illustrating one of the clearest examples of the architect utilizing the machine, Wright had dealt with the same idea early in the century, utilized it in the plans for St. Mark's Tower, a project contemporary with this essay, and in 1940 drew plans for an enormous apartment hotel project embracing the same building system.

How Ideas Grow. Before all I wanted to create a standardization as a basis for the vital power of buildings, as a piece of genuine architecture, but likewise be in a position to arrive at a lively modern architecture with the whole as an expression of a valuable principle which found through this its realization.

I began with my studies in the winter 1921-23 at Los Angeles after having carried them in my mind in their essence during many years. I had the good fortune to consult my master, Louis H. Sullivan, about it shortly before his death. With deep thanks and proudly I remember his words: "I always believed that it would happen. I see in your manner of building the realization of a democratical architecture. Now I know what I have been talking about all these years. I could never have done it myself, but I believe that you would not have done it without me." I confess that I should certainly not have arrived at this without him and his help. This essay is a dedication to him.

A Metal Architecture. The engine shows its best sides in rolling, cutting, coining, stamping, and folding everything it gets hold of. The movements are rather narrowly limited if they are not combined movements as with the Corliss or the linotype.

The easiest movements of all are those of rotation, of pressing or hammering, "lever and shifter" work together with one or with both of this kind of movements. In all these movements we have to reckon, to a great extent, with "rough powers" for which many possibilities of combining or dividing are given until we get something of equal regard as a working brain; in short, the artificial socager. If the human mind associates with these primitive powers the consequences may be terrifying. The will of mankind, deprived of soul, can drive these powers up to the limit of human resistance, even until the extermination of all mankind.

We all know that business has no grandeur of mind! Commercial interests left to themselves would soon doom themselves in the execution of their social existence. They would cease to reproduce because the essential elements of commerce are those of the machine;

they lack the animating "divine spark." The excess of profits which accumulates is lazy and idle, impotent. The machine now represents in the material body of our modern world the same excess: this "profit" is equally averse to labor. Idle and impotent.

The question that always turns up is the one: what does the expounder of life, the architect, do with it? And it may be put forward here again. Indeed, there is a possibility in metal plates to give birth to things which the architects disdain, notwithstanding the fact that they have to use them on account of their cheapness. They use plates as a material of the second class. In the building one has, everywhere, cornices, gutters, draining pipes and covers from lead, zinc, tin, iron, and copper, and also for imitating a great many other and various materials. However, where do we employ plates in their own character for our own benefit? Sometimes, but why not always? It is, indeed, the only really good material which the machine has presented to the industry of house building. Apart from this, we do manufacture a large number of useful things from the same metallic stuff; kitchen utensils, furniture, motor and railway cars, and through its use as a roof cover it keeps actually a great deal of Americans from getting wet in their dwellings.

In the building line these products of the metal-producing industry have been used so far in a most offending manner; in buildings where the architect either never appeared or was not required. Metallic plates are thus used as makeshift by his "highness" the American contractor. Roofs are obviously the problem in building which can be resolved in quite a natural way through the use of sheet metal plates which are easily brought in any required size and form. It is easy to mend or solder plates and thus obtain light yet decorative metallic covers.

The machines, working sheet metal plates, fold, twist, and cut and stamp metals just in the same way as an intelligent child would do with sheets of paper. The finished product can be painted, enameled or galvanized. Copper is, however, the only metal which has through its beauty and durability found a worthy way into the realm of architecture. The green color of the copper in connection with stone or tiles or even wood is always beautiful. Besides this copper shows more resistance than any other material which the architect uses. Japanese sword sheaths furnish proof of how splendidly metals can be used and wrought to advantage by a master hand. Their metallic contrasts and harmonies are inexhaustible. A collection of those wonderful "trifles" of Japanese art and handicraft should constitute the *vade mecum* of each junior or the master himself in working metals. Chinese and Japanese seem to have given a great deal of their subtle genius to such interworking of metals.

They were as famous for skill in making sharp blade edges as through their invention of various textures for iron for decorative purposes.

Valuable metals form a category in themselves. For us, however, the skillful use of lower class metals is of the greatest importance because we are masters in the production of metals, depending upon them in our industries, although we have not been able so far to develop its real beauties in our works. The time is ripe for a building made entirely from copper sheet metal.

1928: In the Cause of Architecture: The Logic of the Plan

FROM THE *Architectural Record,* JANUARY, 1928.

This is the first essay of a series commissioned by the Architectural Record *at a time when Wright's fame was in eclipse and his personal fortunes were at their lowest ebb. The resulting essays may be roughly compared in their influence to Louis Sullivan's* Kindergarten Chats. *Taken as a whole they form a primer of the essential points in Wright's architectural philosophy, especially in relation to the plan and the use of materials. Many of the essays were reprinted in German, Italian and other European publications.*

Architect and Plan. As to the logic of the plan it is easy to see there can be none except as the result of integrated scale; materials and building method clearly articulate. But with all that logically set, all the more, there is the important human equation at work in every move that is made. The architect weaves into every part, as each step is taken, his sense of the whole. He articulates, emphasizes, and finally emerges triumphant with what the man loves.

Terminals. Terminal masses are most important as to form. Nature will show this to you in her own fabrications. Take good care of the terminals and the rest will take care of itself.

Where Is the Plan? In the steel and glass buildings I have designed, there are no walls, only wall screens. The method of the cantilever in concrete and steel yields best to suspended screens or shells in place of outer walls, all may be shop fabricated. The spider web is a good inspiration for steel construction. A slender mechanized fabric for all walls and partitions enters here to give the form and style that is architecture.

Mono-Material Building. The more simple the materials used, the more the building tends toward a mono-material building, the more nearly will "perfect style" reward an organic plan and ease of execution economize results. Not only the more logical will the whole become, but all will emerge with the countenance of simplicity.

Scale and St. Peter's. St. Peter's is invariably disappointing as a great building for not until the eye deliberately catches a human figure for purposes of comparison with the building does one realize that the building is vast. Michelangelo made the architectural details huge likewise and the sense of grandeur the whole might have had, were the great masses qualified by details that were kept to human scale, is lost in this exaggeration of detail, in this degradation of the human figure. A strange error for a great sculptor to have made.

How to Plan. The original plan not as an idea but as a piece of paper may be thrown away as the work proceeds. Probably most of those for the most wonderful buildings in the world were because the concept grows and matures during realization, if the master mind is continually with the work in order that the original plan may be fulfilled.

But to throw these paper plans away is luxury of creation ill afforded by the organizations of our modern method. Even to change them has ruined owners and architects and enriched numberless contractors. Therefore, more carefully than ever, conceive the buildings in imagination, not first on paper but in the mind, thoroughly, before touching paper. Let the building, living in imagination, develop gradually, taking more and more definite form before committing it to the drafting board. When the thing sufficiently lives for you then start to plan it with instruments, not before. To draw during the conception or "sketch," as we say, experimenting with practical adjustments to scale, is well enough if the concept is clear enough to be firmly held meantime. But it is best always to thus cultivate the imagination from within. Construct and complete the building so far as you can before going to work on it with tee square and triangle. Working with triangle and tee square should be only to modify or extend or intensify or test the conception; to finally correlate the parts in detail.

If original concept is lost as the drawing proceeds, throw away all and begin afresh. To throw away a concept *entirely* to make way for a fresh one, that is a faculty of the mind not easily cultivated. Few architects have that capacity. It is perhaps a gift, but may be attained by practice. What I am trying to express is the fact that the plan is the gist of all truly creative matter and must gradually mature as such.

Therefore, the building is wooed and won or lost before anything more tangible than the plan begins.

Beauty in Plan. There is more beauty in a fine ground plan itself than in almost any of its ultimate consequences.

1928: In the Cause of Architecture: What Style Means to the Architect

FROM THE *Architectural Record,* FEBRUARY, 1928.

Style. Style is a consequence of character.

Character. Character is one of our strong words. It is loosely applied to any manifestation of force. Properly, it is used to signify "individual significance."

To be insignificant is to have no "character." Observe that we may use the word "character" for "style" and "style" for "character" with no great inconsistency. The words are not interchangeable, but are applicable to either case. Character is the result of some inward force taking consistent outward form, taking shape consistent with its nature.

From the Inside Out. To make clear to the young architect this "sense of the within" as interior initiative which may now be his it is necessary to show him that any comprehension on his part of the opportunity that is to his hand lies in what may rise from his ground plan.

This interior viewpoint once grasped his own nature will gather force from the idea, and with experience become truly potent as a creative force in our modern life concerns.

What significance as form? This should be the question through which everything in the way of form be sifted in imagination before it is accepted or rejected in his work.

Expression. The building is no longer a block of building material dealt with artistically from the outside, a form of sculpture. The room within, the space to be lived in, is the great fact about the building; this *room* to be expressed in the exterior as *space enclosed.* This sense of the *room* within strongly held as the great *motif* for all architectural enclosure, is the advanced thought of the era in architecture. It is now searching for exterior expression as integral architecture.

The Cornice. The cornice, one of the salient features of classic architecture, is a constructed thing for its own sake. The cornice became fixed in our practice, as it had been fixed in Graeco-Roman life, as the characteristic architectural expression of "culture." The cornice became a gesture (sometimes a fine gesture) but it always was an empty one. What original significance the cornice had was soon lost. It had come down to the Greeks by way of the eaves of a projecting and visible roof. It stayed as "art," that is to say for the look of the thing, centuries after its use and purpose had entirely gone. The cornice was a more or less graceful "lie" authorized as a "thing of beauty"; it became the last word of authority in the language of approved form. This, of course, entirely regardless of *interior* significance.

So the cornice hangs today in the eye of the sun, as dubious an excrescence as ever made shift. It was, in itself, the last word for "exterior" or "classic" architecture. In all but monuments it has disappeared.

The Styles. "Styles" are standardization carried to the logical grave of style in the process we call civilization.

Let no one so unlucky be the cause of a style, or ever increase the number of the peddlers of a style.

Here is a great hope that the era of the great styles is past.

The Soiled Fringe. There is a soiled fringe hanging to every manful effort to realize anything good in this world, even a square meal. But is it so greatly important in this matter of getting the beautiful born or even kept alive?

Standardization—a Tool. Standardization is a form of dying of which to beware. It is something to be watched, for overnight with over-repetition it may "set" the form past redemption and the creative matter be found dead.

Standardization is a mere, but indispensable, tool; a tool to be used only to a certain extent in all other than purely technical or commercial matters or mere matters of method. Standardization is only a means to an end.

Used to the extent that it leaves the spirit free to destroy this static element in the will, on suspicion maybe, used to the extent only that it does not become a style, or inflexible rule, only to that extent is it desirable to the architect.

To the extent that it is capable of new forms or a matter of style, and remains a servant of those forms, it is desirable.

Standardization should be put to work but never master the process that yields the original form.

Variety in Unity. A "style" once accomplished soon becomes a yardstick for the blind; a crutch for the lame; the recourse or refuge of the impotent.

Therefore as humanity develops there will be less recourse to the standardization that is "the styles" and more style (for the development of humanity is a matter of greater creative power for the individual), more of that quality in each that was once painfully achieved by the whole. A richer variety in unity is, therefore, a rational hope in America.

Autobiography of a Form. In the logic of the plan what we call "standardization" is seen to be fundamental ground work in architecture. All things in nature exhibit this tendency to crystallize; to form mathematically and then to conform, as we may easily see. There is the fluid, elastic period of becoming, as in the plan, when possibilities are infinite. New effects may then originate from the idea or principle that conceives. Once form is achieved, however, that possibility is dead so far as it is a positive creative flux.

1928: In the Cause of Architecture: Stone

FROM THE *Architectural Record*, APRIL, 1928.

Gothic Masonry. Stonecraft rose highest in the Gothic era.

But the Gothic builders, then set to work and carved the beautiful construction elaborately and constructed carving in the spirit of the construction to an extent never before seen in the world. No arris was left without its molding. It was as though stone had blossomed into a thing of the human spirit; as though a wave of creative impulse had seized stone and, mutable as the sea, the noble material had heaved and swelled and broken into lines of surge, peaks of foam, human symbols, images of organic life caught and held in its cosmic urge. A splendid song.

The song of *stone?*

No. Because stone was used as a negative material neither limitations respected nor stone nature interpreted. In wood the result was pretty much the same or in iron or in plaster, in the hands of the Goths.

But as a building material stone was *scientifically* used. Stereotomy was a science and such stone was usually chosen as had little to say for itself and so not outraged much by such cutting to the shapes of organic life, as it was subjected to in that time.

We may say that stone was not outraged, but neither was it allowed to sing its own song, to be *itself*. But nearer to that, by the Gothic, than anywhere else since the archaic time of Stonehenge, the Egyptian, the Maya and later the Byzantine culture.

No. It was not the *stone* that inspired the cathedrals of the Middle Ages nor invited them. It limited them.

The Nature of Stone. Stone is a solid material: heavy, durable and most grateful for and so most effective in masses. A "massive" material we say; so, the nobler the masses the better.

Wood into Stone. In most great architectures of the world stone has suffered imitation of the stick. Even in oldest cultures like Greek and Chinese civilization, great constructions of stone imitate wood posts and wood beams in joinery. Imitate literally great wood towering of poles and posts surmounted by beams or wands richly carved to imitate the carvings of the wooden ones that preceded them and could not endure. Undoubtedly the stick came first in architecture, came long before the stone. The ideas of form that became associated with ideas of the beautiful in this use of wood took the more enduring material stone, as yet ignorant of its nature, and foolishly enslaved it to the idea of the ornamented stick.

1928: In the Cause of Architecture: Wood

FROM THE *Architectural Record,* MAY, 1928.

Building Is Architecture. While all building, as things go, cannot be architecture but must be makeshift, architecture should hold forth such natural ways and means for the true use of good materials that, from any standpoint of economical realization of the best the material can give to structure, architecture would put mere building to shame. Stupid waste characterizes most of the efforts of mere builders, always even, or especially when, building for profit in the United States.

True Conservation. Wood grows more precious as our country grows older. To save it from destruction by the man with the machine it is only necessary to use the machine to emancipate its qualities, in simple ways, such as I have indicated, and satisfy the man.

"Will Do Anything a Plastic Will." After we have exhausted the board and the machined interlocking batten, the spread of the figure of the wood flowering over flat surfaces, the combinations of the following backband and the varying ribband, the spindle stick, the flat slab and the rod, the marking strip and the accent block, the ornamental pole, rectangular timbering ornamentally planked, the undressed, interlocking boards on walls and roof slopes, well, then, we have combinations of all these. A variety sufficient to intrigue the liveliest imagination for as long as life lasts, without once regretting the old curvatures and imitations of organic forms, the morbid twists and curious turns of senseless contortions imposed on wood in the name of the "styles" all *mostly* using wood as a makeshift, or if not, using it as something other than wood. We now owe both abuse and opportunity to the machine.

Using Wood as Wood. As a young architect at Oak Park I found the uses of wood I shall describe. Machinery in that era was well under way and the machines plowed and tore, whirled and gouged all wood to pieces in the name of art and architecture. And this the machines did so effectually and busily that the devastation began to be felt in the boundless Usonian forests. Conservative lumbermen took alarm and made the native supply go a little farther by shrinking all standard timber sizes first; one-eighth inch both ways. Then a little farther by shrinking all one-eighth inch more both ways, now still a little farther, until a stud is becoming a bed slat, a board akin to curling veneer.

All standardized sticks both great and small are still shrinking by a changing standard to meet the scarcity due to this deadly facility which the machine has given to man's appetite for useless *things*.

Usonian forests show all too plainly terrible destruction and, bitter thought, Usonia has got nothing of genuine beauty to show for it.

The darkness of death is descending on wood by way of the unenlightened architect and architecture.

The life of the tree has been taken in vain as the stick, the substance of the shapely stick to become imitation à la mode; the precious efflorescent patterns of wood, painted out of sight; its silken textures vulgarized by varnish in the misshapen monstrosities of a monstrous "taste."

The noble forest is become an ignominious scrap heap ready to burn in the name of false culture.

The machine, then, was it, that placed this curse on so beautiful a gift to man? So friendly a material, this brother to the man, laid thus low in murder.

No.

Unless the sword in the hand of the swordsman murdered the man whose heart it ran through. The machine is only a tool. Before all the man is responsible for its use.

His ignorance became forest devastation because his tool, in callous hands, became a deadly weapon effective beyond any efficiency such hands had known before, effective beyond any sensibilities he ever had. His performance with his machine outran not only his imagination which, long since, it vanquished, but the endurance of his own sensibilities, as human, also.

No. Blame the base appetite the machine released upon the forest for the devastation. Blame human lack of imaginative insight for the rubbish heap we have now to show for the lost trees of a continent, a scrap heap instead of a noble architecture.

What should we have had to show if these United States were otherwise? Vain speculation. What may we have to show for what is left if base appetite becomes enlightened desire and imagination awakes and sees?

Well, we may have an expression of the nobility of the *material* itself if nothing else.

We may have simple timber construction, at least overhead, as a scientific art, free of affectation: the wood let alone as wood or as richly ornamented by hand in color or carving.

We may have satin-boarded wainscots, polished board, the joints interlocked by beaded insertion, so that shrinkage is allowed and the joint, as such, ornaments the whole in harmony with its nature, individualizing each board.

We may have plaster covered walls banded into significant color surfaces by plain wood strips, thick or thin, or cubicle insertion, wide or narrow in surface.

We may have ceilings ribbanded in rhythmical arrangement of line to give the charm of timbering without the waste.

We may use flat wood strips with silken surfaces contrasting as ribbons might be contrasted with stuffs, to show what we meant in arranging our surfaces, marking them by bands of sympathetic flat wood.

We may use a plastic system of varying widths, weights of finely marked wood ribbands to articulate the new plastic effects in construction never dreamed of before. The flat strip comes so easily into our hands, by way of the machine, as to give us the "backband" that follow all outlines even in an ordinary dwelling, by the mile for a few cents a foot, cleaning and trimming all the ragged edges.

We may compound composite slabs of refuse lumber glued together under high pressure and press facings of purest flowered wood veneer into glue spread on the surfaces thus made, on both sides, making slabs of any thickness or width or length. Slabs can be cut into doors, great and small. Tops thin or thick. In all preserving the same flower of the grain over entire series or groups of doors as a unit.

We may mitre the flowered slabs across the grain at the edges of the breaks to turn the flowering grain around corners and down the sides and thus gain another plastic effect from the continuity of the flowering.

We may economically split a precious log into thin wide veneers and the flitches suitably "backed," lay each to each, opening one sheet to lay it edge to edge with the sheet beneath it, like the leaves of a book so the pattern of the one becomes another greater pattern when doubled by the next.

We may cross veneer the edges of top surfaces so that the grain of the top carries the flower unbroken down over the ends as it does on the sides.

There is the flat fillet (it happens to be true to wood) to "talk" with, if it is necessary to "explain."

We may use the plain spindle alternating with the thin flat slat or square or round ones in definite rhythms of light and shade, allowing the natural color and marking of the wood to enrich and soften the surface made by them as a whole. With this we may bring in the accent block.

We have the edgewise and flatwise strip or cubical stick and accent block to "ingeniously" combine into screens for light filters or for furniture.

These treatments all allow wood to be wood at its best and the machine can do them all surpassingly better than they could be done by hand, a thousand times cheaper.

Conspicuous Waste. Because of wood, we have the carpenter.

The carpenter loved wood in feeble ways, but he loved his tools with strength and determination. He loved his tools more. Good wood is willing to do what its designer never meant it to do, another of its lovable qualities, but therefore it is soon prostitute to human ingenuity in the makeshift of the carpenter. Wood, therefore, has more outrage done upon it than man has done, even upon himself.

It has suffered more, far more than any of the materials in our category.

Where and when it is cheap and so become too familiar, as it nearly always does in a new country, it soon falls into contempt. The longing for novelty tries to make it something else. To the degree that the carpenter-artist has succeeded in doing this, one might think, Is he the artist-carpenter?

In the carpenter-architect's or architect-carpenter's (Jesus himself was one or the other) search for novelty, wood in his hands has been joined and glued, braced and screwed, boxed and nailed, turned and tortured, scroll sawed, beaded, fluted, suitably furbelowed and flounced at the carpenter's party, enough to please even him. By the aid of "modern" machines the carpenter-artist got wood into Eastlake composites of trim and furniture, into Usonian jigger porches and the corner tower eventuating into candle snuffer domes; or What would you have? He got "woodwork" all over Queen Anne houses outside and inside, the triumph of his industrious ingenuity, until carpentry and millwork became synonymous with butchery and botch work.

Queen Anne! What wood-murder!

And even now, especially now, at this tail end of the passing procession of the "periods" I never see orderly piles of freshly cut and dried timber disappearing into the mills to be gored and ground and torn and hacked into millwork without a sense of utter weariness in the face of the overwhelming outrage of something precious just because that something is by nature so kind, beneficent, and lovely.

Japanese Treatment of Wood. Wood is universally beautiful to man. It is the most humanly intimate of all materials. Man loves his association with it; likes to feel it under his hand, sympathetic to his touch and to his eye.

And yet, passing by the primitive uses of wood, getting to higher civilization, the Japanese understood it best. The Japanese have never outraged wood in their art or in their craft. Japan's primitive religion, "Shinto," with its "be clean" ideal found in wood ideal material and gave it ideal use in that masterpiece of architecture, the Japanese dwelling, as well as in all that pertained to living in it.

In Japanese architecture may be seen what a sensitive material let alone for its own sake can do for human sensibilities, as beauty, for the human spirit.

Whether pole, beam, plank, board, slat, or rod, the Japanese architect got the forms and treatments of his architecture out of tree nature, wood wise, and heightened the natural beauty of the material by cunning peculiar to himself.

The possibilities of the properties of wood came out richly as he rubbed into it the natural oil of the palm of his hand, ground out the soft parts of the grain to leave the hard fiber standing, an "erosion" like that of the plain where flowing water washes away the sand from the ribs of the stone.

No western people ever used wood with such understanding as the Japanese used it in their construction, where wood always came up and came out as nobly beautiful.

And when we see the bamboo rod in their hands, seeing a whole industrial world interpreting it into articles of use and art that ask only to be *bamboo,* we reverence the scientific art that makes wood *theirs.*

The simple Japanese dwelling with its fences and utensils is the *revelation* of wood.

I have chosen to speak of Japan, not in the past tense, in this connection because nowhere else may wood be so profitably studied for its natural possibilities as a major architectural material as in Old Japan.

Proper Uses. We may use wood with intelligence only if we understand wood.

To distinguish it let us say wood is efflorescent.

The crystal is inflorescent or exflorescent.

Wood is the flowering of a process proceeding from the same principle as the crystal, it is true, subject to the same law as stone but having apparently more volition, going further along the way to some ideal freedom in its acts . . . because more is left to the individual of any tree species than is given to any mineral and even to the mineral species itself.

Greater volition and freedom than even the tree seems to know came in the organic matter we know as "animal." And forms even more free than that seem still pending in creation to be, some day discovered by the architect.

Let us say the tree is efflorescence subject to light, imprisoning heat.

The crystal is subject to heat imprisoning light.

The tree in this sense is a flower of light.

The stick becomes the substance of the stalk that upheld or held forth the tree flower to the light of the sun. At once the stick was the fibrous channel that fed it from the ground and the structural post and cantilever beam that held all securely in sun and air.

The stick is the natural post.

It is also the natural beam.

Post and beam construction were, by nature, first wood.

Whenever stone, later, became used as post and beam construction stone became enslaved to wood unless translated to stone as the Egyptians translated it in the Temple of Philae. Sophisticated refinement such as the Greeks wrought upon the stone cannot change or even modify the slavery.

Only such refinement as is wrought by its own stone nature can have validity as great architecture.

The same is true of wood.

Wood, as we may now see, is patterned, textured in endless variety by the inherent nature of efflorescence and, obeying the law of the crystals, achieving color, textures, patterns, endless in beauty, perfect in point of style.

Falling Leaves. The Greeks supposed trees the earliest dwellings of the gods. Zeus spoke his truest oracles through the rustling of the leaves. And although, in the combined voice of all the poets, the falling leaf has been metaphor of everything that dies, the forests correct our faith, for we know now that the race of leaves grow off and do not fall off, and owing to natural science their "speech" is more a marvel of sensibility today than in the twilight of the "Gods."

In a finer poetic sense, too, the leaves fall to a new glory.

1928: In the Cause of Architecture: The Kiln

FROM THE *Architectural Record,* JUNE, 1928.

Our Native Material. Brick is the material we in Usonia know and love best. We probably have brought brickmaking to a pitch of perfection never existing in the world before at any time. And we use it, on the whole, very well. Not only is our range in brickmaking inexhaustible in texture and color and shape, but the material itself is wholly admirable in quality.

Monreale. I remember going to Palermo some years ago to see the mosaics of Monreale. I had just got into the cathedral square and lifted my eyes to that great work when to the left I saw, or did I see, for some moments I thought I dreamed, there against the sky, no, not against it, of it, literally *of the sky,* was a great dome of pure Racca blue. I forgot the cathedral for quite some time in the wonderful blue dome so simple in form; a heavenly thing. I have never recovered from it.

Sullivan and Terra Cotta. Terra cotta was easily this master's natural medium because his sense of beautiful form was the subtle fluctuation modulation of flowering surface, songlike as found in organic plant life; the music of the crystal is seen in his work as minor accompaniment only. And that is the sensibility I think for true use of so-called terra cotta.

The tones of the main theme in this material are those of organic efflorescence, growth as it is performed by plant species. This idea of growth was the theme, invariably, which Louis Sullivan glorified in his system of ornament.

Instead of "orders" he created "species" by himself, and could have kept on creating others endlessly.

This procedure or organic growth intrigued his imagination; inspired him. "Organic" became his God word, as he traced form to function in foliation. The *symbol* of growth to him became the pattern of growth he evolved and expressed in ornament for plastic terra cotta.

Sullivan's Ornament. The only limit to Sullivan's treatment was the degree to which the substance of the pliable clay would stay up between the thumb and finger of the modeler and come through the fire. As a matter of principle background disappeared, but surface was preserved. There was no sense of background, however, as such, anywhere. All his ornamentation was of the surface, out of the material.

What Sullivan Did with Terra Cotta. Terra cotta was a greatest opportunity for the creative artist. Greater, perhaps, than any other material he might choose. Terra cotta is, of course, simply burned clay on the grand scale, any color or glaze for an entire building. Pottery buildings! Earthenware architecture.

Modern terra cotta has known but one creative master, only one, Louis H. Sullivan.

He is dead. His work in terra cotta will live long after him. His was the temperament and imagination that would naturally find in this impressionable material ideal medium for his genius.

Terra cotta lives only as it takes the impression of human imagination: material for the modeler. In the architect's hand it is what wax is in the sculptor's hand.

After the material takes shape, the surface treatments are all a matter of feeling; and they are limitless in quality, color, and style.

But the chief business of terra cotta has been to imitate stone.

Terra cotta would imitate anything else as readily, with gratitude so it seems. It is the misfortune of anything impressionable to be called upon to give imitations. Mimicry is all too human. To imitate is the natural tendency of men. Not of man.

But Louis Sullivan's exuberant, sensuous nature and brilliant imagination took terra cotta, and terra cotta lived. No longer was permission for pattern asked of the styles. Terra cotta for buildings was now *itself* because it was Louis H. Sullivan himself. In it this great master created a grammar of ornament all his own. And notwithstanding certain realistic tendencies, it was an original style of ornamentation out of the man, astonishing in range, never lacking virility.

Into the living intricacy of his loving modulation of surface, "background" (the curse of all stupid ornament) ceased to exist. None might see where terra cotta left off and ornamentation came to life. A fragment of Sullivanian terra cotta, were this civilization at some remote period of time to be excavated, would be found with a thrill. It would mean that a man lived among us at a dead time in art.

The Sullivanian motif was efflorescent, evolute, supported by tracery of geometric motives, bringing up through the clay forms so delicate and varied and lively that no parallel in these respects exists even in ancient times.

We may see, for once, how completely a negative material can be appropriately brought to life by the creative spirit. It is reassuring.

Is there in architectural history another man who out of himself not only created an exuberant type of beautiful architectural relief but furnished it forth, always consistent in style, in amazing variety that could not have ended but with his terra cotta building, inside and outside, as definite a possibility as was the Han vessel itself in its time or as the Greek vase in Greece?

1928: In the Cause of Architecture: Glass

FROM THE *Architectural Record,* JULY, 1928.

Fixtures. Lighting may be made a part of the building itself. No longer any appliance or even appurtenance are needed. But all this may be made, really, architecture.

Crystal City. Imagine a city iridescent by day, luminous by night, imperishable! Buildings, shimmering fabrics, woven of rich glass; glass all clear or part opaque and part clear, patterned in color or stamped to harmonize with the metal tracery that is to hold all together, the metal tracery to be, in itself, a thing of delicate beauty consistent with slender steel construction, expressing the nature of that construction in the mathematics of structure which are the mathematics of music as well. Such a city would clean itself in the rain, would know no fire alarms; no, nor any glooms. To any extent the light could be reduced within the rooms by screens, blinds, or insertion of translucent or opaque glass. The heating problem would be no greater than with the rattling windows of the imitation masonry structure, because the fabric now would be mechanically perfect, the product of the machine shop instead of the makeshift of the topsy-turvy field. And the glass area would be increased only by about 10 percent over such buildings as they still continue to build of masonry.

I dream of such a city. I have worked enough on such a building to see definitely its desirability and its practicability.

Light and Shadow. Shadows have been the brush work of the architect when he modeled his traditional architectural forms. Let him work, now, with light diffused, light refracted, light reflected, use light for its own sake, shadows aside. The prism has always delighted and fascinated man. The machine gives him prismatic opportunity in glass. The machine process can do any kind of glass: thick, thin, colored, texture to order; and cheap; and the machine in the architect's hand can now set it, protect it, and humanize its use completely. A new experience is awaiting architecture. Then why are modern cities still sodden imitations of medieval strongholds? Why are our city families cave dwellers to such an extent?

Glass, the Modern Material. Perhaps the greatest eventual difference between ancient and modern buildings will eventually be due to our modern machine-made glass. For glass, in any wide utilitarian sense, is new.

Once a precious substance limited in quantity and size, glass and its making have grown so that a perfect clarity of any thickness, quality, or dimension is so cheap and desirable that our modern world is drifting toward structures of glass and steel. Had the ancients been able to enclose interior space with the facility we enjoy because of glass, I suppose the history of architecture would have been radically different, although it is surprising how little this material has yet modified our traditional sense of architecture beyond the show windows the shopkeeper demands from his architect and gets, now.

How that show window plagued the architect at first and still teases the classicist. The "show" window has probably done more to show the classicist up as ridiculous in our architectural endeavor in the United States than almost any other single factor that could be named.

Popular demand for visibility makes walls and even posts an intrusion in almost any building to be got rid of at any cost in many cases.

"Architecture," therefore, gave up the first story of city building but started bravely above the glass at the second, nothing daunted and nothing changed. The building apparently stood in midair. Glass did it. Glass will soon abolish the "architecture" of the upper stories too. It is well on toward success in that respect.

Crystal plates have now quite generally taken the place of fundamental wall and piers in almost all commercial buildings; and glass, the curse of the classic, as an opportunity for the use of delicate construction of sheet metal and steel, is a tempting material now about to be explored. As glass has become clearer and clearer and cheaper and cheaper from age to age, about all that has been done with it architecturally is to fill the same building openings that opaque ill-made but beautiful glass screened long ago, with a perfect visibility now, except for the broader use to which the shopman demands that it be put.

The shop! Yes, that is where glass has almost come into its own. But we have yet to give glass proper architectural recognition, even in the shop.

1928: In the Cause of Architecture: Concrete

FROM THE *Architectural Record*, AUGUST, 1928.

Conglomera. Aesthetically concrete has neither song nor any story. Nor is it easy to see in this conglomerate, in this mud pie, a high aesthetic property, because in itself it is amalgam, aggregate compound. And cement, the binding medium, is characterless in itself.

The net result is usually an artificial stone at best, or a petrified sand heap at worst.

Concrete would be better named "conglomera" because concrete is a noble word in itself which this material totally fails to live up to. Concrete, so-called, is a mixture having little quality in itself.

If this material is to acquire either form, texture, or color in and of itself, such must be given to it artificially by human imagination.

A New World. New life, new purposes and possibilities were given to both cement and steel when the coefficient of expansion and contraction was found to be the same in each. A new world was then and there opened to the architect.

Granite Sand and Cement. On the Phoenix plain of Arizona, the ruddy granite mountain heaps, grown old, are decomposing; sliding down, layer upon layer, to further compose the soil of the great plain or mesa of the Salt River Valley. Granite in various stages of decay, sand silt and gravel make the floor of the world here unless "calichi" interferes.

Buildings could grow right up out of the ground as adobe buildings do if this soil, before it is too far rotted, was cemented in proper proportions and beaten into flasks or boxes; a few steel strands dropped in for reinforcement.

Cement may be here as elsewhere the secret stamina of the physical body of our new world. It seems destined to be.

1928: In the Cause of Architecture: Sheet Metal and a Modern Instance

FROM THE *Architectural Record,* OCTOBER, 1928.

Sheet Metal. What is left of the architectural framework of the modern world after concrete and steel have done with it will probably be in some form or other, sheet metal.

Metal Work. The machinery at work in the sheet metal trades easily crimps, folds, trims, and stamps sheets of metal as an ingenious child might his sheets of paper. The finished product may have the color brought up in surface treatment, or be enameled with other durable substances as in enamel color glazing or plating, or as in galvanizing the finished work may be dipped and coated entire. But copper is the only sheet metal that has yet entered into architecture as beautiful permanent material. Its verdigris is always a great beauty in connection with stone or brick or wood, and copper is more nearly permanent than anything we have at hand as an architect's medium.

We now have other rustless metals, by alloy, like monel metal, Allegheny metal and others. All are going to prove invaluable.

But now that all metals may be rolled into sheets and manipulated so cheaply, combinations of various metals may be made as any other combination of materials may be. And will be.

1928: In the Cause of Architecture: The Terms

FROM THE *Architectural Record,* DECEMBER, 1928.

Writing About Building. I would much rather build than write about building, but when I am not building I will write about building, or the significance of those buildings I have already built.

Usonian Romanticism. The fact remains that Usonia wanted romance and sought it. The failure to get it is less significant than the fact that it was sought.

Simple Semantics. The word "poetry." A dangerous word to use. Carl Sandburg once said to me, "Why do you use the words 'poetry,' 'beauty,' 'truth,' or 'ideal' any more? Why not just get down to tacks? Talk about boards, nails, and barn doors."

Good advice. I think that is what I should do. But I won't do it unless I can get an equivalent by doing so. That equivalent I exactly cannot get. The words: romance, poetry, beauty, truth, ideal, are not "precious" words at all, nor should they be *specious* words, as they now seem to be. Elemental human word symbols must be brought back again to our respect. We must again use them significantly if we use them at all, or we ought to go to jail.

1928: In the Cause of Architecture: The Meaning of Materials

The Limited Palette. Work wherever possible in mono material, except where the use of sympathetic extra materials may add the necessary grace or graceful necessity desirable; or unavoidable.

Each material *speaks a language* of its own just as the line and color speak or perhaps because they do speak.

Each has a story.

Song. Each material has its own message and, to the creative artist, its own song.

Materials. The country between Madison and Janesville near Taliesin, my home and workshop, is the old bed of an ancient glacier drift. Vast, busy gravel pits abound there, exposing heaps of yellow aggregate, once and everywhere else sleeping beneath the green fields. Great heaps, clean and golden, are always waiting there in the sun. And I never pass on my way to and from Chicago without an emotion, a vision of the long dust-whitened stretches of the cement mills grinding to impalpable fineness the magic powder that would "set" it all to shape and wish both bill and gravel endlessly subject to my will.

Nor do I ever come to a lumber yard with its citylike, graduated masses of fresh shingles, boards and timbers, without taking a deep breath of its fragrance, seeing the forest laid low in it by processes that cut and shaped it to the architect's scale of feet and inches, coveting it *all.*

The rock ledges of a stone quarry are a story and a longing to me. There is a suggestion in the strata, and character in the formation. I like to sit and feel the stone as it is there. Often I have thought were monumental great buildings ever given me to build I would go to the Grand Canyon of Arizona to ponder them.

When in early years I looked south from the massive stone tower in the Auditorium Building, a pencil in the hand of a master, the red glare of the Bessemer steel converters to the south of Chicago would thrill me as pages of the *Arabian Nights* used to do with a sense of terror and romance.

And the smothered incandescence of the kiln. In the fabulous heat, baking mineral and chemical treasure on mere clay to issue in all the hues of the rainbow, all the shapes of imagination and never yield to time, subject only to the violence or carelessness of man. These great ovens would cast a spell upon me as I listened to the subdued roar deep within them.

The potter's thumb and finger deftly pressing the soft mass whirling on his wheel as it yielded to his touch, the bulbous glass at the end of the slender pipe as the breath of the glass blower and his deft turning decided its shape—its fate fascinated me. Something was being born.

Colors; in paste or crayon, pencil; always a thrill. To this day I love to hold a handful of many-colored pencils and open my hand to see them lying loose upon my palm, in the light.

Mere accidental colored chalk marks on the sunlit sidewalk, perhaps, will make me pause and "something" in me harks back to "something," half remembered, half felt, and as though an unseen door had opened and distant music had, for an instant, come trembling through to my senses.

In this sense of earth! Deep buried treasure there without end. Mineral matter and metal stores folded away in the veins of gleaming quartz. Gold and silver, lead and copper, tawny iron ore; all to yield themselves up to roaring furnaces and flow obedient to the hands of the architect; all to become pawns to human will in the plan of the human mind.

And jewels! Happy discoveries. The gleam of mineral colors and flashing facets of crystals. Gems to be sought and set; to forever play with light to man's delight, in never-ending beams of purest green, or red or blue or yellow, and all that lives between. Light! Living in the mathematics of form to match with the mathematics of sound.

Crystals are proof of nature's matchless architectural principle.

All this I see as the architect's garden, his palette I call it, to humble the figure.

Materials! What a resource.

1928: In the Cause of Architecture: Composition

Cosmetics. In most modern structures you may see the triumph over architecture of "art and decoration." These structures are modern, but they are not new. They are not even yet architecture. Not until the abstraction finds proper use as method and motif for true building, and its pattern becomes the constitution of construction as well as its colorful imaginative features, not until then will we have the nobility of a truly genuine architecture.

And when the mind is disciplined by this power to see in the abstract the actual "patterns" of nature; yes, in this case the very *patterns* of steel construction, the skeleton will become an important feature and, in its proper place, will not be paraded as a discovery for its own sake. The skeleton is a novelty just now. Architects are discovering that bones have picturesque effects. To skin the bones is, therefore, an architectural pursuit at the present moment.

A more serious endeavor than "make-up," certainly.

But the method of creation is still to come in this effort with steel.

Only as the principle of construction: cantilever, hanger, post, or beam, does steel find expression in natural pattern (yes, all these elements of architecture have their creative pattern) and not until that natural pattern becomes a plastic, rhythmic fabric adapted to human needs with complete repose, not until then, I say, will this "modern" crusade result in architecture.

We are now, A.D. 1928, at the two extremes.

Art and decoration is insisting upon "make-up." Its own.

The bone yard is insisting upon the skeleton articulate.

The one school gaily disposing of the matter with feudal surface and mass.

The other school painfully rattling the bones ignored by the first, and in the name of the machine turning the matter inside out, putting barren boxes on top of stark posts; so glassing them in that one may see that they are boxes on top of posts and be sure to make no mistake about that whatever.

This fact for the moment they seem to regard as architecture. It may be a beginning.

Beautifully dressed is the first, for the sake of the dress.

Stark, naked "necessity" is the other, for the sake of the necessity.

Messieurs!

The machine does not need nor heed your compliments. Instead the machine needs honest work to do, not merely by way of exposing its bones. No, no more than "on its face," it needs a more becoming "make-up."

Lay lip stick and rouge aside!

Drag no skeletons to light to murder repose unless to convict the murderer of murder.

Let us practice method that builds the building naturally as a significant entity in itself, perfected by the machine perhaps, but not *for* the machine nor *as* a machine. Never will art and decoration nor the sensational rattling of bones take the place of integral architecture unless the people of America lose their vision or fail to find it.

Elements. Any of the accepted masterpieces of the time, the place, and the hour may be analyzed into at least several distinctly different things arranged together showing clearly now the structure was not born but made.

Nature Still. Machine-made mimicry and mummery have had their day and overtime, notwithstanding the novelty they may stage and restage for our entertainment. Let us learn to see within, at least far enough to grasp essential pattern in all created things. And method in creation will come freely to him who learns to see in the abstract. Study the geometry that is the *idea* of every form: a quail, a snail, a shell, a fish. They yield their secret readily, and are easier to grasp than dogs and horses and humans because they are a little nearer origins, a little more primitive. Take for analysis the more simple, obvious things first.

Then take the texture of the trees.

Learn the essential pattern that makes the oak and distinguishes it from the essential *pattern* that makes the pine.

Then make *new* ones. Try after this, the curling vine, flowing water, curving sand.

Then try the flowers, butterflies, and bees.

A chrysanthemum is easy.

A rock or a rose is difficult.

And I do not mean to take the obvious surface effects that differentiate each, but to go within to find the essential geometry of pattern that gives *character* to each. That is the proper study for an architect who would find method and get legitimate "effects."

Try this method and gradually discipline your power to see.

Get patiently to the point where you naturally see this element of pattern in everything. Make it your favorite "intrigue."

How much richer this vision will make your world you can have no idea until you develop this disciplinary power. Your world becomes manifold; rich with significance; infinite in variety; and imbued with principle. It is easier then to believe in God. If you want to.

This essential pattern mastered in the abstract, now try to connect it as form with what function you may discover by search it may fit.

Learn the reasonableness; admire and appreciate the wisdom that cast it in the form it has for what it is, and learn to see why it is what it is. That study is the study of architecture.

These are proper kindergarten studies for an architect. And I promise you a habit of thought arising from such eye-minded exercises as to make constructive effort natural and spontaneous.

Things begin of themselves to proceed from generals to particulars; to *build,* to develop, to emerge and take inevitable form, forcing nothing, imposing not at all. *Lying* never.

Deception in this realm is unthinkable because it is unnatural. In that realm destiny is inherent in every chosen motif and finds another destiny in your hands guided by your imagination to your heart's desire.

1928: In the Cause of Architecture: Purely Personal

The Japanese Influence. I knew nothing of Japanese architecture until I first saw it in 1906.

Le Corbusier. Le Corbusier, at least, is no sentimentalist.

The "Old Sentimentalist." An emotional being imbued with much sentiment, I am therefore called names. A "new traditionalist" for one. Soon I may be called an "old sentimentalist."

Indeed, that, I suspect, is what the premature historians already hint when they refer to me as a "romanticist." At any rate, unashamed, I am searching for this poetic development that I call the sound body of architecture, a search based not upon sentiment but upon principle.

Depth. The essential element that alone can guide either surface or mass to life is *depth.*

Virtue of the Lean and Hard. I should not be too unhappy were France, our fashionmonger, in the school of "surface and mass" to set a fashion among us for a generation or two. Lean, hard plainness, mistaken for simplicity, has the quality of simplicity to a refreshing extent, wherever all is fat or false. It *is* aristocratic by contrast. I say this fashion would be good for what ails the United States in architecture. This cowardly, superficial artificiality might well meet antidotal superficiality. Any transient influence in the direction of simplicity is welcome.

But I shall continue to resent "eers," "ists," or "isms," and particularly resist the *"ist."*

Skeleton and Body. The organic elements of building are wholesome, I find. The proper organs of architectural expression should always be appropriately in place, *all of them.* Were the ceiling planes revealed by stripping my buildings to mere third dimension surface, they would startle the "new" by unsuspected resemblance to their recent "discoveries." The "new" delights in surface effects but discovers the "skeleton" necessary and cannot see it wholly lacking in effect in their present day architecture as it was wholly lacking in ours before the days of the pioneers.

Now a good skeleton in architecture is indispensable but only for the purpose of a sound body. So I have been working with these organic developments that contribute to the sound body, believing that poetry of architecture, therefore, the art of architecture to be inherent in surface and mass only when both are organically the expression of the constitution of the whole building. In themselves they are nothing—again.

Architectural Haberdashery. To a real pioneer, it was an unfortunate but sadly accepted fact that the commercial machine, owing to its deadly facility, in these United States, would have to find such ready-made architectural clothes to wear for some time. The necessary "outfit" was discovered at the Columbian Fair and has served as may be seen. But never for one moment during the 34 years since the borrowed garments first began to be worn has there been a doubt in my mind that the practical expression concealed by such cheap expedients would slowly emerge to eventually render the expedient not only unnecessary but absurd. Any true organic expression of underlying practical nature is of slow growth. But it is a sure growth. One may look within and already see transplanted forms, dying or dead. What little we have built on our soil by way of principle will not die. It is all the "architecture" we have; as always before on earth where architecture is the record of human life, such building survives and is the ultimate triumph.

1928: Fiske Kimball's New Book

FROM THE *Architectural Record,* AUGUST, 1928.

This review of American Architecture *marks the beginning of Wright's struggle against his premature historians, critics and obituary writers. From the publication of Lewis Mumford's* Sticks and Stones *in 1924 grew a healthier view of architecture, one unfortunate aspect of which was a tendency to view Wright in the trinity of Richardson, Sullivan and Wright, and to regard his work as concluded. Although Wright has since been able to combat this tendency with his actual buildings, at this period he was largely limited to words.*

"American Classic." The title to Mr. Kimball's new book should have been "Architecture in America." According to him American architecture has passed out and all we have left is what McKim, Mead, and White and the plan factories initiated by Daniel H. Burnham have borrowed from Europe (the classic); and have used to successfully conceal the ways and means by which it had its being.

I learned from the genial writer in the early chapters of his book, and enjoyed his glowing pages until I got to the matter of which I know considerable, beginning with the chapter "What Is Modern Architecture?" Here Fiske Kimball allows nature quite enough rope to hang herself and awards the "victory" to the sophist Greek and his elegant abstractions in doing this, without shame, in the machine age. He does this apparently with both eyes wide open, quite gaily unconscious of the fact that he pleads the old mime of "Art for art's sake." Therein is he a good Greek.

There is no objection in anyone's doing this so well as Fiske Kimball does it. But, easy to see, he doesn't really believe it, as does no one else of his caliber today.

His real sympathies all the while are really with us; Mr. Sullivan, the modern Europeans, and myself. He writes much better and more sympathetically in his obituaries of Mr. Sullivan (and myself) than of his triumphant bona-fide heroes of the "American classic," which may only be, after all, his sentimentality getting the better of his generosity.

The "American classic" (a choice phrase of his) is lawless. It is without logic or philosophy, that is, and defiant of cause and effect. At best it is what a very wealthy client of mine, president of a great company, accused me of some years ago. Visiting Taliesin, he looked about honestly delighted and astonished. He said, "Well, I've heard a great deal about this place, but hang it, I ain't heard the half." He looked out, looked in, and looked around and turning to me said suddenly, "After all there ain't nothing to it, is there? It's just taste, ain't it?" Well, I plead not guilty. But there you have Fiske Kimball's brief for "American classic."

"It's just taste, ain't it?"

1928: Towards a New Architecture

FROM *World Unity,* SEPTEMBER, 1928.

With this little-known review of Le Corbusier's brilliant tract begins the counter-attack against the European modernists whose work was popularized in 1931 by the Museum of Modern Art exhibition. Wright tried here, and on numerous occasions during the next ten years, to point out the errors in the "International Style." Perhaps the most forceful single essay was "The Cardboard House," given as a lecture at Princeton in 1930.

America and Le Corbusier. All Le Corbusier says or means was at home here in architecture in America in the work of Louis Sullivan and myself, more than 25 years ago, and is fully on record in both building and writing here and abroad.

The Third Dimension. In this matter of art, the Frenchman has seldom got inside. He has usually discovered the surface "effects" best suited to the time, the place, and the hour. It is no small virtue in him and the trait has heaped honors upon his nation for centuries.

But that "flair" is no longer good enough. In this architectural matter France may for once find herself behind. America's minority report, already handed in a quarter-century earlier, goes deeper and the French movement may soon lose its two dimensions ("surface and mass") within the three that characterize the American work. The third dimension we already have, to be added to the two of France, is *depth.*

It is this quality of *depth* that alone can give life to architecture.

1929: Surface and Mass—Again!

FROM THE *Architectural Record,* JULY, 1929.

The Architecture of Model Builders. These young critics, I believe, intrigued by the science and philosophy of the great art, love architecture as a mysterious essence. They see in "surface and mass" abstractions by "great and gifted" Europeans inspired by French painting, the truth. But I know these abstractions repudiate the third dimension, ignoring depth of matter to get surface effects characteristic of canvas and pigment as painting but not of architecture no matter howsoever stark or begot by gas pipe, thin slabs, and naked steel work. "Materials" may now be used as "decorative cliché" too. Witness the concoctions of wire, lead pipe, plumbing fittings, brass keys, bits of glass and wood of this school. Sophisticated, ingenious, cleverly curious, they smell of the dissecting room, affect me as cadavers in a morgue.

These walls artificially thin, like cardboard bent, folded, and glued together, are frankly likewise dedicated *not to the machine but to machinery!* Therefore they cannot live.

Notes for the Critics. Do I make excursion into the feeling of an oriental race and, no lessening of grasp upon organic architecture, build their building by means of their own handicraft, dedicate the building to them, their life and land as a kind of oriental symphony?

A wail! I have been false to the mode of the machine I had proclaimed and championed.

Should I have proclaimed that superficial "mode," now of Paris, from Tokio housetops by means of oriental *handicraft* no matter how false the circumstances? Not for a moment was the machine forgotten by me, but it was in abeyance while I took off my hat to the Japanese people in their home and the destructive force that was their immemorial enemy was conquered by integral building. I showed them that architecture may be "symphonic" in more sound senses than one.

This exception proved many rules to me, but it broke more and still confounds my solicitous critics.

I design a Negro schoolhouse in the South; make it theirs, in point of life and color, form too, departing nowise from integral building. The mode of the machine deserted again to be humane. This is license, say the same critics.

I build a home for myself in southern Wisconsin: a stone, wood, and plaster building, make it as much a part of my grandfather's ground as the rocks and trees and hills there are.

Well, this architect has again "lapsed into the picturesque."

On Midwestern prairies I build, in three dimensions, houses that proclaim the prairie's quiet level, the third dimension evident as unbroken roof planes likewise lying in similar repose, as human *shelter.*

The floor planes too all in evidence to give scale to the whole affair.

Now, "the Gothic" has been put to bed on its side!

The effort in California and Arizona? Harassed by vexation of industrial confusion, forced lying, handsore and heartsick with makeshift tools, I finally found simple mechanical means to produce a complete building that looks the way the machine made it, as much so at least as any woven fabric need look. Tough, light, but not *"thin,"* imperishable, plastic, no necessary lie about it anywhere and yet, machine-made, mechanically perfect. Standardization as the soul of the machine here for the first time may be seen in the hand of the architect, put squarely up to imagination, the limitations of imagination the only limitation of building.

Yet, unhappily, my critics, having once seen, it seems, must continue to see Egyptian, Maya, Chinese, Japanese, Persian, Moorish. Not one motif of the sort can they fairly fix in these buildings for such were never in my mind.

Only because these desert buildings, too, are naturally elemental in form, as they are, can they verify even resemblance.

Did I prefer them lean, sun defiant, ascetic? They might be so, and please my critics.

Here in principle in all my buildings, but subservient, servant, not *master,* is the machine.

But why should the product look like machinery?

"The Rule So Broad." Although a pupil of Louis Sullivan, I have never been his disciple. He has himself gratefully acknowledged this publicly. Had I been his disciple I should have envied him and in the end have betrayed him.

Unjust then as untrue to quote from his autobiography, "The search for the rule so broad as to admit of no exception," as mine when the "exception" still, as always, interests me most, as necessary to prove any rule both useful and useless. That trait enables most critics to fail to penetrate the variegated surface of what I've tried to do.

1930: Poor Little American Architecture

H.-R. Hitchcock. I warn Henry-Russell Hitchcock right here and now that, having a good start, not only do I fully intend to be the greatest architect who has yet lived, but the greatest who will ever live. Yes, I intend to be the greatest architect of all time. And I do hereunto affix "the red square" and sign my name to this warning.

Criteria for Critics. I do not say no man should write about building who has not himself built something worth building. I do not believe that a man should drink a tub of dye to know what color it is. But it is my feeling that any man who writes about building should know something about building in particular, other than some aesthetic he may have imbibed abroad or at home and subscribed to as such.

A Guide to Misunderstanding. Were I really to know Henry-Russell Hitchcock, as with almost all my detractors, I should have to like him and would, perhaps, admire him. And probably were he someday to stop prowling around among photographs and so change his habits long enough to actually see my work, he, too, would be in the same embarrassing position concerning both my work and myself.

Bad Photographs. Not long since dropping into the offices of the *Architectural Record* on business concerning a book (being, I believe, the last "prolific writer" on architecture in the whole world, to attempt one) I casually picked up a black engraving of a man; hat, the typical French Mansard, beard, French, although the young woman at the desk (her smile was most engaging) said the actual color of the beard was not typically French.

That is how I learned what Henry-Russell Hitchcock looked like and all I know about him except that I have been told he occasionally comes over from Paris to teach young ladies at Vassar what they should think about architecture, and that he is addicted to photographs for criticism. So I am as qualified to write about him as he is to write about me. I know him by black engraving and his "aesthetics." He knows me by some bad photographs of my work, because there have never been any other kind.

1930: The Profession

This appears to be an early draft of the article "American Architecture as a Profession" published in the American Architect, *December, 1930.*

The Old Boys. The old fellows are gone, "done in" by time and the circumstance we sometimes stupidly call progress. But the firm or the plan factory that takes their place in the immediate present is no more than a passing makeshift while the country gets its eyes open and looks to itself.

Something important in the long run, more important than all else beside, the essentially human values, have been overlooked or deliberately left out. Important omission for this reason:

Man is going to conquer the machine. The machine is not going to conquer man, even though in all this, it may seem to have him down. We see in all these makeshifts now in use in architecture the work of the minions of the machine: mechanization, standardization, merchandising. "Sell it" or sink it, yes, and sink with it.

Machine overproduction glorifies salesmanship. "The stuff must be got rid of."

But soon, individuality will be doubly desirable and infinitely more treasured in America just because of this issue between the man and the machine, just as genius is now at a premium in Russia; for reasons not so dissimilar as one might think glancing superficially at the matter.

I don't know just what procedure is going to evolve out of this convolute "progress" to enable the man of ideas, technique trained and adequate, to get these ideas into the form of practical, beautiful buildings for the human joy and use of tomorrow, where there is so little or none today.

Had I just one guess, I should say this man in need now would have more in common with the composer-conductor of an orchestra. The orchestra and therefore that new architectural office is modern.

Modern industrial and, therefore, economic affairs are becoming daily more "orchestrated," meaning more dependent upon each other if not better correlated, in this country. The characteristic building enterprise that is attractive to bondholders today is attractive and successful most often on account of its size and importance, but on account of its size and importance it is now out of all human scale.

So the architect's employer today is more likely to be a corporation than a man or any except the extraordinary individual. More important, therefore, that this corporate aggregate, with its inherent weakness in initiative, and the mediocrity of its "committee decisions" center upon the architect competent to create. That can only mean center upon the supreme individual, however he happens to be "hooked up" or "hooked in" to the corporate aggregation.

All the more important, too, it becomes, to insure performance of the "piece" (or building) *according to design,* and just as greatly conceived. Details being more than ever consequential to *invention.* It is indispensable in fact, as things are, to have conception really natural to new materials and economic methods. Lines of least resistance in industry must now be followed to insure maximum human benefits, nor does that mean entirely biggest immediate net profits to the landlord. To be short, the architect being more important than ever, it is imperative today that he seriously qualify for his job, "profession," or "profession" be damned.

Qualifying would mean knowing industrial conditions well, knowing modern tools and methods even better, and knowing best of all their relation to the specific human purposes of any building project. Here again, say, as the composer-conductor we have in mind knows his score, knows his instruments, knows his players, and knows their possibilities in relation to the human desire for music.

It is true that the modern architect on any creative basis, except in circumstances extraordinary, can no more be compounded of several men today than he could have been in the old order.

Imagine several men together leading that orchestra.

Well, architecture today is a great orchestration of materials, methods, and men. The architect must be correlated to it all, but he must also rise above it all. When he does so, machine conditions will only have extended his opportunities, however he may choose to divide his responsibilities. A creative "modern" architecture would probably mean financial ruin to the architectural "firm" as now organized, and certainly the end of the plan factory. The plan factory knows it, or will, soon. The old triangle unluckily sponsored and fostered by the A.I.A.: "owner, one; architect, two; and contractor, three"; that formed the basis of architectural practice has proved about as satisfactory "service" as the triangle that forms the prevalent pattern of the popular sex play or novel.

That triangle gives rise to the same demoralization in getting good building built.

The architect usually sits where the unlucky husband sits in the domestic triangle, about as happily circumstanced. And the building comes out of the imbroglio much as the illegitimate child.

The commissioned builder is too often a competitor of the commissioned architect, easier for the client to understand him and, therefore, to depend upon him to the detriment of the real issue, the building, if the architect knows his own work. Various other modifications of the triangle have arisen with serious drawbacks for the owner, architect, and contractor; or all together.

No system will be adequate to modern conditions that does not give to the architect complete control of his design and assure control to him until final completion of the building. Anything else in the way of "system" cannot cope with modern conditions, however the architect may have made shift to stay with his conception in the past.

The old system was too often comparable to one (keeping our composer-conductor figure in mind) in which that conductor would be subject to the stupid ambition or avarice of his concert meister or his paymaster or perhaps even his piccolo player.

Since great corporate enterprises are taking the place of individual enterprises, business interests do like the man who will enter into their game, and go to jail with them or for them if necessary. A man who will play cricket according to the rules, and above all, who will stay put.

"Business" wants a "safe man," as it calls this one, meaning one also who, if he has to be bought, will not only *stay* bought, but like it, and believe in it for the sake of the byproducts to which all are cheerfully resigned.

It doesn't matter much how much of an architect this fellow is, if he can make a popular picture of his building it is enough.

The great corporation itself is the broker builder and merely "uses" him.

Well then, and why not the great corporation actually the builder, as a matter of fact, and directed by a real architect, "profession" or no "profession"?

A.I.A. The A.I.A. should modernize and become frankly a commercial organization like a labor union. Organize to maintain a fair wage or fee and keep the architect on the job in his true capacity as such. Let ethics go where they can be practiced without betrayal when commercialization or selfish ambition shows itself the real boss of the situation.

Engineer and Architect. We need the "engineering architect." Profession or no profession. An architect not only familiar with shopwork and factory conditions in America but an architect who can sense the human benefits actually to be derived from mechanized production that might make our living in a machine age less destructive to individuality, not more and more destructive. The engineer can no more accomplish this than a professor of mathematics can make music.

1930: The Logic of Contemporary Architecture as the Expression of This Age

FROM THE *Architectural Forum,* MAY, 1930.

What Cannot Be Torn Down. Twentieth century America must pay a ghastly price for nineteenth century grave robbing in architecture, a price that staggers reason, and pay it all back for lack of a simple sense of Tradition that would allow America to live its own life, and by so doing greatly honor that greater tradition.

Imagination. It takes creative imagination to see stone as stone; see steel as steel; see glass as glass, and to view traditions as tradition.

Ornaphobia. The taste for mediocrity grows by what it feeds upon, therefore, the public of this Republic is more than ever likely to find the love of commonplace elegance that curses it, and that was gratified by the sentimentality of the ornamental now pleased by the ornamentality of affected simplicity or again reacts in the sterility of ornaphobia.

Expression. It is no exaggeration to say that the *expression* of this machine age has so far been *repression.* How about the wasted timber resources, lost trees of a new continent to merely rot or burn as "millwork"? How about the butchery by machinery of every traditional form ever borrowed and worn to win the contempt of the civilized world, especially of the Beaux-Arts, that was supposed its advocate? How about neglect and insult by way of traditions to great new materials, and the separation in consequence of engineering and architecture, and the great change in human thought the ideal of democracy represents left without any interpretation whatsoever in architecture?

"Embarras de Choix." If great life is sure of great art, and it is, how can America fail of great life once this confusion of ideas, arising perhaps from the babble of tongues and the embarrassment of the riches of a great but antiquated inheritance passes, and the great immediate facts of the life that is her destiny stand out clearly before her people?

Definitions of Architecture. Architecture is the scientific art of making structure express ideas.

Architecture is the triumph of human imagination over materials, methods, and men to put man into possession of his own earth.

Architecture is man's great sense of himself embodied in a world of his own making. It may rise as high in quality only as its source because great art is great life.

Essential Romance. Romance is immortal.

Industry in the machine age can only become a machine without it. Modern architecture itself will become a poor, flat-faced thing of steel bones, box outlines, gas-pipe, and hand-rail fittings, as sun receptive as a concrete sidewalk or a glass tank. Without romance the essential joy of living as distinguished from pleasure is not alive. The new romance is that reality.

Pure Functionalism. Why should architecture or objects of art in the machine age, just because they are made by machines, have to resemble machinery? Because they were so made might be the best of reasons why they should not. Nor is there good reason why forms stripped clean of all considerations but function and utility should be admirable beyond that standpoint. They may be abominable from the human standpoint. Let us have no fear, therefore, of liberalism in our art of architecture nor in our industries. Dogma is still, as always, deadly.

1930: To the Young Man in Architecture

One of two lectures delivered at the Chicago Art Institute in the winter of 1930-31 and subsequently published by the Institute under the title Two Lectures on Architecture. *The selections given here have been drawn from the manuscript of the lecture as delivered. The published lectures were so completely revised that it is difficult to believe they are the same lectures. Similar thoughts were expressed in the article "Advice to the Young Man in Architecture" printed in the* Architectural Record *in August, 1931. At this time the Taliesin Fellowship was just coming into being and Mr. Wright became increasingly concerned with the problems of the young architects who gathered about him.*

The Shape of Things. Due to the very principles at work as limitations in our mechanical or mechanized products today, you may see coming in the best of them a new order of beauty that, in sense, *is* negation of the old order. In a deeper sense, a little later, you may be able to see it, too, as a liberal scientific re-affirmation of ancient order.

Architectural Education. Any architect should be radical by nature because it is never good enough for him to begin where others have left off. Current traditions in architecture have proved unsafe. They are the propaganda of the dead, as you may now see in this land strewn with the corpses of opportunity. It is no more trustworthy, this propaganda for the dead, than the propaganda for the living. Neither can have much to do with organic architecture.

No; the workings of principle in the direction of integral order is your only safe precedent, now or ever.

So the actual business of your architectural schools should be to assist you in the perception of such order in the study of the various architectures of the world; or else schools exist only to hinder and deform the young. Merely to enable you, young man, to make a living making plans for buildings is not good enough work for any school. And you may see by this definition of order that the "orders," as such, have less than nothing at all to do with the case of modern, that is to say, organic architecture. And too, you may see how little any of the great buildings of the ages can help you to become an architect except *as you look within them* for such working of principle as made them new in the order of their own day. As a matter of course, the particular forms and details appropriate to them became eccentricities to you, fatalities should you attempt to copy them for yourselves when you attempt to build.

Center and Circumference. As the hod of mortar and some bricks give way to sheet metal, the lack seam, and the breaker; as the workman gives way to the automatic machine, so the architect seems to be giving way either to the engineer, the salesman, or the propagandist.

I am here to assure you that the circumference of architecture *is* changing with astonishing rapidity but that its *center* remains unchanged, the human heart.

Exuberant Waste of Nature. Architecture was never old and will ever be new. From architecture the main current, little streams detach themselves, run a muddy course to be regathered and clarified by the great waters as though the little rills and rivulets had never been.

All art in our time is like that, and we witness only the prodigal waste nature sponsors when she flings away a million seeds to get a single plant, seeming in the meantime to enjoy her extravagance.

Nature's real issue, no doubt, in the life of the mind is no less wasteful. And she may enjoy her extravagance in the million fancies we have for one idea; millions of celebrations for one thought; a million buildings for even one small piece of genuine architecture.

1930: Terra Cotta

To the National Terra Cotta Society, Chicago.

The terra cotta manufacturers regarded Wright as Sullivan's heir, and they regarded Sullivan as their god. As Wright has pointed out, terra cotta was not a favorite material of his. Yet he has trenchantly observed, "When Sullivan turned to other materials—they were all terra cotta." Wright has steadfastly maintained that Sullivan's greatest achievement was his ornament, and has pointed out that his qualities most admired by modern critics were those less characteristic of Sullivan than of his partner, Dankmar Adler.

Henry Ford. I went down to Henry Ford's plant the other day and I saw a beautiful building which Albert Kahn had built. It really was a fine thing. Eight hundred feet long, beautifully lighted. The sun was shining in it, and over about half of the shining surface of maple flooring was planted with wonderful machinery, with men working at the machines. But the captain himself was out somewhere not to be found, playing with a reproduction of Liberty Hall, extending it by thousands of square feet to use it as a museum in which he was going to put the row of 100 old glass chandeliers I saw hanging nearby in the engineering building together with the other old things he had gone around the East to buy. Old things, reprehensible enough in themselves, and now worthless, to put into this great museum which Mr. Ford is going to give to the American people. And this is a man we had some right to look forward to and to look forward with. He has gone "a-slumming" too.

I do not know why such aberration should come over the country now. Ford is a man from whom the future had a right to expect something beside sentimentality. He is a man of common sense. He is a man that really has contributed a good deal to our country. He has successful ideas. His proposition for Muscle Shoals was one of the best things that I have heard of as a solution of the excess machine increment from this great tool, the machine which this man has now in its hand. What to do with the man at the machine? Ford's proposal was for the decentralization of industry. If he could get Muscle Shoals he was going to have lots of little factories. He was going to split up the big factory. He was going to put the men back on the ground. He was going to give every man a few acres of ground for his own.

In the summer the men would work on the ground. In the winter they would go to work with their machines in the factory, the machines in the factory giving such facility that they need only work at the machines for 5 or 6 months of each year.

Well now, here is a man to whom we have a right to look for salvation running around slumming, paying out machine increment for a reproduction of Liberty Hall, only making the toy thousands of square feet bigger; rummaging around to find all the old cast-off things that he calls American, but which are not. They are Georgian. They were brought over to this new freedom by the Colonials because they had none other or better to bring. And this is to be his personal "bequest" to the future. And I believe it was an architect who sold him the idea. It would be.

Confronted by a collapse like this, How are you going to blame Rockefeller for his Gothic "monster," or these other big boys in industry for amusing themselves likewise? How are we going to blame you terra-cotta boys for anything at all? How is anybody going to *blame* anybody for being silly when the best we have set a precedent for silly?

Analogy. Here is my hand, a human hand. As I move its members, the fingers, it changes expression, doesn't it? It may express almost anything you want to express and almost anything as you feel, but what makes it expressive? Nothing but the flowing continuous line and the continuous smooth simple surface. If you were to take off the flesh and the skin and reduce the hand to a skeleton and were to see the bones and all their joinings, then you would get back toward this other thing: ancient architecture, where you would have the structural element at work instead of the plastic sense of the whole supreme.

Practical or Expedient? "It is not practical," you say, "He is not practical," they say, but usually you all really mean *not expedient.* That is quite American; this universal worship of the expedient. I think it is one of the things, and perhaps the one thing most seriously the matter with our country, this worship of the expedient; being willing to "get by," to accept, to promote, to undersell the practical with the expedient.

Terra Cotta. Now, I suppose having gone so far into what is wrong with you I ought to be able to tell you what to do. I can't tell you what to do, but I will tell you some few things inevitable to you. I do not know much about your material because it has not been a favorite material of mine. It was a favorite material of the old meister's, and probably for that reason I have reacted. I was needed somewhere else so I have not used much terra cotta. But one thing terra cotta *can't* be, boys, is *stone;* and I think another thing it *can't* be is *wood.* I think it has got to be *itself,* and I think if it is going to be itself you have got to eliminate the masonry joint. I do not think you can cut and trim pieces of terra cotta as pieces of stone are joined and put mortar into the joints and get away with it. I think that is folly because you have got a *plastic* material, don't you see? The moment you stultify it by trying to make it a cut and butt and *set* material like stone, you haven't yet got to the nature of the thing.

1931: Two Lectures on Architecture

PUBLISHED BY THE ART INSTITUTE, CHICAGO.

Idealists. The absorbed idealist, egocentric-inventor in the realm of the thought-built, has a hard time with us socially, financially, and with peculiar force, morally. In addition to the instinctive fear for the safety of the tribe, in our form of social-contract the man with an idea seems to have become an invidious reflection upon his many fellows who have none. And certain effects belonging naturally to the idealist—such as belief in himself as having caught sight of something deeper, wider, higher or more important just beyond, mark him. He, all unsuspecting, will appear soon on the "path" peculiar to his own individuality in ways the poor fool, less absorbed, would have realized as unimportant if true, and have kept under cover. Ridicule from his many fellows, safely in the middle of the road, is always ready. And now it is only the incurably *young* person, in our country, who ever attempts to break through all down the line—and is laughed out of countenance, laughed out of a job, and eventually out of house and home.

Ideas and the Crisis. America is likely to bankrupt life by commercial, political and utensil-machinery. No! No political device, no device of organization, no device of salesmanship, no mechanical device can help our country much further on beyond. Only ideas can help her now.

Birth of the Skyscraper. An idea came into American practice when Louis Sullivan, absorbed egocentric, came into the little room where I worked beside him, pushed a drawing board with a fresh sketch on it over on my table, turned, went back into his office without saying a word and gently shut the door behind him. There it was, . . . the Wainwright Building of St. Louis, the first "skyscraper" as a tall building in its own right. Up to that time tall buildings were got by piling one cornice building on top of another cornice building.

There had been no vision of the tall office building's innate character and purpose as tall. But here, delicately indicated in pencil on manila-paper, a frail trace of human thought that might have faded or blown away overnight, was the thing we call an idea.

Though unaware of its origin, now you all behold the consequences of that prophecy, for every true idea is *prophecy.* An idea is a glimpse of the nature of the thing as more workable or "practical" as we say (we like that word "practical," but abuse it) than found in current practice or custom. An idea, therefore, is an act expressing in terms of human thought implicit faith in the character of Nature, something for lesser men to build and improve upon.

A fancy or conceit trifles with appearances as they are. An idea searches the *sources* of appearances, comes out as a form of inner experiences, to give fresh proof of higher and better order in the life we live. Finally . . . an idea is salvation by imagination.

Ideas at Work. A single glimpse of reality may change the *world* for any of us if, from the fancies and conceits of mere appearances, we get within the source of appearances. By means of human imagination at work upon this source, untold new life may find expression, for, with new force, ideas do actually fashion our visible world. A new order emerges to deepen life that we may become less wasted in anxious endeavor to go from here to somewhere else in order to hurry on somewhere from there. Any true conception as an idea, derived from any *original* source, has similar consequences in all the fields of our common endeavor to build a civilization.

The Prairie. I loved the prairie by instinct as a great simplicity, the trees and flowers, the sky itself, thrilling by contrast. I saw that a little of height on the prairie was enough to look like much more. Notice how every detail as to height becomes intensely significant and how breadths all fall short! Here was a tremendous spaciousness sacrificed needlessly, —all cut up crosswise and lengthwise into fifty foot lots, or would you have twenty-five feet? Salesmanship parcelled it out and sold it without restrictions. In a great new free country, everywhere, I could see only a mean tendency to tip up everything in the way of human habitation edgewise instead of letting it lie comfortably flatwise with the ground. Nor has this changed much today since automobilization made it a far less genuine economic issue and a social crime.

Point of View. I saw a building primarily not as a cave, but as shelter in the open.

1931: Hell-bent is Eclecticism

Eclecticism. At this psychological moment in our history, as a people, there is nothing deeper needed than culture; capacity to help America draw the line between the curious and the beautiful, which truly is the line of civilization itself. Any and every civilization as a culture has been built upon better foundations than eclectic "taste," furnished by academic institutions.

1931: American Architecture Today

TO THE MICHIGAN SOCIETY OF ARCHITECTS AND THE GRAND RAPIDS CHAPTER OF THE AMERICAN INSTITUTE OF ARCHITECTS.

Protestantism. We are a very young Nation. No protestantism is going to last with us very long. We want affirmation.

We are not satisfied to keep on protesting.

My European Colleagues. I have the greatest respect for my European colleagues. I think that in Europe are perhaps a dozen who are among the greatest architects and among the greatest men who have lived in our time.

I believe they are doing magnificent work. I think they got some original inspirations from us, here in America. I think they use them pretty well. Better than we ourselves do. And what does it matter that for the moment ornaphobia takes the place of ornamentia?

Of course, the protestant has never been beautiful, but he *has* been useful. And I believe Le Corbusier and the group around him are extremely useful. Extremely valuable, especially as an enemy. Able to demonstrate the depravity of our own very best ornamentia.

And I think that for us to build any more ornamental buildings, as such, is just criminal waste, now. But, on the other hand, some of the so-called mechanistic buildings in the name of the straight line and the flat plane have become fetish or a fad, dogma in the name of aesthetics. You get not much nearer to ultimate truth with these new buildings than with the old ornamental buildings. Because when you get below the surface, no matter how plain "modernistic" is, it is still merely ornamental.

The Gas Station. Keep your eye on the little gas station. That is the advance agent of decentralization; a new integration made by the advent of the automobile.

Murals and Sculpture. This architecture of the future is the only hope the sculptor and the painter have. They got a divorce from architecture when architecture became moribund. They could not hang around there to die, so by way of the Renaissance, they tried to set up for themselves. And they have been having a very good time ever since. But they have been getting nowhere in particular.

They both naturally belong with the architect. The interior ideal of which I spoke, when put to work, is the ideal that makes a building natural, a true expression of contemporary life. There is the painter's chance. There is the sculptor's chance. Both cooperatives of the modern architect.

Skyscrapers. I think that a tall building may be a beautiful thing.

I do not see why we should not have tall buildings. But I would be hanged before I could see why we should have any more big monuments to landlordism, to swell the rent roll, add to congestion and contribute to all that is subversive and that defeats the purpose of human life, wherever the attempt to build any more may be made. You are witnessing in the skyscraper a collision between the mechanistic factor and the mechanistic device; between the automobile and the skyscraper. On which would you bet?

You will have to take one or the other.

I would take the automobile.

Wouldn't you?

Louis H. Sullivan. The essential contribution of Louis Sullivan was one of heroism, one of faith in an ideal, an architectural ideal which after all is an expression of that life within, of which we have just been speaking. But his work was tentative. He got on the wrong side of the social ledger. He abused himself. But he was more mightily abused by his own country. He was wasted and thrown away by ignorance, not designedly. Simply run over by the juggernaut of selfish ambition and greed which increasingly characterizes our great country. And the significance of his work lies in the fact that he, fundamentally, courageously like a prophet set about his ideal and did his "damnedest" until he died.

The fact that Louis Sullivan's buildings were imperfect manifestations of his own ideal is no weakness of his, nor to be regarded as such by anyone. An ideal that can be wholly realized by any man in a lifetime is not worth striving for as an ideal. But his work in behalf of that ideal is forever valuable to his country. For God's sake let us be grateful. He, the first in American architecture, was true to his country to the death. Architecture to him was really the life and beating heart of this country. Now, what does it matter that we can build better buildings today than the buildings he built? Every great worker, every great man must be taken in true relation to the time in which he worked and sweated and was bled. And by any standard whatsoever brought, by intelligence, to bear upon his work or his life, he was a great man. He was a genius.

Space Enclosed. The interior space itself is the *reality* of the building. The room itself must "come through" or architecture has not arrived in the modern sense.

The Dead Hand. I don't think it would be too much to say that in America today, there is not a single public building and very few private buildings owned by the very rich, that could be characterized as a thought-built, genuine product of prophetic American thought or of true American life. We have had with us dead things that we have sentimentally taken as live traditions.

Vulcan and Eupalinos. Architecture is now blacksmithing, iron work, engineering. Most of you have been busy putting such architecture as you had on the outside of these new things, putting it all over the surface. I do not blame you so much because that superficiality had been going on for nearly five centuries before we took hold here in this country.

1931: I Will

I Hope. The old fair killed architecture for America. The next one will bury the corpse.

Organic architecture may then flourish on American ground.

I hope.

1931: Radio City

This appears to be an unpublished article written in the heat of the famous Radio City controversy. A violent attack on the intense concentration of office space and population originally contemplated secured important compromises in the final design, and produced the first significant protest against the skyscraper.

What Is Modern? Modern (really a la mode) is a protest against the sentimentality that ignores reality to find comfort and respectability in sentimental make-believe.

Apply this to our buildings:

And a hotel won't look like an office building.

A railway station won't look like a palazzo.

A gas station won't look like a Colonial diminutive.

A school won't look like a factory.

A factory won't look like a museum, etc.

To be modern simply means that all materials are used honestly for the sake of their own qualities and that the materials also modify the design of the building.

For the instance in hand, a steel building won't look like a masonry building. In the purpose of the structure itself, in the way it is built, and in what makes it stand there where it is: modern architecture is found and developed into an outside.

Architecture is not made on the "outside" of anything as the functioneers shamelessly say they make it after the thing is all arranged and set up. *Radio City!* Take off a chunk of New York anywhere you please, of similar area, where congestion is greatest and you will have another and perhaps a better Radio City, on its own old-fashioned terms of old-fashioned composition, lacking only the little park down there in the dark.

Landlords Know. Waste "pays."

Private Concerns. "Mr. Rockefeller is not building a monument," said Doctor Corbett, apologizing for the new model for Radio City.

No, Mr. Rockefeller is in need of money. And space makers for rent are arranging the little drama for him. When that is all right they will talk to you about architecture. If you want to talk about it.

But why talk about it?

That is only the public's concern.

Neither Mr. Rockefeller nor his doctors are concerned, unless *afterward.*

The typical situation in our great united experiment—sacrosanct.

1931: Raymond Hood

The skyscraper's most distinguished creator is given a severe but good-natured going over in this review. Hood was the last of the really gifted eclectics in the true sense of that word. He seems always to have regarded modern building as "just another style."

Architecture as Business. So "The *success* of a building is measured by the degree of satisfaction to its occupants, and if it pays, and if it is acceptable to the public," Mr. Hood?

"Architectural ability," Mr. Hood says, "lies in the production of a 'successful' building on these lines." We have here a certain feature of an architect's ability, certainly. But again going a little beyond Mr. Hood by these terms, present popularity is the test of all art. The intelligence of the purchasers or tenants today (they may not know what art is, but they know what they like) is not only tomorrow but becomes the horoscope and horizon of all art and architecture whatever. Apparently, in common with his landlord, Mr. Hood often mistakes such success for architecture. And as contemporary thought runs. His mistake *is* good business for a short time.

Purport 6. Concerning construction: "The several acceptable types of building construction," Mr. Hood goes on, are those which provide for commercial contingencies. "Because," he says, "no one can tell what is going to happen to the building." So, something like the sideboard converted into the folding bed seems to be the ideal here. Any landlord would like that because, as I gather from the language of this section of his "credo," construction should be "mixed" as much as possible. The more mongrel construction is, the easier it is to tear the building down, or to make it over into something else.

Thus sound engineering passes out, and the makeshift comes in with Mr. Hood to take its place.

This is one reason, I suppose, why Mr. Hood's "architecture" is designed to go on outside or on top of the construction in any style preferred by the client. It all has to come off again anyway.

Purport 7. In "publicity" as a feature of architecture Mr. Hood has a lively and timely interest. "Publicity" has influenced all his designs, he says. Expert in this, he cites examples of his success. All of which seems sensible expediency and might account in no small degree for his career.

Magnitude is such an advertising feature, it seems, and so are "hanging gardens," meteorology especially. And "height." Whereas I grew up in the belief that architecture might be great in the little and little in the great. But Ray talks a little too much like an advertising expert, who, somehow, got into architecture. And as the "contemporary thought" of which he speaks, runs, this should be praise for him, not blame.

Careerists. Architecture can be no form of expediency whatever. Architecture is "pot and pan" only as pots are pots and pans are pans. And it is self-advertising only as one of the lowest attributes of its character; a misfortune due to our commercial circumstances.

Any good architecture is the genuine expression of the realities of life by way of genuinely practical building. The integrities are the stake of architecture and not the pretensions and lies of life that make money to make life lie "smooth."

And finally let me express the belief that in our country such architecture and architectural careers as Ray Hood's—we have hardly any other kind—are only proof of how shallow is any demand for integrity of any kind in this culture we have made impotent by way of too much "good taste," and too little sincerity.

Wherever principle concerns a purpose, career is a poor substitute for creation.

Limitations of the Eclectic. No one born and bred eclectic can be a modern architect, in any practical application of the exacting term, if, indeed, he can ever be one. Such an eclectic is not capable of more than another exploit of some preferred original.

The Chicago Fair. Being myself born in, trained, and having lived all my life in what we have now turned to, over page, as Mr. Hood did overnight, I believe it not only indiscreet on his part, but impossible (his eye on the "public") for him to build good buildings by way of this latest fortuitous election on his part. Architecture must be born and not made. It grows slowly. Unfortunately there is not yet enough modern architecture ready made to go around the eclectic's circle in this World's Fair. Then what shallow effrontery for a man, clever as Raymond Hood is clever (I should not be criticizing him here unless he were), suddenly to seize it for show purposes and the self-advertising of a group of American architects.

I know by the internal evidence of the Hood language, no less than by the way he does what he does, that he cannot know what organic architecture is as distinguished from any other kind except as to classifying certain effects or surface appearances. Nor do I believe he feels it necessary to care what it is. Were it expedient (he would say practical), he would build a Gothic church tomorrow. As he has himself said, he would build a classic temple for any purpose if such were opportune. He would build anything a likely client wanted, and so he is the beaux-ideal American architect. In other words architecture, Beaux-Arts or modern, to Ray is just one more expediency.

Architecture to his kind is no spiritual conviction for which he would suffer defeat and fail, if need be. But modern architecture must be now a feature of "success" as his apostasy alone would indicate. And there are many like him as there are eclectics engaged in designing pictorial prevarication in the name of advertising.

1931: Taste and Autobiography

Autobiography. Listen to any man you meet and you will see that nothing is more natural than autobiography, and usually, nothing more tedious. Every man you meet is either intensely, modestly, offensively or charmingly autobiographical. Women are less so. They have learned the wisdom that makes them natural biographers. Too often, heartless ones.

1931: For All May Raise the Flowers Now for All Have Got the Seed

FROM *T-Square,* FEBRUARY, 1932.

As the dogmas of the "International Style" became more firmly intrenched Wright redoubled his efforts to clarify the distinction between the new views and those he had long held. Founded in large part upon his own early work, Wright believed that the new "architectural nudism" had at best a negative value. This essay is typical of the controversies that seethed during the years before modern architecture in the United States got out of the copybook stage.

Disciples. What creative mind wants emulation?

What he architect wants disciples? Not one.

He wants work.

The man wants to see the principles he loves, live while he lives.

He wants life to go on growing, not by emulation, but by depth of individual experience. Not by *peddling,* but by *working.*

On Being Alive. I often have occasion to reflect upon the disadvantage I offer, by being alive and more productive than ever, a living reproach to callous or flighty disciples or perhaps callow apprentices now full fledged and eager to fly. As somebody said at the "League" last year—was it "Little Napoleon number three" who said it?—"We always come to the realization that Frank Lloyd Wright is alive with a kind of shock."

Motives. It is another serious weakness of our American system that the national mind seems never to believe that a man may be actuated by principles to speak his own mind, loving principle more than himself and willing to eat the dirt thrown into his mouth every time he opens it rather than let the principle in him go by default. No. The instinct of the salesman immediately places him as not "having got his." To a salesman, all men are salesmen. So where financial interests have any concern in architecture (and where are they not concerned?), it is all the man's socioeconomic life is worth to voice dissent where money is tied up or tied in. There is but one voice where there is "investment." Hence, the default or the combined ballyhoo of salesmanship to drown the voice.

The Kimono and the Derby Hat. I loved Japan and reverently took off my hat to its nativity when asked there to build a building. The Japanese are oriental, not occidental, hard as they may try to be occidental. They are trying pitifully hard, but there is a chasm between the races where art is concerned wholly in favor of the oriental.

Yet, see all the internationalists busy over there encouraging that ambitious, "industrious little nation" to belie and stultify itself by an aggravated architectural version of the derby hat, kimono and Boston gaiters. Tokio is becoming a profane sight in consequence. To anyone who loves these sensitive, ambitious people who call Tokio capital, here is deplorable butchery.

The East still thinks the West knows what it is about and promptly gets after whatever the West is after, too quick to grab and fall in line. Japan's national weakness.

Some day the East will learn that the West itself is a formula chaser or an imitator, instead of a culture builder. Any formula derived from its experimental civilization can only be a brand or a fraud upon the East.

The Japanese will some day wake to curse the abuse they were encouraged to practice upon themselves.

The Japanese house, a perfect expression of organic architecture, is being made over into a western garage, instead of being organically developed into a suitable place for the same life rising from its knees to its feet.

Nudism. The cause of an organic architecture runs well beyond the yardstick and plain plaster by which international style busybodies, in their extremity, obscure a simple issue as "modern."

A bee in their bonnets.

They are doing some harm, I believe, and unless there is enough vitality in the great cause of architecture itself to rebuke and shake them off, they intend doing not only more but all the harm there is in them. It may not be so much in the long run, but it discourages all true creative initiative meantime in this country of mine.

1931: Apology for the Decorator

One of several speeches, articles and book reviews dealing with the position of the interior decorator in the modern movement, and the general relationship between decoration and architecture, only a few of which have been included here.

Interior Desecration and Its Remedy. The discouraging thing to me, and I am sure to anyone who thinks at all, in this latest repetition by way of competition, is not that the new mode is here. In common with others I have waited long enough to see these more simple appearances in our country, but I have worked all along for the end of sentimental make-believe, for an *organic* simplicity, still far away.

But so far as any real grasp of the significance of such forms as modernism is taking goes, this hoped-for reality is more lacking in the "modernistic" than it was lacking in the other borrowings.

The greater shame lies in this fact, that here at last is something that might be really different. It is in this latest eclecticism that America really has something to lose by imitation.

There was no principle at work in the great "styles" so far as our life went or now goes and so not so much to lose.

But there *is* a principle at work behind the original appearances from which the "modernistic" is deriving its thankless "style." There *are* underlying forms that are appropriate to our age and our kind of life. Those underlying principles and forms can save the day for our art and industry only if designers and decorators would abandon "desecration" long enough to get down to these principles and learn the technique that is able to work them, independently.

Picturizing. The amount of money that passes through the hands of the surface decorator, "in" or "out," in the course of a year in these United States is colossal. A staggering total. I do not know, nor does anybody, just what the total of millions is, but it is only fair to admit that nearly all is spent with intent to make something beautiful. A picture of some kind is aimed at and often very pretty pictures result. These pretty pictures are the poison of the future. The better the meretricious picture is, the greater the stumbling block on the path.

The good-looking "picture" is about all architects as decorators, or decorators as architects ever think about except the more and more important business of selling the picture to the inhabitant for a price. Given enough overstuffing and cushions and free floor space the pictures can be made fairly habitable, although, as we all know quite generally, they are incongruously inhabited.

1932: Why I Love Wisconsin

FROM THE *Wisconsin Magazine*, 1932.

I love Wisconsin because my staunch old Welsh grandfather with my gentle grandmother and their 10 children settled here nearby. I see the site of their homestead and those of their offspring as I write. Offspring myself, my home and workshop are planted on the ground grandfather and his sons broke before the Indians had entirely gone away.

This Wisconsin valley with the spring-water stream winding down as its center line has been looked forward to or back upon by me and mine from all over the world, as home.

And I come back from the distant, strange, and beautiful places that I used to read about when I was a boy, and wonder about; yes, every time I come back here it is with the feeling there is nothing anywhere better than this is.

More dramatic elsewhere, perhaps more strange, more thrilling, more grand, too, but nothing that picks you up in its arms and so gently, almost lovingly, cradles you as do these southwestern Wisconsin hills. These ranges of low hills that make these fertile valleys of southwestern Wisconsin by leading down to the great sandy plain that was once the bed of a mightier Wisconsin river than any of us have ever seen.

I doubt if that vast river flood were more beautiful then, however, than this wide, slow-winding, curving stream in the broad sand bed, where gleaming sandbars make curved beaches and shaded shores to be overhung by masses of great greenery. Well, it is not quite like any of the more important rivers of the world. It is more what specialists in scenery would call "picturesque." It is, however, unique.

So "human" is this countryside in scale and feeling. "Pastoral" beauty, I believe, the poets call it. More like Tuscany, perhaps, than any other land, but the Florentines that roamed those hills never saw such wild flowers as we see any spring, if the snow has been plentiful. The snow usually is plentiful and the cold too. The kind of cold that has always tempered the man of the North as a conqueror of the South.

And the Wisconsin red barn! Wisconsin barns are mostly all red, and everywhere make a feature of the landscape missing in most States. A farmstead here is somehow warmed and given life by the red of the barns as they stand about me over the green hills and among the yellow fields with the sun on them.

And then Wisconsin is a dairy State. That means herds of pure Holsteins or Guernseys, or what have you, occupying the best ground anywhere around, making pictures that go with the one made by the red barn. Wisconsin, fond of passing laws, should pass another law compelling every farmer to paint his barn red. Another that will compel him to pasture his cows by the highway and his pigs back behind the barn.

I've found out, too, that we are known abroad as a "progressive" State. They know about Ross and Commons, Reinsh and Glenn Frank: names that help to make Wisconsin scientific, agrarian and political to the outside world. The name of La Follette distinguishes our political history, I find, wherever I go. And I, too, always speak of Wisconsin as "progressive" when I talk about her away from home. Not understanding very well just what the word means, I suppose, any more than other Wisconsin people, in general, do. But that is what Wisconsin would like to be anyway, and what she means to be. Which is most important after all.

A good solid State, our State. Physically very beautiful, a veritable playground for humanity in summer as Arizona is in winter.

Next to Wisconsin, "gathering of the waters," Arizona, "arid zone," is my favorite State. Each very different from the other, but something individual in them both not to be found elsewhere.

I am glad, too, Wisconsin is an Indian name. European people interested in architecture have learned to say Wisconsin, in Japan, in Germany, in Holland, Austria, and Switzerland more often probably than any other American name except New York.

Just now on my table is a Lloyd's Reisebureau advertisement proposing excursions to America from Switzerland. The program is given by days, what is to be seen each day. When the "West" is reached, "Dienstag und Mittwoch" are to be devoted to the "Landhausen Wright."

Taliesin has received architectural pilgrims from all over the world. They have helped Taliesin a lot and the pilgrims have gone home and written in European newspapers and magazines and books, about America as they discovered it hidden away in a rural nook in southwestern Wisconsin.

In this rural nook in southwestern Wisconsin is our busy workshop. Out of it have come plans for buildings that have established new ideals in life and architecture and carried new principles in engineering into effect. They will never again build buildings in earthquake zones as they did before the Imperial was built in Tokio.

They will never again build the skyscraper quite so wastefully and foolishly whenever St. Mark's Tower is completed.

They will not long continue to make little scene paintings of houses in Arizona and California as they now do after San Marcos in the Desert grows up out of the desert as an indigenous human plant.

The American people only need to know they *can* build *real* buildings. We would like to hold and consolidate all these gains for Wisconsin as the Cardinals hold and consolidate their football gains on the gridiron. We are trying to do this by establishing a larger industrial workshop near here for the young people who want to be American artists; something in which the State university itself might well take an interest. Students are awakening to a lively interest in this matter. But that interest on the part of a great university might, after all, stultify our own enjoyment in a fresh endeavor and get us mixed up with senators and assemblymen and committees and regents and wear us all away with nothing done. Our social system is like that, unfortunately; yes, even in Wisconsin.

Why does any real progress have to overcome so much resistance? Why do we need, always, so many first-class funerals in order to get anything sensible done, if it is "unusual." Some day Wisconsin will be so progressive that she will consider the fine arts not only essential as science, politics, or farming, but even more fundamental to any State that would live "above the belt."

Getting back to why I love Wisconsin. . . .

I love Wisconsin because of her Meiklejohn experiment at the University, whether it succeeded or not. And because of every sincere forward-looking experiment the State itself has ever made; because of her courage; her love of independence; her true belief in individuality as essential to immortality. I love her because she will spend her money to grubstake prospectors for future benefits to her posterity, even though some of her too, too substantial citizens call her foolish for that—and I love her because she has not so very many snobs.

I love her because she has so few highbrows. They are men educated far beyond their capacity, so my old master Louis Sullivan used to say. And I love her because most of her was for the temperance of the Declaration of Independence instead of for the prohibition that violates temperance.

Without taking myself too seriously, I hope I love her because I, too, am by birth and nature a Wisconsin radical. Radical is a fine word meaning "roots." Being radical I must strike root somewhere. Wisconsin is my somewhere. I feel my roots in these hillsides as I know those of the oak that have struck in here beside me.

That oak and I understand each other.

Wisconsin soil has put sap into my veins. Why, I should love her as I loved my mother, my old grandmother, and as I love my work.

1932: The Traffic Problem

FROM THE *New York Times.*

Decentralization. Centralization was the ideal of monarchy . . . the individual unit compelled to revolve round about a common center.

Integration is the ideal of democracy . . . many units, free in themselves, functioning together in freedom.

Monarchy has fallen. Our capitalist system, if it persists as a form of centralization, stands to fall. Electrified mechanical forces that are building our modern world now are, by nature, turning upon centralization to destroy it. And that means that the city is destroying itself.

Centralization, whether as the city, the factory, school, or farm, now has the enormous power of the machine-age setting in dead against it. It is in the nature of universal or ubiquitous mobilization that the city spreads out far away and thin.

It is in the nature of flying that the city as we know it disappears.

It is in the nature of universal electrification that the city has never been.

Centralization by way of the city has had a big day and a long day. It is not dead yet. But it is no longer a necessity or a luxury. Mobilization of the human animal, volatilization of human thought, voice, and vision make the city as troublesome interference to life as "static" is troublesome to radio.

1932: The Frozen Fountain

FROM THE *Saturday Review of Literature,* MAY 21, 1932.

A review of Claude Bragdon's book, which attempted to create abstract rules of architectural form.

Systems of Proportion. Proportion is nothing in itself. It is a matter of relation to environment modified always by every feature, exterior as well as interior. Le Corbusier, hard as nails and sane as a hammer up to this point, goes as superstitious as a milkmaid lost in the mist of a moonlit night.

But in meticulous, abstract, geometrical analysis there will always be fascinating room for the astrological, geometrical mind. And sometimes the long arm of coincidence will find a pretty circumstance in the hand. I should say the laws lie deeper and in the realm of relativity. Were the abstraction so easily made I should distrust the validity of the laws.

1932: Books

Literatures. Mine is a catholic taste which probably means a hearty appetite, and I find much to admire in books that do not touch my own work. When I get to ones that do I find too much pretended or missing, just as I probably would if I were more developed in the fields in which I am still ignorant enough to enjoy without too close questioning.

But, to me, the greatest literature, after all, is not words but notes. Bach, Handel, and Beethoven, and sometimes the Negro spirituals, Stravinsky, Scriabin, and "jazz." Music gives me more than ever now.

Yes, I find too much pleasure in all literature, script or music, ever to qualify as a model of any kind.

1932: America Tomorrow

FROM THE *American Architect,* MAY, 1932.

Role of the Architect. If this machine age needs an architect at all it needs him in the same place now he occupied in former civilizations and that place was interpreter of the industry of his epoch and the builder of the buildings natural to their day.

Now it may be that the buildings natural to our day may be only plain or fancy masks, and that a masquerade is all our undercultured, overeducated people have coming to them. In that case the function of an architect is merely that of a decorator and chiefly important to women who do not know what architecture is, but do know what they like.

1932: The Designing Partner

Wright's love of colored crayons probably derives from his Pestalozzi kindergarten training.

Colored Pencils. I went alone into the deserted working rooms with time to reflect a little. Looking about over the drafting boards I wondered what, at the moment, would please me most. The most pleasurable thing I could imagine was that I might go into some shop where fine colored pencils were kept and gather several of every color I had ever seen and perhaps see some never seen before. Perhaps a more gorgeous red, a truer blue, a warmer green. And I would lay them all out in a row, abuse the white paper on the board at which I sat; and sit looking at them, several of each and every possible color. Enough to use and last sometime, for once. I suppose the recent scarcity of some of the most desirable colors, because we use those most and can't buy more at the moment, led up to this organic desire. But I love colored pencils. They are intimately associated with my sense of happiness, and have been since childhood.

Designers. The designer is a happy fellow. Ordinarily the happiest of all but it is hard for me to see him as a "partner."

Nevertheless, most of our architectural "firms" are made up of a designer, and a builder or a business getter, or of all three.

And I wonder how the thing works out. Is the designing partner a happy fellow working for the builder and business getter, or is it the other way around?

It is hard to think of a real designer managing a partner. It is easier for me to imagine a partner managing the designer.

1932: Contribution to a Symposium

The Horseless Carriage. You will be able to drive a motorcar up to the new house and not spoil the picture. You can't do that to the fashionable ones now if you are sensibly eye-minded.

Every Man His Own Architect. When we come to understand architecture as the essential nature of all harmonious structure we will see that it is the architecture of music that inspired Bach and Beethoven; the architecture of painting that is inspiring our modern painters as it inspired Mantegna or Velasquez; that it is the architecture of life itself that is the inspiration of the great poets and philosophers. And if by any chance, or by the grace of whatever gods may be, we should ever again have a statesman in this country, he would be the architect of a social order that would be a fit basis for the architecture that is going to give new and more livable form to our homes, forms that will express a broader and better life than we have ever known or any existing as history.

Landlords and Pseudism. Do not imagine, however, that the landlord is going to be allowed to "handle" the new home of the new era as he has handled the old one in the era that is passing. There would be no chance for the new home in his hands. To tell why would be too long a story.

At the moment it is enough to know that in spite of the landlord human habitation is about to find new forms and new effectiveness.

I know we can't have a great architecture while it is only for the landlord.

I know we must have architecture out of the man and for the man, and that we may have it by way of such modern improvements as machinery has already made or will soon be making. If not we will go spiritually bankrupt.

I know these new forms will bear the same relation to the old forms as the sunlit strand to the cave, and we will have houses more delightful than pseudo tudor, or pseudo classic, or Camden Gothic, or Mediterranean or anything the Colonials had with them or on them when they came over. I know the new houses will be more satisfying than the tons of commonplace elegance we cherish now between a cellar and an attic.

Modern houses are going to have as genuine significance as enclosed space as, once upon a time, houses had as sculpture in Greece and Rome.

1932: What is the Modern Idea?

FROM *Physical Culture,* JUNE 24, 1934.

Our Power. The ancient power that built such civilizations as have died, still lives.

The ancient cities are dead because of the exterior ideals of external life that prevailed, and when imposed upon life caused that life to grow old and die.

But the same power, multiplied now by the leverage of machine power, may build a civilization in America that will live because of this *interior* ideal of an interior life externalized as the great architecture of a great life that we have now come to call the modern idea.

The Modern Ideal. Walls that as solid walls served feudal thought and life are vanishing.

The heavy bulks of building material, hollowed out as caves to live in, are disappearing with the fortifications that protected the might of the feudal estate.

No free man in America need "box up" or "hole in" for protection any more in any building or in any city.

If our country is as free as our ideal should make it, why not make ideal freedom come true? We have no longer need in America for master or slave however disguised, nor for lord or serf. So, there is no longer need for the exaggerated defenses of a foregone, outlived, human entity in any of its forms.

In this age of democracy may we not be allowed to live, no longer as the savage animal man was once compelled to live, but believing in the free being man may be?

So the modern idea is to seek the spaciousness, openness, lightness, and strength that is now logical and that will scatter urbanism (the city) into the regional field just as inadvertent disease is absorbed into the circulation of a healthy body.

The modern gifts of glass; the modern gifts of steel in tension; the modern gifts of electromagnetic sciences: all began a new era for man. All are simple, natural agents of a new freedom for mankind. They are at work. No power can turn them aside.

Every man will soon have facility to roam the sky or ground and live with the perfect freedom of vision that will relate him to the ground and all that the ground should mean to the human life of which he is the whole as he is a part.

His supermaterial, glass, as he has it now, is a modest but direct means to this liberation.

The supermaterial, steel, as he may see it tense in the strand as John Roebling used in the Brooklyn Bridge to usher in a new era. The strand is direct means to this liberation.

The textile as a shimmering robe to clothe interior spaciousness within shells of glass and metals, all the nuances of imagination entangled in the pattern of its meshes is, among others, another means to this end. All are humble materials, but all are potent when grasped by the modern idea.

And working with these for twentieth century freedom are the new factual forces of the new order: mobilization, teletransmission, ubiquitous publicity, the armed and mighty power of the machine.

Freedom of the Highway. Modern thought grasps the new means of today to enlarge space in the scheme of human living and create an appropriate sense of space in human life itself. Life is learning to see itself as free.

Modern life is beginning to see the extended highways as the horizontal lines of human freedom in our human life here on this earth.

By way of this release of these new powers and this new sense of freedom you will soon see the death of the city.

1932: The House on the Mesa

A description of a luxurious country house in Colorado which appears to have been written in answer to an inquiry from Fortune.

House on the Mesa. The style of this fireproof house grows naturally from practical space arrangement definitely related to practical modern construction. The scheme of construction is the cantilever slab hung from above by cantilever beams projecting from the masonry chimney mass. The light enclosing copper and glass screens hanging from the cantilever slabs are offset to place the opening sash in the horizontal ledges. This general type of construction and the offset concrete-block wall to allow ventilation at the floor levels, gives the house its individual grammar.

The sweep of the mesa with the magnificent views of the Rocky Mountains is felt and reflected in the general arrangement and, as a foil, comes the sheltered bathing pool pouring into the "lake for swimming," its surrounding glass planes sequestered by the surrounding masses of trees.

The house itself, as a whole, becomes a complete garden, open or sheltered at will. A good time place. It has what might truthfully be called twentieth century style.

1932: What Does the Machine Mean to Life in a Democracy?

FROM *Pictorial Review.*

The publication of The Disappearing City *outlined the plan for Broadacre City, a distinguished addition to the long line of architectural utopias of the last half-century. In this plan, the basic ideas of which are well summarized in this selection, many of Wright's leading ideas have been brought into simultaneous focus. The most important of these may be found indexed here under such headings as decentralization, skyscrapers, motorcar, traffic, land, housing and Broadacre City. An exhibition with detailed models showing the typical development of Broadacre City has been widely displayed.*

I now realize that organic architecture is life and life itself is organic architecture or both are in vain.

The principles that are working in one are working in the other. We are sacrificing the greater human efficiency to put all into the lesser but ubiquitous machine efficiency. It is useless to go on working for the landlord on any general basis of a great future for a noble architecture. The landlord is not intrinsic. What perversion to allow land to hold the improvements instead of the improvements holding the land.

All is more or less makeshift where life itself is concerned, as long as the basis upon which life and architecture must function is not free. The valiant special case alone is free. Out of my own sense of an organic architecture and observing the principles of that architecture at work as the law of natural change in our own country comes a basic outline of a future city growing from the ground up to utilize for the human being the forces that built the whirling vortex from the top down.

The vortex was built on the space measurement most appropriate to the man on his legs or sitting in some trap behind a horse. The plan, even so, was faulty. But how utilize that plan now when the standard of space measurement has changed to the man seated in his motor car, vicarious power in the throttle at his feet, his hands on a steering wheel, not to mention the cigar in his mouth? One mile has little advantage to him over ten miles. But he bulks in space requirements, movement aside, 10 to 1, as compared with his former self.

We have been too tolerant of re-form. It is true form we should now be seeking. It has never been had by any alteration upon any old building nor will it be had by any alteration upon an old order. It will grow from the ground up as nature always grows her forms; roots in the soil that is nature. And that means a new layout for a new city upon free ground for a new sense of freedom in space.

In the present city cruelty, misfortune, and poverty may be mitigated and should be. Meantime, honor to those so engaged.

But we have learned enough from the specialization that is centralization to go to the root for construction and by way of evolution work with the law of beneficent change. The generalization that is integration is that change. Why longer try to hold against it what we have? "To have and to hold" is all very well when having and holding *with* nature, both are disastrous when holding *against* nature. And in line with that normal law of change, as I have observed its working throughout our country, will come the disappearance of the Moloch that knows no god but more: the big city, the big establishment, the big fortune, the big business. Except as bigness is in a general group of individual units and not in any particular overgrown unit, it is no longer humanly economic. All will be absorbed into the body of the whole country, circulation once more healthy and efficiency again genuine where humanity is concerned.

The important new factors, electrification, mobilization, modern architecture, have been taken for granted by high and low, therefore, they have had no intelligent recognition in our industrial plan or in our culture. But factitious increment as a premium put upon centralization has not been wholly wasted because the mechanical factors of our age have been more rapidly developed to a higher degree of efficiency than would ever have been possible otherwise. This mechanical power, as leverage, should be utilized. But the time has gone by when this efficiency can justify the immense cost of its inefficiencies to life itself.

The time is here when something must be done with these new powers in a larger way, for humanity, to relieve the cruel centrifugal pressure inordinate centralization has become. These new resources and humanity, fast growing apart as enemies to destroy each other, wasting each other meantime, are both by way of each other capable of a new form.

And the new form is openly thrusting at the old in all these factors. Their new forces are beginning to decentralize the city, subdivide the immense aggregates, and build up individuality in order to reintegrate all in larger unity. An entirely new space measurement demanded by volatilizing of thought, voice and sight, the widening of the horizon of physical movement by means of the motor car and a true individual freedom in the life of the United States. Compelled by the organic forces of these new resources, our big cities are already splitting up into several centers; our big mercantile establishments are already building distributing centers on the edges of the big cities; our big manufacturers have already confessed that the big establishment is no longer necessary; the motorbus and motortruck have already cut the wasteful back and forth haul of the too many competing railways to the heart. The new centers of distribution serving mobilization, the gas station one of them, are rapidly growing in importance and range, especially Middle West and South, Southwest and West. Manhattan alone lost hundreds of thousands of citizens last year.

So greatly has mobilization already changed human values, modified human character, and altered the circumstances that most of our equipment is obsolete when it is built. Almost all our present architectural and structural equipment is obsolete or old. The machine age, while exaggerating them, has made the old arrangements of which the city was the most important already invalid and soon inoperative.

Decentralization is inevitable.

It is therefore time not to dream of the future but to realize the future is now and here. It is imperative to go to work with it, no longer foolishly trying to stand against it.

Supersense is soon common sense.

To decentralize is already common sense, needing only to realize the forms that best express it in our daily life. Those needed forms are all organic architecture, organic economics and an organic social contract.

Our pioneer days are not over, but the frontier has shifted. Our forbears took life in their hands and, efficient, went in their covered wagons to clear the ground. It seems they blazed the way for an efficiency that could only become exaggerated centralization by way of a rugged individualism; an exaggeration of their own great qualities. The heroic sacrifice of the original pioneers was forerunner to this type of selfish domination we now see as exaggerated centralization.

This later pioneering, our inheritance, is now the frontier to be cleared away again by the forces of a more humane, because a more organic, culture. Only by regaining appropriate humane use of the new resources derived from pioneer "success" may democracy flourish. "Excess" as "success" must perish into opportunity for all to live as the bravest and best.

No longer should men be compelled to live (would they succeed at all) according to the baser qualities of their natures, but "success" according to their better selves. And survive.

On this new frontier, however, is scraping off the too full bushel while ignoring the sources that overfill it, statesmanship? Then the tinker is the best maker, the imitator the best creator, and vicarious power the best power.

Politicians are not statesmen. A statesman is an architect of an organic social order. The *reforms* proposed and effected by our governing powers are little shifts or make shifts in the rules of the game that have all been tried; but no interpretation in the changed circumstances of the ideal we have professed and have ignored, has been tried.

Have we, then, really lost that ideal?

There is no question whatever as to the rightmindedness and humane instincts of humanity, when humanity is free, but . . . in what does this freedom actually consist?

Let us discuss that as intelligently and frankly as we do science, biology, for instance, and this fundamental cause to which we have dedicated our country and ourselves may come a little nearer realization.

What *is* the meaning of life in a democracy, developed machine power a factor, as distinguished from life in other forms of social contract? What is true human efficiency? What is true human economy?

Let our bravest and best seek the answer and they will find it in life as organic architecture, as I have found it in organic architecture as life.

The present basis for life is inorganic, unsound and therefore dangerous just as such architecture as we have is inorganic waste. The inorganic has had a sporadic increase but has no possible life because it lacks the correlation essential to growth. Centralization is *ingrowing*. Even with all its increase it has no interior, informing, expanding principle of life. Its efficiencies are all too narrow.

Inorganic, our economic system, our social system, our arts, our religion, our politics are absurd. Our status quo a strong arm. Our fortunes false.

We have drifted into exaggeration and toward impotence by way of a vicarious use of a vicarious power to make money as, itself, another vicarious power. Let us have an intelligent interpretation of our own ideal, democracy, and then honest appraisal of our direction as we stand. And then? With what we have accomplished let us go in the direction we intend.

1933: First Answers to Questions by *Pravda*

Architects of the U.S.S.R., having tried and rejected European modernism, were strongly attracted to Wright's work. This is the first indication of the interest that was to lead to the trip to the U.S.S.R. in 1937.

Economics of "Traditional" Architecture. In the epoch now painfully closing disguised as "economic depression," architecture was only a bad form of surface decoration; landlord bait for tenants. If the profession of architecture has any future at all as such it must get the buildings more directly and sensibly out of nature for the native. An entirely new set of ideas more in keeping with the principles of architecture are needed before thinking men can be inspired with sufficient confidence to go on building any more buildings. Capital will only spend money to make money and there is no more to be made in the old building way.

A View of U.S.S.R. I view the U.S.S.R. as a heroic endeavor to establish more honest human values in a social state than ever existed before. Its heroism and devotion and its plight too move me deeply. Russia is a great hope. But I fear that pseudo-machine worship used to defeat pseudo capitalism may become inverted capitalism in Russia itself, and again prostitute the man to the machine because heart beats that are human are not like the ticking of a watch. Creative art, creative in its masterful use of principle, is essential in any upbuilding of any social order worthy to be called organic and likely to continue. Individuality is a precious asset of the human race where, free from wilfully exaggerated personality, it stands upon a common basis fair to all. And it is a quality that should be rewarded according to its human value. This just reward is no less the problem of Russia even now, as I see it, than of every other sincere attempt to free all the people to be ruled by their own bravest and by their own best whether from within or from without.

"Safe" Education. The educational system of the country has for many decades been breeding inertia. It aims to produce the middle-class mind which is a mind able to function only in the middle of the road, boulevard preferred. It is the "safe" mind for the system as set up.

1933: The Chicago World's Fair

FROM THE *Architects' Journal,* JULY, 1933.

The Virtues of 1893. To see the Chicago "Progress" Fair of 1933 is to remember its original, the Columbian Fair of 1893, and to realize how much better the Columbian Fair was in every respect—even as novelty. At the Columbian Fair the provincials of the United States saw, for the first time, architecture as coordination on the grand scale. Thrilled by its orchestral effects the provinces aided by the group of eclectics responsible for that ensemble went heavily pseudo; and imagined they went "classic."

There was some excuse for their debauch of sanity by way of academic taste because they yet knew nothing of the scientific organism of architecture. The building to them was a picture. The pictorial in any form was the art they knew. They were victorian. And there was much to be said for the eclecticism of 1893 as a picture, especially for the United States. The architecture of the fair became epidemic and five times since the same thing has broken out in various parts of the country modified somewhat each time but the thought unchanged.

There was only retrogression in the repetition and each was confessed a failure. No progress.

1933: In the Show Window at Macy's

FROM THE *Architectural Forum,* NOVEMBER, 1933.

M.M.A., New York City. The Moscow of Modern Art.

1934: What Shall We Work For?

Immortality. Immortality lies here and now in what we call creative energy. Then why not work for immortality? There is where today is born and tomorrow lives above mere pleasures and where the old, whatever their years may be, can never come. And when death comes to cut you down and "they" come to shove you 6 feet under ground, you will scarcely know the time has come if you work for immortality. History proves this by way of her creative individuals; those workers indicative of innumerable men that history never recorded because it did not know them. Creative work is never otherwise than of youth, by youth, for youth, for all time, whether time ever knows it or not.

Selfhood. "What to work for?" Certainly not for popular acclaim or favor. It is necessarily treacherous; treacherous because it can never be really certain of anything; able to judge others only by its own reflection.

Work for the esteem and good will of our fellow professionals then? Not for one moment. The brighter your light burns the less the little candles they are holding up will be visible and they will soon be trying to blow yours out, thinking that in twilight or darkness theirs may be seen. What hope from such?

For money? Well; where money is the only certainty of safety or power, such as it certainly is in a capitalistic system of the present stripe, perhaps so. But look at what has happened to money!

Utter money mindedness failed to save its devotees. It always will.

And so, back and forth we might go through the stock and shop of the mental and spiritual equipment of our time and find nothing at all worth seriously living and working for.

Then, I ask you to what may a sensible man devote his creative energies and yet look himself in the face as a man? The first answer coming to my mind is youth, the future in another word. But "youth" is a spirit and the future is always now.

If by "youth" the young in years is meant; then, no. The young are unspeakably cruel. The vices of their parents are all lying within them unqualified, making faces at the self-discipline that alone can make them worthy of any great sacrifices or fit them for any dedication to anything more than help to their own selfishness. For them, hope. Not trust.

In what then to place one's trust as a worthy objective for creative energy?

Place it in nothing at all outside one's own best self. Nor place it within one's self either, unless there is something beside selfishness there. Selfishness is selfhood degenerate. It is that very lack of quality that makes individuality mere personality and reduces character to an empty sounding box.

But is there any such thing as unselfishness? Yes, there is selfhood. Selfhood is whole-minded and noble. Selfishness is narrow-minded and ignoble. The difference lies in that the one is a quality with life in it while the other is the quality gone sterile; seedy but no seed.

Selfhood is youthful; selfishness is senile.

"By Their Works." There in the creative mind we have a fountain of energy that does not dry up as bones become brittle and the hair shines whiter or thinner or not at all. Any work of any lifetime truly animated by principle will leave fresh ideas upon the drawing boards every morning, give impetus to better ways of achieving them by inventing new construction until the carcass that contained the immortal mind as a lead casket contains precious jewels is shoved into the usual profane box and planted under ground. And the later work of any such spirit as that will be the greatest work; ripened by the only valuable tests on the only real proving ground; the proving ground of intimate experience. We speak of immortality; it lies here and now and is found in this quality we call creative.

The oriental knows this. The Asiatics preserve thought as a quality of immortality accruing to creative individuality and so venerate and continually cherish it as the precious residue of life experience. Age is a qualification. And as it is in the life of the individual so it passes on as a rare asset into the life of the oriental nation. Perhaps, for this, China and Japan are said to be the paradise of the very old and the very young. Perhaps, for this, too, they may be rated as unprogressive nations. Time is yet to tell.

1935-1938: Taliesin

1935: Organic Architecture

FROM THE *Architects' Journal,* AUGUST, 1936.

In this paper Wright dealt with the period 1893-1920. He appears to have planned a second paper on the period since, but there is no record of this having been written or printed. At the risk of some repetition nearly all of this paper has been reprinted here because it summarizes a great deal of what has been said before in a new perspective.

The typical American dwelling of 1893 was crowding in upon itself all over the Chicago prairies as I used to go home from my work with Adler and Sullivan in Chicago to Oak Park, a Chicago suburb. That dwelling had somehow become typical American architecture but by any faith in nature implicit or explicit it did not belong anywhere. I was in my sixth year with Adler and Sullivan then, and they had completed the Wainwright Building in St. Louis, the first expression of the skyscraper as a *tall* building. But after building the great Auditorium the firm did not build residences because they got in the way of larger, more important work. I had taken over dwellings, Mr. Sullivan's own house among them, whenever a client came to them for a house. The Charnley house was done in this way. I longed for a chance to build a sensible house and (1893) soon free to build one, I furnished an office in the Schiller Building and began my own practice of architecture. The first real chance came by way of Herman Winslow for client. I was not the only one then sick of hypocrisy and hungry for reality. Winslow was something of an artist himself, sick of it all.

What was the matter with this typical American house? Well, just for an honest beginning, it lied about everything. It had no sense of unity at all nor any such sense of space as should belong to a free people. It was stuck up in thoughtless fashion. It had no more sense of earth than a "modernistic" house. And it was stuck up on wherever it happened to be. To take any one of these so-called "homes" away would have improved the landscape and helped to clear the atmosphere. The thing was more a hive than a home just as "modernistic" houses are more boxes than houses. But these "homes" were very like the homes Americans were making for themselves elsewhere, all over their new country.

Nor, where the human being was concerned, had this *typical* dwelling any appropriate sense of proportion whatever. It began somewhere way down in the wet and ended as high up as it could get in the high and narrow. All materials looked alike to it or to anything or anybody in it. Essentially, were it brick or wood or stone, this "house" was a bedeviled box with a fussy lid; a complex box that had to be cut up by all kinds of holes made in it to let in light and air, with an especially ugly hole to go in and come out of. The holes were all "trimmed"; the doors and windows themselves trimmed; the roofs trimmed; the walls trimmed. Architecture seemed to consist in what was done to these holes. "Joinery" everywhere reigned supreme in the pattern and as the soul of it all. Floors were the only part of the house left plain after "Queen Anne" had swept past. The "joiner" recommended "parquetry" but usually the housewife and the fashionable decorator covered these surfaces down under foot with a tangled rug collection because otherwise the floors would be "bare." They were "bare" only because one could not very well walk on jigsawing or turned spindles or plaster ornament. This last limitation must have seemed somehow unkind.

It is not too much to say that as a young architect, by inheritance and training a radical, my lot was cast with an inebriate lot of criminals called builders; sinners hardened by habit against every human significance except one, vulgarity. The one touch of nature that makes the whole world kin. And I will venture to say, too, that the aggregation was at the lowest aesthetic level in all history. Steam heat, plumbing, and electric light were the only redeeming features and these new features were hard put to it to function in the circumstances. Bowels, circulation, and nerves were new in buildings. But they had come to stay and a building could not longer remain a mere shell in which life was somehow to make shift as it might.

When I was 11 years old I was sent to a Wisconsin farm to learn how to really work. So all this I saw around me seemed affectation, nonsense, or profane. The first feeling was hunger for reality, for sincerity. A desire for simplicity that would yield a broader, deeper comfort was natural, too, to this first feeling. A growing idea of simplicity as organic, as I had been born into it and trained in it, was new as a quality of thought, able to strengthen and refresh the spirit in any circumstances. Organic simplicity might everywhere be seen producing significant character in the ruthless but harmonious order I was taught to call nature. I was more than familiar with it on the farm. All around me, I, or anyone for that matter, might see beauty in growing things and by a little painstaking, learn how they grew to be "beautiful." None were ever insignificant. I loved the prairie by instinct as itself a great simplicity; the trees, flowers, and sky were thrilling by contrast. And I saw that a little of height on the prairie was enough to look like much more. Notice how every detail as to height becomes intensely significant and how breadths all fall short. Here was a tremendous spaciousness needlessly sacrificed, all cut up crosswise or lengthwise into 50-foot lots, or would you have 25 feet? Reduced to a money-matter salesmanship kept on parceling out the ground, selling it with no restrictions. Everywhere, in a great new, free country, I could see only this mean tendency to tip everything in the way of human occupation or habitation up edgewise instead of letting it lie comfortably flatwise with the ground where spaciousness was a virtue. Nor has this changed much since automobilization has made it no genuine economic issue at all but has made it a social crime to crowd in upon one another.

By now I had committed the indiscretion that was eventually to leave me no peace and keep me from ever finding satisfaction in anything superficial. That indiscretion was a determination to search for the *qualities* in all things.

I had an idea (it still seems to be my own) that the planes parallel to the earth in buildings identify themselves with the ground, do most to make the buildings belong to the ground. (Unluckily they defy the photographer.) At any rate, independently I perceived this fact and put it to work. I had an idea that every house in that low region should begin *on* the ground, not *in* it as they then began, with damp cellars. This feeling became an idea also; eliminated the "basement." I devised one at ground level. And the feeling that the house should *look* as though it began there *at* the ground, put a projecting base course as a visible edge to this foundation where, as a platform, it was evident preparation for the building itself and welded the structure to the ground.

An idea (probably rooted deep in racial instinct) that *shelter* should be the essential look of any dwelling, put the low spreading roof, flat or hipped or low gabled, with generously projecting eaves over the whole. I began to see a building primarily not as a cave but as broad shelter in the open, related to vista; vista without and vista within. You may see in these various feelings all taking the same direction that I was born an American child of the ground and of space, welcoming spaciousness as a modern human need as well as learning to see it as the natural human opportunity. The farm had no negligible share in developing this sense of things in me, I am sure.

Before this, by way of innate sense of comfort, had come the idea that the size of the human figure should fix every proportion of a dwelling or of anything in it. Human scale was true building scale. Why not, then, the scale fixing the proportions of all buildings whatsoever? What other scale could I use? This was not a canon taught me by anyone. So I accommodated heights in the new buildings to no exaggerated established order nor to impress the beholder (I hated grandomania then as much as I hate it now) but only to comfort the human being. I knew the house dweller could seldom afford enough freedom to move about in built-in or built-over space, so, perceiving the horizontal line as the earth line of human life (the line of repose), this, as an individual sense of the thing, began to bear fruit. I first extended horizontal spacing without enlarging the building by cutting out all the room partitions that did not serve the kitchen or give needed privacy for sleeping apartments or (as in the day of the parlor) serve to prevent some formal intrusion into the intimacy of the family circle. The small social office I set aside as a necessary evil to receive "callers," for instance. Even this one concession soon disappeared as a relic of the barbarism called "fashion"; the "parlor."

To get the house down to the horizontal in appropriate proportion and into quiet relationship with the ground and as a more humane consideration anyway, the servants had to come down out of the complicated attic and go into a separate unit of their own attached to the kitchen on the ground floor. They liked this compulsion, though the housewife worried. Closets disappeared as unsanitary boxes wasteful of room and airy wardrobes out in the rooms served instead.

Freedom of floor space and elimination of useless heights worked a miracle in the new dwelling place. A sense of appropriate freedom had changed its whole aspect. The dwelling became more fit for human habitation on modern terms and far more natural to its site. An entirely new sense of space values in architecture began to come home. It now appears that, self-conscious of architectural implications, they first came into the architecture of the modern world. This was about 1893. Certainly something of the kind was due.

A new sense of repose in flat planes and quiet "streamline" effects had thereby and then found its way into building, as we can now see it admirably in steamships, airplanes and motorcars. The age came into its own and the "age" did not know its own. There had been nothing at all from overseas to help in getting this new architecture planted on American soil. From 1893 to 1910 these prairie houses had planted it there. No, my dear "Mrs. Gablemore," "Mrs. Plasterbilt," and especially, no, "Miss Flattop," nothing from "Japan" had helped at all, except the marvel of Japanese color prints. They were a lesson in elimination of the insignificant and in the beauty of the natural use of materials.

But more important than all, rising to greater dignity as idea, the ideal of plasticity was now to be developed and emphasized in the treatment of the building as a whole. Plasticity was a familiar term but something I had seen in no buildings whatsoever. I had seen it in Lieber Meister's ornament only. It had not found its way into his buildings otherwise. It might now be seen creeping into the expressive lines and surfaces of the *buildings* I was building. You may see the appearance of the thing in the surface of your hand as contrasted with the articulation of the bony skeleton itself. This ideal, profound in its architectural implications, soon took another conscious stride forward in the form of a new aesthetic. I called it *continuity.* (It is easy to see it in the "folded plane.") Continuity in this aesthetic sense appeared to me as the natural means to achieve truly organic architecture by machine technique or by any other natural technique. Here was direct means, the only means I could then see or can now see to express, objectify and again bring natural form to architecture. Here by instinct at first (all ideas germinate) principle had entered into building as the new aesthetic, "continuity." It went abroad as "plasticity." They began to call it, as I myself often did then, "the third dimension." It was only a single phase of "continuity" but a phase that has come back home again to go to work on the surface and upon the novice. It will do him no harm as it is. But were the full import of continuity in architecture to be grasped, aesthetic and structure become completely one, it would continue to revolutionize the use and wont of our machine age architecture, making it superior in harmony and beauty to any architecture, Gothic or Greek. This ideal at work upon materials by nature of the process or tools used means a living architecture in a new age, organic architecture, the only architecture that can live and let live because it never can become a mere style. Nor can it ever become a formula for the tyro. Where principle is put to work, not as recipe or as formula, there will always be *style* and no need to bury it as a "style."

Although the wrap-around window, originally a minor outward expression of the interior folded plane in my own buildings, and various other minor features of the work of this period intended to simplify and eliminate "parts" are now scattered around the world and have become the rather senseless features of various attempts at formula, such as the sporadic "international" and other attempts characterized by plain surfaces cut into patterns by simple large openings, nevertheless, the ideas behind these earlier appearances, the fundamental ideas that made them genuine expressions of architecture, have been altogether missed. The nature of materials is ignored in these imitations to get block mass outlines. The reverse of the period wherein mass material outlines tried to ignore the materials. But it is the same mistake.

The word "plastic" was a word Louis Sullivan himself was fond of using in reference to his scheme of ornamentation as distinguished from all other or any *applied* ornament. But now, and not merely as "form following function," came a larger application of the element called plasticity. "Form follows function" is mere dogma until you realize the higher truth that form and function are one.

Why any principle working in the part if not working in the whole?

I promoted plasticity as conceived by Lieber Meister to *continuity* in the concept of the building as a whole. If the dictum, "form follows function," had any bearing at all on building it could take form in architecture only by means of plasticity when seen at work as complete *continuity*. So why not throw away entirely all implications of post and beam construction? Have no posts, no columns, no pilasters, cornices or moldings or ornament; no divisions of the sort nor allow any fixtures whatever to enter as something added to the structure. Any building should be complete, including all within itself. Instead of many things, *one* thing.

The folded plane enters here with the merging lines, walls and ceilings made one. Let walls, ceilings, floors now become not only party to each other but *part of each other,* reacting upon and within one another; continuity in all, eliminating any merely constructed features as such, or any fixture or appliance whatsoever as such.

When Louis Sullivan had eliminated background in his system of ornament in favor of an integral sense of the whole he had implied this larger sense of the thing. I now began to achieve it.

Conceive that here came a new sense of building on American soil that could *grow* building forms not only true to function but expressive far beyond mere function in the realm of the human spirit. Our new country might now have a true architecture hitherto unknown. Yes, architectural forms by this interior means might now grow up to express a deeper sense of human life values than any existing before. Architecture might extend the bounds of human individuality indefinitely by way of safe interior discipline. Not only had space come upon a new technique of its own but every material and every method might now speak for itself in objective terms of human life. Architects were no longer tied to Greek space but were free to enter into the space of Einstein.

Architectural forms might *grow* up? Yes, but grow up in what image? Here came concentrated appeal to pure imagination. Gradually proceeding from generals to particulars in the field of work with materials and machines, "plasticity" (become "continuity") began to grip me and work its own will in architecture. I would watch sequences fascinated, seeing other sequences in those consequences already in evidence. I occasionally look through such early studies as I made at this period (a number of them still remain), fascinated by implications. They seem, even now, generic. The old architecture, always dead for me so far as its grammar went began literally to disappear. As if by magic new effects came to life as though by themselves and I could draw inspiration from nature herself. I was beholden to no man for the look of anything. Textbook for me? "The book of creation." No longer need any more to be a wanderer among the objects and traditions of the past, picking and choosing his way by the personal idiosyncrasy of taste, guided only by personal predilection. From this hell I had been saved. The world lost an eclectic and gained an interpreter. If I did not like the Gods now I could make better ones.

Visions of simplicities so broad and far reaching would open to me and such building harmonies appear that I was tireless in search of new ones. In various form researches, with all my energy I concentrated upon the principle of plasticity working as continuity. Soon a practical working technique evolved and a new scale within the buildings I was building in the endeavor to more sensibly and sensitively accomplish this thing we call architecture. Here at work was something that would change and deepen the thinking and culture of the modern world. So I believed.

Nevertheless, it was some years later that I took the aesthetic "continuity" into the physical method of constructing a building. Then the changes came along slowly because, to eliminate the post and beam as such (the old order), I could get no help from the engineer. By habit, engineers reduce everything in the field of calculation to post and girder before they can calculate anything or tell you where and just how much of what. Walls that were part of floors and ceilings all merging together, reacting within upon each other, the engineer had never met in buildings. And so the engineer had not yet enough scientific formula in any handbook to enable him to calculate at all for continuity. Even slabs stiffened and used over supports as cantilevers to get planes parallel to the earth, such as were now necessary to develop emphasis of the "third dimension" (as I myself had been calling it), were yet new. But the engineer soon mastered the element of continuity, which we call the cantilever, in these floor slabs. The cantilever thus became a new feature in architectural form. As used in the Imperial Hotel in Tokio it was one of the several features that insured the life of that building in the subsequent terrific temblor. After that "practical" demonstration a great new *economic stability* had entered building construction proving the new *aesthetic* not only safe but also *sound economics of structure*. Form and function were one.

From some laboratory experiments being made at Princeton by Professor Beggs which I saw while there delivering the Kahn Lectures in 1930, it appears that aesthetic "continuity" at work in the practice of physical structure is concrete proof of the practical usefulness of the aesthetic ideal in designing architectural forms and, I hope, may soon be available as structural formula in some handbook. Welding instead of riveting steel is one new means to this new end and other plastic methods are constantly coming into use. But that and other possibilities (they will, I hope and believe, never need) are ahead of our story.

There were then no symbols at all for these ideas. But I have already objectified most of them. Were architecture bricks, my hands were in the mud of which bricks were made.

An idea soon came from this stimulating simplifying ideal (ideas breed, especially in actually making them work) that in order to be consistent, or indeed if all were to be put to work as architecture successfully, this new element of plasticity should have a new *sense* as well as a new *science* of materials.

It may interest you to know (it surprised me) that there is nothing in the literature of the civilized world upon that subject. Nothing I could find as *interpretation* in this sense of the nature of materials. Here was another great field for concrete endeavor, neglected. So I began, in my fashion, to study the nature of materials. Life is short. Lieber Meister had not reached this study. All materials alike were to receive the impress of his imagination. I began to learn to see brick as brick. I learned to see wood as wood and learned to see concrete or glass or metal each for itself and all as themselves. Strange to say this required uncommon sustained concentration of uncommon imagination (we call it vision), demanded not only a new conscious approach to building but opened a new world of thought that would certainly tear down the old world completely. Each different material required a different handling, and each different handling as well as the material itself had new possibilities of use peculiar to the nature of each. Appropriate designs for one material would not be at all appropriate for any other material. In the light of this ideal of building form as an organic simplicity almost all architecture fell to the ground. That is to say, ancient buildings were obsolete in the light of the idea of space determining form from within, all materials modifying if indeed they did not create the "form" when used with understanding according to the limitations of process and purpose.

Architecture might, and did, begin life anew.

Had steel, concrete, and glass existed in the ancient order we could have had nothing like our ponderous, senseless "classic" architecture. No, nothing even at Washington. Such betrayal of new life and new opportunities as ours has been would have been impossible to the ancients, the Greeks excepted, and we should have had a practice of architecture by the eclectic wherein tradition was not a parasite nor an enemy but a friend because the ancestors would have done the necessary work for us that we seem unable to do for ourselves. We would then have been able to copy the antique with sense and safety. Myself with the others.

Now there can be no organic architecture where the nature of synthetic materials or the nature of nature materials either is ignored or misunderstood. How can there be? Perfect correlation, integration, is life. It is the first principle of any growth that the thing grown be no mere aggregation. Integration as entity is first essential. And integration means that no part of anything is of any great value in itself except as it be integrate part of the harmonious whole. Even my great old master designed for materials all alike. All were grist for his rich imagination and he lived completely as artist, all to the contrary notwithstanding, only with his sentient ornament. Contrary to the ideas formed of him by word-wise but superficial critics, in this he created out of himself a world of his own, not yet appreciated at its true worth. How could it be yet? In this expression he went beyond the capacities of any individual before him. But all materials were only one material to him in which to weave the stuff of his dreams. Terra cotta was that one material. Terra cotta was *his* material, the one he loved most and served best. There he was master. But I honored him when I carried his work and thought further along by acting upon this new train of ideas, and the acts soon brought work sharply and immediately up against the tools that could be found to get these ideas put into new forms of building.

What a man does—*that* he has. You may find other things on him but they are not his.

What were the tools in use in the building trades everywhere? *Machines* and the automatic process, all too many of them. Stone or wood planers, stone and wood molding shapers, various lathes, presses, and power saws, the casting of metals and glass; all in commercially organized mills. The kiln; sheet-metal breakers; presses; shears; cutting, molding, and stamping machines in foundries and rolling mills; commercialized machine "shops"; concrete mixers; clay breakers; casters; glassmakers themselves; and the trades-union versus capital; all laborer's or employer's units in a more or less highly commercialized greater union in which craftsmanship had no place except as survival for burial by standardization. Quantity production or standardization was already inflexible necessity either as enemy or friend. You might choose. And as you chose you became master and useful, or a luxury and eventually the more or less elegant parasite we call an "eclectic": a man guided only by instinct of choice called "taste."

By now I did not choose by instinct. I felt, yes, but I *knew* now what it was I felt concerning architecture.

Already, when I began to build, commercial machine standardization had taken the life of handicraft. But outworn handicraft had never troubled me. To make the new forms living expression of the new order of the machine and continue what was noble in tradition did trouble me. I wanted to realize genuine new forms true to the spirit of great tradition and found I should have to make them; not only make forms appropriate to the old (natural) and to new (synthetic) materials, but I should have to so design them that the machine (or process) that must make them could and would make them better than anything could possibly be made by hand. But now with this sense of integral order in architecture supreme in my mind I could have done nothing less unless I could have commanded armies of craftsmen as later I did command them in the building of the Imperial Hotel; a building in no sense a product of machine method. By now, safe inner discipline had come to me; the interior discipline of a great ideal. There is none so severe. But no other discipline yields such rich rewards in work, nor is there any man so safe and sure of results as the man disciplined from within by this ideal of the integration that is organic. Experience is this man's "school." It is yet his only school.

As I put these ideas to work in materials, lesser ideas took flight from this exacting ideal. But always in the same direction. They went farther on each occasion for flight, which was each new building I built, until great goals were in sight. Some few of the goals have been partially realized. You may see the "signs and portents" gathered together in various exhibition galleries if you can read drawings and models. The photographs are poor because the depth planes cannot be rendered by photography. But a number of the buildings are scattered or mutilated and unfortunately most of the best drawings are gone. The best buildings, too, were never built and may only be studied by the record. But later designs and models all exemplify in some material or grouping of materials, or idea of arrangement, these early objectives. Lieber Meister had been searching for "the rule so broad as to admit of no exception." For the life of me I could not help being most interested in the exception that proved the rule. This may explain "inconsistency" in performance and apparent departure from original objectives.

A group of young Chicago architects were gathered about me as disciples and friends in the early days, about 1893. They were my contemporaries and all learned from me to speak the new language. I wrote a little and later I tried to stem the tide of imitation. An instance was the paper read at Hull House some 30 years ago on "The Art and Craft of the Machine." Occasionally, then an indifferent lecturer, I lectured. But talking isn't building, as I soon saw where any "school" as they called it (and later had names for the branches) had actually *to build.* Among these contemporaries the more ambitious began to call the new dwellings that appeared upon the prairies from 1893 to 1910 "the prairie school." I suppose this was modern architecture's first gallery. None knew much of Louis Sullivan, then, except by such work as he had done. And to a certain extent they imitated him too; imitating his individual ornamentation as the feature most in view. Some years later C. R. Ashbee came over to the United States and Kuno Francke of Harvard came to Oak Park. Both, in turn, saw the new work on the prairies and carried the tale of it to Europe in 1908. Some 15 or 20 years later a Swiss (in France) was to rediscover a familiar preliminary aesthetic; the affirmative negation declared by the Larkin Building, widely published at the time when it was built and recorded by an article in the *Architectural Record,* March 1908. But already (1910) in my own work the ideal of an organic architecture as affirmation had gone far beyond that belated negation that it was at work in Europe itself.

Before trying to put down more in detail concerning goals now in sight, popular reaction to this new endeavor might be interesting. After the first "prairie house" was built, the Winslow house in 1893, which only in the matter of ornamentation bore resemblance in respect to the master (in the Charnley house I had stated, for the first time so far as I know, the thesis of the plain wall given the nature of decoration by a well-placed single opening which is also a feature of the Winslow house), my next client said he did not want a house "so different that he would have to go down the backway to his morning train to avoid being laughed at." That was one popular consequence. There were many others; bankers at first refused to loan money on the "queer" houses, so friends had to be found to finance the early buildings. Millmen would soon look for the name of the plans when the plans were presented for estimates, read the name of the architect and roll up the drawings again, handing them back with the remark that "they were not hunting for trouble"; contractors more often than not failed to read the plans correctly, so much had to be left off the buildings. The buildings were already off the main track. The clients themselves usually stood by interested and excited, often way beyond their means. So, when they moved into their new house, quite frequently they had no money left, had borrowed all they could and had to drag their old furniture into their new world. Seldom could I complete an interior because the ideal of "organic simplicity" seen as the countenance of perfect integration (as you have already read) naturally abolished all fixtures, rejected the old furniture, all carpets and most hangings, declaring them to be irrelevant or superficial decoration. The new practice made all furnishings so far as possible (certainly the electric lighting and heating systems) integral parts of the architecture. So far as possible all furniture was to be designed in place as part of the building. Hangings, rugs, carpets, were they to be used (as they might be if properly designed), all came into the same category. But the money matter generally crippled this particular feature of the original scheme, as I have said, and made trouble in this process of elimination and integration.

Nor, theoretically, was any planting to be done about the houses without cooperating with the architect. But, of course, it was done more often than not. But no sculpture, no painting was let in unless cooperating with the architect, although more often than not pictures were "hung." This made trouble. For no decoration, as such, was to be seen anywhere. Sculpture and painting were to be likewise of the building itself. But in the Midway Gardens built in Chicago in 1913 I tried to complete the synthesis: planting, furnishings, music, painting, and sculpture, all to be one. But I found musicians, painters, and sculptors were unable to rise at that time to any such synthesis. Only in a grudging and dim way did most of them even understand it as an idea. So I made the designs for all to harmonize with the architecture; crude as any sketch is crude, incomplete as to execution, but in effect sufficiently complete to show the immense importance of any such attempt on any architect's part and show, indeed, that only so does architecture completely live. A new ideal of ornamentation had by now arrived that wiped out all ornament unless it, too, was an integral feature of the whole. True ornament became more desirable than ever but it had to "mean something"; in other words *be* something organic in character. Decorators hunting a job would visit the owners and, learning the name of the architect, lift their hats, turn on their heels, leaving with the curt and sarcastic "good day!" meaning really what the slang "good night!" of the period meant. This matter of integral ornament is the rock upon which a later generation of young architects splits and wisely decides to let it alone for the time being.

The owners of the early houses were, of course, all subjected to curiosity, sometimes to admiration, but were submitted most often to the ridicule of the "middle of the road egotist." To that ubiquitous egotist there was something about the owner too, now, when he had a house like that, "the rope tie around the monkey's neck."

Well, I soon had to face the fact that a different choice of materials would mean a different building altogether. Concrete was just coming into use and Unity Temple became the first concrete monolith in the world, that is to say, the first building complete as monolithic architecture when the wooden forms in which it was cast were taken away. No critic has yet seen it as it is for what it is except to realize that here, at least, was *something*. They might not like the temple but they were "impressed" by it. Meanwhile, the Larkin Building at Buffalo had just been built a consciously important challenge to the empty ornamentality of the old order. The phrases I myself used concerning it in the issue of the *Architectural Record* in 1908 devoted to my work, put it on record as such. "Here again most of the critic's architecture has been left out. Therefore, the work may have the same claim to consideration as a work of art, as an ocean liner, a locomotive, or a battleship." The words may have escaped the Swiss "discoverer"; he was young at the time.

Plastered houses were then new. Casement windows were new. So many things were new. Nearly everything was new but the law of gravity and the idiosyncrasy of the client.

And simple as the buildings seemed and seem to be to this day because all had character and the countenance of principle, only the outward countenance of their simplicity has ever taken effect and that countenance is now being variously exaggerated by confirmed eclectics for the sake of the effect of a style. The innate simplicity that enabled them and enables them to multiply in infinite variety has not been practiced. I have built 187 buildings, planned and detailed about 37 more that have not been built, and all together they do not classify as a style. Nevertheless, all have "style."

As reward for independent thinking put into action as building and first plainly shown in the constitution and profiles of the prairie houses of Oak Park, Riverside, and other suburbs and Chicago and other cities, Unity Temple at Oak Park and the Larkin Administration Building in Buffalo, an entirely new sense of architecture for anyone who could read architecture had emerged. A higher concept of architecture. Architecture not alone as "form following function" in Lieber Meister's sense but architecture for the spirit of man, for life as life must be lived today; architecture spiritually (virtually) conceived as appropriate enclosure of interior space to be lived in. Form and function made one. The enclosed space within them is the *reality* of the building. The enclosed space comes through as architecture and may be seen in these exteriors I have built as the *reality* of the building I wanted to build and did build and am still building in spite of all opposition and the supreme obstacle, pretentious ignorance. This sense of the "within" or the room itself (or the rooms themselves) I see as the great thing to be realized and that may take the new forms we need as architecture. Such a source would never stultify itself as a mere style. This sense of interior space made *exterior* as architecture, working out by way of the nature of materials and tools, transcends, as a fertilizing motive, all that has ever gone before in architecture. This clarifying motive of the whole makes previous ideas useful only as a means to the realization of this far greater concept of architecture. But if the buildings I have conceived upon this basis still seem enigmatical, most of all they must seem so to those who profess the "modernistic." A chasm exists between the usual profession and performance, because growth, where the quality we now call organic is concerned, must be slow growth. Eclecticism may take place overnight but organic architecture must come from the ground up into the light by gradual growth. It will itself be the ground of a better way of life; it is not only the beautifier of the building; it is as a circumstance in itself, becoming the blessing of the occupants. All building construction naturally becomes lighter and stronger as fibrous "integument" takes the place of "solid mass." Our arboreal ancestors in their trees seem more likely precedent for us at the present time than savage animals who "hole in" for protection. But to properly put it on a human level, a higher *order* of the spirit has dawned for modern life in this interior concept of lived-in space playing with light, taking organic form as the reality of building; a building now an entity by way of native materials and natural methods of structure; forms becoming more naturally significant of ideal and purpose, ultimate in economy and strength. We have now coming clear an ideal the core of which must soon pervade the whole realm of creative man and one that, I know now, dates back to Laotse 500 B.C., and, later, to Jesus himself. The building era that Louis Sullivan ushered in is developing beyond the limitations that marked it, aside from his splendid elemental fluorescence, into the higher realm where as a human creative ideal throughout all culture it will make all form and function one.

Not much yet exists in our country; no, nor in any country outside plans and models; to exemplify steel and glass at its best in the light of this new sense of building. But a new countenance—it is the countenance of principle—has already appeared around the world. A new architectural language is being brokenly, variously, and often falsely spoken by youths, with perspicacity and some breadth of view but with too little depth of knowledge that can only come from continued experience. Unfortunately, academic training and current criticism have no penetration to this inner world. The old academic order is bulging with its own important impotence. Society is cracking under the strain of a sterility education imposes far beyond capacity; exaggerated capitalism has left all this as academic heritage to its own youth. General cultural sterility, the cause of the unrest of this uncreative moment that now stalls the world might be saved and fructified by this ideal of an organic architecture: led from shallow troubled muddy water into deeper clearer pools of thought. Life needs these deeper fresher pools into which youth may plunge to come out refreshed.

Light. More and more, so it seems to me, light is the beautifier of the building. Light always was the beautifier of the building in the matter of shadows but now especially needs these deeper satisfactions; needs a more worthy human ego for that tomorrow that is always today because of yesterday.

The Deeper Sense of Building. Inevitably this deeper sense of building as integral produce of the spirit of man is to construct the physical body of our machine age. But that in itself will not be enough. Unless this construction were to enable a broader, finer sense of life as something to be lived in to the full, all resources of time, place, and man in place to give us an architecture that is inspiring environment at the same time that it is a true expression of that life itself, the ideal will again have failed.

These gestures being lightly called "modernistic," what then is this new lip service, in shops, studios and schoolrooms? What are these pretentious gestures, this superficial association of ideas or this attempted academic rationalizing of this new work of mine? Why is the true content or motivating inner thought of this new architecture as organic architecture so confused in their hypocritical manifestations? Why is there so little modest, earnest effort to profit honestly by cooperation in these researches and, understanding such proofs as we have, honestly use them, such as they are? Why not go ahead with them for growth instead of continuing to exploit them for a living or for a passing name? This self-seeking of some transient fame? "Publicity" is the only fame such shallow ambition may know, and like all such ambitions only the "advertising" that will be dead with yesterday's newspaper.

1935: The Bad Lands

To Robert D. Lusk: *The Evening Huronite*, Huron, S. Dak.

In this letter and the following article on Arizona are ideas which should add new layers of meaning to Wright's constant use of the words "nature" and "natural." His imaginative response to nature, as shown here, stands with our best traditional literature of travel and topographic description.

Dear Bob: I have been laid up for 3 days but am fit once more. You are a good soldier and I too hope I can come out to see you all again. I am writing a note to "Spitz" thanking him.

Publicity might be such a worthy power in a place like the U.S.A. if it were in the hands of worthy men; well, like you, of course. Or anything else? But think of Hearst *et al.!*

Speaking of our trip to the Big Bad Lands, Black Hills, and Spearfish Canyon: I've been about the world a lot and pretty much over our own country; but I was totally unprepared for that revolution called the Dakota Bad Lands. From Mitchell, Paul Bellamy was driving a fair seventy over the brown Dakota prairie to reach the Bad Lands before sunset. About four, afternoon, something came into view that made me sit up straight and look at Bellamy to see if he saw what I saw. "Oh," said he, "you've seen nothing yet." But I had. What I saw gave me an indescribable sense of mysterious otherwhere—a distant architecture, ethereal, touched, only touched with a sense of Egyptian, Mayan drift and silhouette. As we came closer a templed realm definitely stood ambient in air before my astonished "scene," loving but scene-jaded gaze. The streamline working on a vast plateau of solid cream white clay, something like "calichi," had sculptured this familiar world into one unfamiliar but entrancing.

Endless trabeations surmounted by or rising into pyramid (obelisk) and temple, ethereal in color and exquisitely chiseled in endless detail, they began to reach to infinity spreading into the sky on every side; an endless supernatural world more spiritual than earth but created out of it. As we rode, or seemed to be floating upon a splendid winding road that seemed to understand it all and just where to go, we rose and fell between its delicate parallels of rose and cream and sublime shapes, chalk white, fretted against a blue sky with high floating clouds; the sky itself seemed only there to cleanse and light the vast harmonious building scheme.

Of course I am an architect and that ride through the land of pure line and evanescent color affected me strangely. Here was the element, architecture, cut of the body of the ground itself, beggaring human imagination, prostrating the simplicities of man before the great cosmic simplicity. Reverence, yes, awe. Deep satisfaction, harmoniouslike great music drifted over the senses until a new sacred realm was born of light, delicate color and ever changing but immaculate form wherein not even the senses could touch bottom, top, nor sides of its vast repose.

Here, for once, came complete release from materiality. Communion with what man often calls "God" is inevitable in this place. It is everywhere around him and when the man emerges to the brown plateau and looks back, as I did, the sun now setting, a pale moon rising in darkening rose and blue sky as rays of last light drifted over, linking drifting water lines of dark rose in pallid creamy walls, gently playing with the sky line, with mingled obelisks, terraces, and temples more beautiful than thought, eternal, who knows, a strange sense of inner experience will come to him of a crisis in his perception of what he has termed beauty. He will leave that place a more humble, seeking soul than when he went in to this pure appeal to his spirit. He will know baptism in its higher than sectarian sense.

Let sculptors come to the Bad Lands. Let painters come. But first of all the true architect should come. He who could interpret this vast gift of nature in terms of human habitation so that Americans on their own continent might glimpse a new and higher civilization certainly, and touch it and feel it as they lived in it and deserved to call it their own. Yes, I say the aspects of the Dakota Bad Lands have more spiritual quality to impart to the mind of America than anything else in it made by man's God.

I turned to Bellamy and finally said, "But how is it that I've heard so little of this miracle and we, toward the Atlantic, have heard so much of the Grand Canyon when this is even more miraculous?"

"Oh," said he slyly, "we are not on the through line to the coast."

"Never mind," I said, "all the better eventually." And we drove on to the famous Black Hills which the fame of Borglum's work had already brought to my attention.

Next day, Bellamy again at the wheel, from fine little Rapid City, well set in low hills (what could not that town do for itself if it knew how to live accordingly), several of us drove up another finely laid-out road that seemed to know what the region was all about, through scenery I had often heard of as beautiful. But a more flesh and blood kind of beauty. The beauty that appeals surely to a human being because he is human and brother to the tree and respects individualistic rock formations. Here they are great but not too great. All has the charm of human scale which many great Western scenes lack, and invites the wanderer to enter into the spirit of it all and rest. No home for man the Rocky Mountains; no, nor perhaps the Bad Lands, yet; but an ideal home; these Black Hills. Do not think from this that the Hills are unexciting. They are exciting but they stir a different region of the soul; we call it the heart probably. There are stone needles, stone spires, stone piles and stone blades, artificial lakes, tall beautiful pines, wooded gorges, more free standing and sculptured rock masses in nature's own style than one has ever seen before grouped in one area. So it seems fitting that some hand of man should brush aside the realistic veil of a stained weathered rock and let the mind of man himself envision his own greatness and his fate alongside the titanic handiwork of nature. Human nature, let us hope eventually nature's higher nature, found its hand for this in Gutzon Borglum's masterhand and the face of the great leader of his country. The noble countenance emerges from Rushmore as though the spirit of the mountain had heard a human prayer and itself became a human countenance. The countenance haunts you as you ride rises; winds and falls with you as freight through depths of pine woods; huge rocks standing about you, themselves statues of a more elemental thought than Gutzon Borglum's: the cosmic urge.

We passed by a quiet land-locked lake (Stockade Lake) that seems to be there with a man-made white sand shore to invite you to get out and stay and rest and drink in the breath of the pines as the breezes print themselves on the surface of the placid water. This Black Hills country has charm, inviting you to get out and go about or stay about. It is a lingering kind of human satisfaction for the soul, hungry of a tired body, the recreation of any jaded mind compelled to live by the abacus, money.

You may think all this the feeling of the moment, a mood, and because I was in good company. But no! I am an old soldier of the spirit, a veteran in time, place, and man. I could not be mistaken. Go and see.

We wound on upward to Sylvan Lake, a gem spot in the Hills where South Dakota plans to entertain her guests. It may be that South Dakota sees a body of water so seldom that her citizens overvalue it for the lake is artificial and small, but what a setting! Here a sweeping mountain resort, with the lake as a vignette seen below, could be a masterful thing of the kind, woven in with the great rich rock and tree foreground, framing the vistas of this spot; another and a higher kind of nature understanding well and loving the earth from which it springs, loving it too much to imitate it.

Harney Peak loomed to one side. Turning from the little rock-defended, rock-bound lake your gaze travels away along blue ridges ornamented by great rock piles to distant blue mountain tops, as far away as the human eye can go beneath the clouds. Round about you, rugged strengths, forest depths, primeval earth at best; well, an architect is speaking.

There was a hotel there once but nature disposed of it in her inscrutable way, for cause. It was ugly.

Notwithstanding the expenditure of riches, so far, there were wonders left for tomorrow. And "Spitz," as I felt like calling him by now, came with Ted Lusk's car to drive me to

Spearfish Canyon. I felt a little dull toward Spearfish. I had seen two marvels unique in the scenery of the world. I felt headed in for an anticlimax and said so. The boys said, no. These South Dakota boys by now had me where I believed that they knew their stuff. They couldn't have built those superb roads in the Bad Lands and Black Hills if they didn't know. So I patiently waited and visited with "Spitz" as we rode away. We stopped at Homestake, of which everyone has heard, and saw how a primitive gold mining operation has been turned over to the power of the machine and remains primitive just the same. The resources of machinery couldn't change the original steps or even the original way of mining except to cut down the manpower involved. By afternoon we got in by Spearfish, a mountain torrent beginning a canyon 26 miles long. Not very interesting at first, I had seen so many; the Western States are full of them as everyone knows. The road here is haphazard as hazard was and is none too good. "Spitz" drove well, fortunately. And the stream itself was something but after a half-hour things began to happen. We would be headed straight for gigantic white walls trabeated in ledges from which pines sprouted and grew in precisely the manner of the pictorial dreams of the great Chinese painters, the greatest painters who ever lived. We were in the land of the Sung and Ming masters. Whoever knows their idealizations of nature in the Chinese landscape painting of those great periods, and they were mostly landscapes, can see the character of the Spearfish ensemble.

Great horizontal rock walls abruptly rising above torrential streams, their stratified surfaces decorated (it is the word) with red pine stems carving stratified branches in horizontal textures over the cream white walls, multiplied red pine trunks and the black green masses of the pine rhythmically repeating pattern, climbing, climbing until the sky disappeared or was a narrow rift of blue as the clear water poured over pebbles or pooled under the heavy masses of green at the foot of the grand rock walls. Well, here was something again different. As different as could be from Bad Lands or Black Hills or anything I had actually seen, a stately exposition of what decorated walls on enormous scale can do and be. The Chinese predicted and depicted it. This continued for miles and miles without palling or growing in the least stale. We drove out, finally, and turned away from Spearfish town to get back, two architects drunk with primal scene painting, to Gutzon Borglum's little dinner. A third type of earthly marvel was now added to the two. All unique and unparalleled elsewhere in our country.

But now came an unexpected experience. That drive from the Canyon "Spearfish" to Rapid City. Does anyone who knows California and Arizona know that in the softly modeled brown surfaces of South Dakota binding these three wonders together is a terrain greater in charm than any to be found in either? A sweep of modeling and a tender color (it is early September) and a variety of aspect matchless anywhere?

No, I shall be burned for a heretic when I make the statement. But I should be thanked as a prophet and hailed as a discoverer by that jaded public who have "seen everything" and stick to the "through lines." The greatest scenic wonders of the world I know now are touched on grand safe highways but not on railroads. My hat is off to South Dakota's treasures and the men who made them.

We got back in time for a whisky; no, soda, thank you; and Gutzon's little dinner where some Rapid City folk were gathered together to welcome a stranger. He, Gutzon Borglum, of course, is master in more than one medium. The way he handled his dinner, the guests (among them Congressman Harry Gandy), and handled me too, was a masterpiece. Ask anybody there. Gutzon broke down. I like him for it, and anyway, I like those South Dakota folk; I want to see them all again sometime if I can.

Go to South Dakota, but drive there. It is so near to us all and yet I never knew, nor had ever heard much about its southwestern treasure house until Gutzon Borglum went out there to work and Senator Norbeck invited me to see it.

I hope the noble inheritance, for that is what it is, won't be exploited too much and spoiled as lesser beauty spots in our country have been spoiled and will not continue to be marred by the nature imitator with his "rustic" effects, piled boulders, peeled logs, and imitation of camp style primitive gabled buildings. Nature seeds from man not imitation but interpretation. It is quite another story, as you may learn.

1935: To Arizona

I, too, have discovered this America that is Arizona. It will seem strange to the small group of fortunate people who intelligently live here that anyone in their Nation should have to "discover" Arizona after seeing the Grand Canyon. But the remarkable beauty peculiar to this southern Arizona region is quite undiscovered by the grand-average American, or for that matter, by the upper American. This I believe is about to change, and the inevitable boom accompanying such discoveries of the picturesque and climate in the United States will probably come, a rubbish heap, to set Arizona backward a decade or two. That doesn't matter so much, if Arizona clings faithfully to its desert beauty and takes care of it. The desert with its rim of arid mountains spotted like the leopard's skin or tattooed with amazing patterns of creation, is a grand garden the like of which in sheer beauty of space and pattern does not exist, I think, in the world. This great desert garden is Arizona's chief asset. Of course, water poured on certain portions of it will make oases of citrus trees, grapefruit, oranges, lettuce, and melons and they will be rolling east to market just as they do in other arid States. But the American people need not come rolling in here for things like that. They will come because this desert has extraordinary beauty all its own and come to breathe the incomparably pure air here on account of the desert. They will come to get away from weather, come to play, and some of them to stay in the invigorating sunshine. All of Arizona is not a large enough playground for the United States so it may well remain caviar to the general, and prosper mightily.

Compared to the clean, intoxicating air, sweeping vistas and astonishing plant life especially created in the crannies and on the ranges of this desert garden, all else in Arizona is insignificant—even if considered by way of the realtor as "property." Los Angeles has oversold by billions a winter climate wholly inferior to this one of the Salt River Valley which lay quietly undiscovered behind the mountain ranges that cut it off from the too well-known California coast until, now, Californians are coming here to winter.

Here in the Salt River Valley is winter climate in unexampled perfection, due almost wholly to the vast surrounding desert. I dread to see this incomparable natural garden marred, to be eventually spoiled by the candy makers and cactus hunters and careless fire builders and period house builders as well as Indian or Mexican "hut" builders, who will soon destroy the beautiful natural plant growths of the more accessible parts unless the people manage somehow to stop them.

To take the life of one desert plant that is naturally otherwise is to betray this greatest gift nature has yet given in trust to any people. Those who come here to live must eat. They must go out and dig irrigation ditches to earn more money, to make them strong to go out and dig more ditches. And date palms and fig trees, grapefruit, and orange groves are all desirable and beautiful things in themselves where they belong but not to be compared in money-getting value to the noble sahuaro, the wicked cholla, the desert spring called the bianana, the golden paloverde, mesquite, and greasebush, the ocatillo and the ironwood's violet profusion under the canopy of Arizona blue.

For the architect what a marvel of construction that sahuaro! Or the latticed stalk of the cholla! Nature, driven to economize in materials by hard conditions, develops, in the sahuaro, a system of economy of materials in a reinforcement of vertical rods, a plaiting of tendons that holds the structure bolt upright for six centuries or more.

Study the stalk of the cholla for a pattern of latticed steel structure or the structure of the stem of the ocatillo that waves its red flags from the tops of a spray of slender plaited whips 15 feet long.

What a building that would be with a sense of those streamlined spaces in its plan, walled like the sahuaro, textured like it, too, by the nature of its construction. For the desert is no place for plain, hard walls; all is sculptured wind and water. All is patterned and textured in the desert, the rocks and reptiles no less than cacti. A desert building should be nobly simple in outline as the region is sculptured, and have learned from the cactus secrets of straight-line patterns for its forms playing with the light and softening the building into its proper place among the organic desert creations, each heightening the beauty of the other. We do not yet understand pattern for one thing because it is an attribute of a very high and older civilization. We now try to think ornament useless or we continue to go wrong with it by trying to emphasize with it when nature intended it to soften, conceal, and harmonize. Nature herself always does just that very thing with it as you will see if you will go to school to the desert.

But nature never "sticks ornament or sheer pattern on." She gets it all out of the inside by way of the way it grows. It is always *of* the thing. Plain house walls that defy the sun and jump out to your eyes from the desert forty miles or more away are not true desert buildings in any cultivated sense. The Indian Hopi house is no desert house in this sense. Even were it no base imitation for us, it is too loud. The projecting poles soften it with shadows a very little; the Indians got that far with it. But the Indian learned from the desert when he made pots or mats or beadwork or clothed himself. He got something of the spirit of the desert into all those things as we may see. The rattlesnake, the Gila monster and the cacti taught him. Architecture, the great art, except on primitive terms, was beyond him as music and literature were. The fine arts are in themselves a finer civilization, or ought to be as they once were. The broken or dotted line is the line for the desert; not the hard line nor the continuous knife edge. And in that comes a new type of structure for the spaces. You will see that the desert abhors sun defiance as nature abhors a vacuum. Sun acceptance as a condition of survival is everywhere evident. That means organic pattern integral ornament in everything. Sun acceptance in building means the dotted line and wall surfaces that eagerly take the light and play with it, break it up, or drink it in until the sunlight blends the building into place with the creation around it. Man's imagination is none too lively but the task is not too great to harmonize his building masses with topography and typify his building walls with the nature creation they consort with, by taking the abstract designs inherent in all desert growth and weaving them quietly in good order into the abstract fabric of his own work whenever he makes anything. That is to say, make the essential spirit of the thing, however or whatever it is, come through as object.

The human threat to the beauty of the desert garden might be avoided if the builder as architect would only go to school to the desert in this sense and learn the harmonious contrasts or sympathetic treatments for his walls that would, thus, "belong."

Is this organic expression too difficult for us at this stage of our development? Well, then, plant trees and vines, water them and cover your walls with them. Trees and vines native to the conditions here. Be quiet at any cost. Blot out your intrusion as you best can.

I believe that the Arizona "drains" and "washes" and the grand square miles of desert floor out here are worth more eventually even in terms of the gold standard than the irrigation ditches, although not so quick to the department stores, I admit. And I must admit also that the irrigated oases to a certain extent are necessary to the life that is coming into the desert to remain. But I hope Arizona won't, as California did, get the cart before the horse. I hope ranching and the vigorous enterprise in drinking and eating won't go far enough to in any degree spoil the desert garden that will soon bring wealth to the various Arizona pioneers just as it already brings beautiful life to millions of faded, jaded dwellers, refugees from our American cities. The cities are all slums by comparison. This conservation of desert creation should be even more important to government than the conservation of the forests, important as any conservation of water in the mountain streams.

Should the legislature of the State neglect to protect its true reserves in this respect, eventually, yes, even its greatest financial resource, the Federal Government should take them over and protect them or future Arizona may yet curse its short-sighted, short-lived legislators.

Arizona, too, already needs less salesmanship and more statesmanship as less building and more architecture.

1935: Skyscraping

Monuments. To some of our people exaggeration will always mean greatness, because they know no better grandeur. To such the skyscrapers will be the great monuments marking the spot where pride once stood to declare that progress is necessarily commercial, twentieth century gravestones. Not milestones on the road to progress *as we would like to believe.*

1935: New Architectural Sculpture

Bertram Goodhue. Goodhue of course was not a modern architect in any true sense. This by internal evidence anyone may see to whom modern architecture is more than merely architecture, à la mode. He was converted too late.

1935: Form and Reform

The P. A. To write books about art is now anybody's pastime. Paint a little, carve a little, compose a little, get some little something built somehow and then write something about it. That is the prevailing fashion. To publicize soon and do it continuously is the secret of such success as most of our modernistic artists, themselves graduates from the ranks of advertising experts, know.

That is the mode. So the American public gets almost all it knows or can stand of art that specious way.

1935: Louis Sullivan

FROM THE *Saturday Review of Literature,* DECEMBER 14, 1935.

From this severe review of Hugh Morrison's book on Sullivan I have omitted a great many points made previously in this collection and referred to in the index.

Adler. "Form follows function." Has it occurred to no one, then, that Dankmar Adler, not Louis Sullivan, deserves the credit for that dogma?

It was Adler's contribution to his young partner when he was teaching him practically all the young man knew about architecture below the belt. As an architect Louis Sullivan went to school not to the Beaux-Arts but to Dankmar Adler.

Out of his association with Adler came Sullivan's whole sense of building as a functional experience in function.

1935: These Critics

"One does not need to bake a loaf of bread to judge of its excellence" is becoming a stock phrase in the critic's mouth. Lewis Mumford used it first, I believe.

But let's look this gift horse (the critic) in the mouth and see what's in this phrase that seems to be all the teeth he has.

Bread may as a matter of course lie well within a critic's power of apprehension and so his judgment of bread be valid when a building or a symphony might be far and away beyond him, but let's look at him where his bread goes.

Some of him like bread white and fine made only of the inner part of the kernel. Others like coarse bread made of the whole kernel. Others like it mostly bran (the outer shell). The white-bread contingent can't see the case for brown bread at all. The brown bread contingent sees the white bread clogging the intestines as an inert mass. Here we soon have two "schools." Schools of preference and some thought, mind you. And another school is forming that rejects bread entirely as inedible with meals. Excellent bread is not excellent; too much starch anyway, say they; "conviction" is here.

Now as to the way of baking the bread. Some say white bread should be made like French bread, light and crusty. Some say that it should be as near like angel food cake as possible. In another school some say graham bread should be heavy, made with molasses. Others like Boston brown bread. Still others say this bread should be mixed with other flour and made light as possible. All disagree as to matters of yeast. So there is salt-risen bread; bread with no yeast at all which seems to me most excellent. And how about the outer crust?

It is evident, then, that even in this bread business the critic may go pretty far afield in this matter of excellence and is no more to be trusted with the matter of bread excellence than where he is concerned with excellence of the building or the symphony. He can only say which bread he prefers and how he prefers it, say which school of thought he believes to be right by way of his own familiarity with the taste of bread and his outside view of it, or other views he has collected.

But he becomes a champion of white bread, brown bread, black bread or no bread at all and proceeds to tell you about it in a book. All doubts removed (and, if he is good at it, including your own) automatically implying that bread excellence should be related to his broad view of bread because he has the proper view. He will not hesitate to tell you who the best bread baker is. Not being a good bread maker himself nor concerned with the chemistry of its effects he has looked over the whole matter and elected the bread that pleased him. He is eclectic and elects the bread by way of taste, taking up with some school of thinking concerning bread as food or as not food, basing his selections upon other preferences similarly made.

Now an independent thinker enters with a deeper interest in bread.

This thinker will not be put off. What is the nature of bread? He goes into bread making to find out, makes bread himself in order to experiment with the action and reactions of different grains and yeast and methods of developing bread from them as good food for good human beings. He learns the chemistry of the stomach, the secrets of the palate and really knows, eventually by inside experience, what good bread would be for a good human being. And his labor is mostly in vain because the bread consumer says: "I may not know what bread is but I know what I like."

And the critic says (by the way, what is he if not gratuitous): "I don't have to know bread to know excellent bread. I have a broad perspective of bread" (meaning he sees the entire surface). He says his "broad view" makes him a better judge of the excellence of bread than anyone else.

According to this conviction concerning himself and bread, he judges.

So the man who went inside to master the principles involved: this independent thinker who learned the nature of bread as good food for the good human being by learning the nature of the process, the nature of the human stomach and the nature of "taste"—idiosyncrasies aside—is waved aside by this critic as "emotionally" committed to his own bread.

Now such as this is most criticism as the current critic proceeds to arouse popular recognition of the bread that by means of his broad view of bread surface he has selected or elected.

Various bread opinions begin to flourish as the various critics "judge." New schools are formed, blows are struck and nobody comes any nearer to the nature of bread than before.

Meantime the independent partaker of the nature of bread by way of a breadth of experience has been set aside as "narrow" in his appreciation of bread because not only breadth but *depth* of view is his possession. He does not elect or select. He knows!

The critic's head, then, is really the critic's bread. And bread continues to be bread.

1935: The Two-Zone House

FROM *Taliesin,* PUBLICATION OF THE TALIESIN FELLOWSHIP.

In answer to a challenge by Dorothy Johnson Field, who later amplified the same ideas in The Human House, *Wright designed the two-zone house discussed in this selection. Mrs. Field's main point: a house has two centers, a center of activity and a center of quiet.*

New facilities make it desirable to lay aside the provincial squeamishness that made the American parlor, and designedly make a beautiful circumstance to take the place of the kind of kitchen that should now go where the parlor went sometime ago. With modern kitchen appurtenances what used to be the kitchen can now become a high spacious "work studio" opening level with the garden. Therefore the zone of activity may be a natural get-together-place in which to live while at work. In this "two-zone plan" the utility-stack has economically standardized and concentrated within it all appurtenance systems entering into modern house construction: oil burning boiler and fuel tanks—air compressors, oil and gasoline supply for car, heating and air conditioning units, electric wiring and plumbing, vent and smoke flues. This enlarged hollow chimney—about six by eight feet on the ground—is accessible from the coat-room and so placed that only one short run (the horizontal pipe or wire run to the study), is necessary. Each bathroom, entire, is a one-piece standardized fixture directly connected to the stack. Kitchen sink, ranges and refrigeration likewise. Here as the nexus of the arrangement is a complete standardization in factory-production of the wasteful tangled web of wires and piping at present involved in the construction of the ordinary dwelling. Thus the cost of about one-third of the usual home is here reduced to a certainty and one-half or one-third of the cost is saved.

The car-port has been "entered" as integral feature of the dwelling, convenient and not the gaping hole it usually is as built in now. The features that distinguish the two-zone house from the norm of the early one-zone house given out from the same source about 1901 are the utilities concentration called the utilities-stack, the development of the kitchen into the real living room completely furnished as part of the whole, and the segregation of space called the study. A third zone—call it the slumber zone—is introduced as mezzanine with balcony opening into the living room or "work room." While the children are young, each member of the household has a dressing room and "sleeps out." When they grow up, by a few simple changes in the mezzanine each has a private room. Here are self-contained economies for the family as a self-contained unit in society, more natural and yet more orderly than is possible under conditions popular at present.

This germ-plan would easily adapt itself, as indicated, to the several standard conditions of the small house in suburb, town and country. The suburban house is shown lighted largely from above—to avoid the more or less indecent exposure most suburban houses suffer from because they try to be little country houses on lots 50 feet wide on the street. The town house is tall, all rooms having high ceilings. The entire house is to be hermetically sealed from dirt and noise and air-conditioned, with opportunity to go out to view the passing show on occasions, but viewing only when moved; and also opportunity to live outside, "up top" where greenery can see the sky. The utility-stack and bathrooms, work room, segregated study and segregated slumber rooms of this townhouse all keep to the scheme of the suburban house.

The country house keeps to the same scheme. Its outer walls are mostly a matter of metal and glass screens and the plan is opened wide to sun, air and vista. More a spreading good-time-place is possible in country life.

The designs could utilize different materials by modifying structural details, only. The simple type of exterior we have indicated would lend itself either to synthetic sheet, to slab construction or to wood frame with plastered metal covering. Were brick or stone to be used the walls would be thicker reducing floor space somewhat without any other necessary changes because the upper story is, in every case, mostly glass and would need the protecting roof planes for protection. The roofs in suburb and country also might be utilized if surroundings and circumstances made it desirable. There is no basement. It has disappeared. The main floor is made directly upon a concrete mat laid over dry filling, well drained.

This two-zone suburban house, complete with standardized utility-stack built in synthetic sheets of metal, wood and plaster, or other materials should not cost over six thousand dollars for garage, three bedrooms, two bathrooms and commodious living quarters. Probably where conditions are favorable and prefabrication possible such a house could come within a four thousand dollar cost limit where no slabs would be taken from the appropriation by "financing" charges or too large a profit taken by the system.

The servant has no domicile in a house of this type. The whole idea of "servant" would vulgarize the kind of life suited to the house. Outside help—coming in at stated times—being more professional, and should be all the labor the modern housewife would need with her modern labor saving devices and a proper regard for bringing up the young to accept normal responsibilities in the household.

1936: An Architect Speaking for Culture

Speaking of—and for—culture, what would you say was the matter with a great new country (most powerful on earth) that put its Supreme Court to work where it was lost in a monstrous monument to Rome and not see it as ridiculous; where government marked its public buildings with a symbol of authority that always was false architecture: the dome. A country whose better folk dwelt in little stage settings pleased and proud to imitate foreign dwellings; whose art institutes were museums directed by picture brokers; and whose museums were really its art institutes; where "learning" was housed in pseudo cathedrals and higher teaching was stale, pseudo academic post mortem; a country where the church was an alibi; whose popular music was a gift from the Negro and the photograph was the great medium of popular expression; whose businessmen pulled up and let down by wires were got up into feudal towers of fake masonry to go to work for a living, and the busier they were up there the more often they had to come down to destroy what they had done in order to keep on being busy, meanwhile going on building more towers; a country where the channels of news and policy were popular entertainment privately owned and no one could do anything about it. A country where every several to seven years government must take hand over the people and tax the future to feed the present, else its workers would starve. A country where cultural endeavor must be false or stand square against the current of available ways and means, sincerity being a quality for heroes; where one of the greatest of inventions, the radio, was a peddler in the parlor and, in order to peddle there, made the country's finest talent a huckster. And society did nothing about it. A people unable (because it had never learned by honestly trying to be itself) to make any proper use of its strength in order to make its enormous strength a blessing, helplessly allowing its powers to become an unmitigated curse. This people so busily ingenious that apparatus multiplied, and the necessity for anything except more machines to run more money-making machinery was beside the mark; where the push button was becoming the symbol of power whether of hostess, wife, overlord, or the citizen; therefore, a country wherein all power was becoming vicarious; proxy being, the machine.

In short, a country trying to outwit life and take a short cut to somewhere, with no idea whatever where; a country mistaking nervousness for emotion, restlessness for energy, believing progress to consist in getting all work done by machinery.

What beside sex and more of it; harder and harder liquor; more and better selling, wisecracking and town crying; more and swifter travel, would you say the infallible eventual recourse of such a country would be?

Overriding all its minorities, it would be war, wouldn't it? More war and bigger and better, or revolutionary, wars; the final war a war between the sexes, probably fought with bigger and better guns.

That nation would be without art, no matter how inventive and industrious it might be, and so with no cultural power whatever to reproduce itself. Looked at impartially you would say such a country would go under as the shortest lived civilization in the history of the world.

The tragedy of our unpreparedness to meet life on any true basis is clearly seen in an emergency like the present when government must step in to perform the functions that a democratic society should perform for itself, and civilization must again see freedom of choice and speech set aside to make "jobs." A progressive people must stand by to see the fruits of labor politically characterized by mediocre groups rather than by the super common sense of art; and see the nation's bravest and best quite idle, equality of meals the emergency forcing the country to stay down, rather than the highest good by means of which the country ought to be inspired and enabled to rise. Our Government, and it is our own fault, is where it must put a premium upon the mediocre, as it imagines, "in order to live." And perhaps that is the only thing any government so politically founded and minded as ours can ever do. But if so, see only the travesty of an ideal of democracy, originally the expression in government nearest to the ideal of an organic architecture! Now that the time has come to atone for success such as ours, instead of democracy we see a sort of "mobocracy" as the nearest possible approach.

So, where our culture is concerned we are a fat gaseous aggregation; too much of everything; no good digestion of anything wholesome.

Too much education, mostly the wrong kind in the wrong places.

Too much money, most of it in the wrong places.

Too much food, most of that in the wrong places at the moment.

Too much machinery, the right kind in wrong.

Too much science, even in the right places.

Too much salesmanship of mechanical artifice in the name of art.

No indigenous art because of too little concern for the present or future of human sensibility; property rights being no longer human rights. Our ambitions have been satisfied to climb upward upon the miseries and credulities of mankind.

This country was and still is the world's white hope for a better future, but it is evident now that some true center line is needed for a life line here in the United States. Somebody in Usonia must go to work. And that somebody is the creative artist.

Any civilization wherein exaggerated urbanism rules the mind, as it rules ours, is sure to lose sight of its birthright, the ground. No art of any life heretofore or hereafter begins or ends anywhere else. We have neglected our ground as the basis for our culture and tried to get culture from the pavements and factories of the world. The factors and their factories have had whip hand over our art and culture, so why, indeed, wonder that our cultural endeavor should take on the character of the factory; the knowledge factory, news factory, war factory, picture factory, relief factory, as well as the shoe factories?

But well-planned decentralization by way of intelligent new use and fresh interpretation of the machine and the ground itself, does loom ahead and sanity may be restored to culture if we will begin to plan for more human use of our new machine advantages instead of letting their present owners go on to further use *us* and by so doing destroy themselves as well.

The house will not go to the factory for prefabrication; no, the factory will go to the house. And when it does go, in the hand of the competent architect, great economies and fresh new beauty will be the beneficial result by way of integration of society.

The best thought for the best way, with the least expenditure where *human* values go, will be the new criterion for *building* or *living* or being, anywhere in our great country.

This simply means that no house is "a machine for living" except as the heart of man is a suction pump. But it does mean that the house, if it is a home, is the epitome of the entire resource of this expert mechanical era; those resources put to work to secure more life for more individuals as individuals than life ever held for the individual before. More freedom, better quality, more colorful in effect so far as individuality goes. I tell you *that* must be the true nature of true American democracy when it becomes honest.

Organic architecture has already declared war upon the box and the box man and upon housing à la mode, no matter if the housing be by government, and declares that to go on making by machinery (which only means with more deadly facility) more houses planned by the old order of thought for the old conditions however the old types may be modified can only stultify progress and be the same kind of waste Henry's old Model T was just because Henry left off thinking at the engine and saw the old buggy as good enough to ride in.

The old type of dwelling, Colonial or of any other period, is not fit for the new machinery of production and can't be made so by all the fixing or fudging that mechanics or the mechanically minded can do, no matter who sells it to whom or where sold. The old house must be thrown away entirely and a new one more fit to live in, conceived in the spirit of organic architecture.

Or again we may find these houses we are building in the name of progress dumped upon some future junk pile together with academicians, politicians, assorted grandomania, sky-scrapers, domes and pediments, pseudo cathedrals, rocking chairs, professors, chewing gum, private ownership of public needs, "equality of meals" government, pampered sons and daughters of pampering parents, slum "housing," grade crossings, "subsistence home-steads," street cars, football, and 6-day bicycle races, magazine covers (except the *New Yorker*), all town criers except Alex Woollcott, the frying pan, prize fights, Balaban and Katz theaters, motorcycles, funerals, radio announcers, gangdom, and Radio City, grand opera, "Grand" hotels, radiators, newspapers, barbed wire, lawyers and in-laws, "selling" on the air, the virtuoso, the expert, the fond mother, the doting father, the Army, the Navy, the newspaper factory, teetotalers of every kind, the cocktail, Sir Joseph Duveen, all "directors," the Fourth of July, Christmas cards, all but one or two varieties of gasoline, cockeyed hats, high heels, "dessert," porches, pie clubs, and parrot clubs, the time bound wherever found, the white collarite, all tips on American soil, anything dated (especially dated people), easel pictures on walls, germs, vitamins, and flies; all ists, isms, ites, and finally "relief!"

1936: Room for the Dead

To the Convention of the Memorial Craftsmen of America, Chicago.

Unpopular words, these, and one can well imagine the stony silence that greeted the speaker after they had been said. Wright's ability to make talks to such groups without compromising or tempering his remarks shows rare courage. Like most of the speeches since 1930, this was given informally without notes; the text here is taken from stenographic transcription.

Lots for the Dead. I think these places we call cemeteries should be more pleasurable to the living as habitations for the dead, less dead to the living.

But how to make them less dead?

Let's talk it over.

The first general curse on habitation for the living is placed there by the "realtor." It is the "lot," the interminable row of "lots," whereas an acre of ground to every house is the only sensible minimum now, if it never were before. Likewise, the realtor comes first to the cemetery, too. He seems to get everywhere first. The citizen, alive, gets a lot two by twice in some long row, and, dead, he gets another, as long as he is tall and as wide as he is long, when he is moved down and out. Or is moved out and down.

There is no sense in this realtor's curse in either case, and I believe if the resting places of the quick and resting places for the dead are ever to be made more beautiful, ground and plenty of it must be more sensibly and generously measured out for that purpose. The matter of improvement begins right there, and there is nothing much to do until the realtors are rounded up and most of them taken out and shot at sunrise.

Room for the Dead. These places we call burying grounds should be places to which we might go with no repulsion or dread, a blessing, too, instead of a curse on life. And, I believe, this is all a matter of *design;* appropriate spaciousness in the first place, an intelligent use of materials in the next place. A fine sense of the whole, dominant

If we are to be regimented in rows 50 feet o.c. while we are alive, for God's sake give us enough room to lie in, gracefully separate, and beautifully informal in arrangement when we are dead. This in order to have a little freedom to look forward to and a better sentiment toward death than we now seem to have. Not that this would do us any good after we are dead, but because it would do us all some good while we are alive to see our loved ones better treated at the last.

Individualism of Clients. A great handicap always, to the architect who works in terms of organic architecture, lies in this fact that everyone looks at any house he has done in the light of what he or she (the spectator) would want and not at all in the light of what it was the possessor of the house desired. To illustrate this let me assure you that of the 200 or more clients I have built houses for, each thinks his house my *only* real success and discounts most of the others.

Where It Begins. So to eliminate artist individuality as inspiring element in favor of the test tube and the mechanical laboratory would be to reduce art to an affair of the brain; music to mathematics, architecture to engineering, poetry to rhyme, philosophy to intellectual cerebration, religion to ritual, etc. That is to say to leave the human heart and mind, typified by the creative artist, out of its own.

An Architecture by Rules. The "style internationale." It soon became a formula any tyro could cliché and it soon became abhorrent to the feelings of the free man everywhere. Only academies and governments could ever look upon such narrow abstraction with tolerance. And in this case they would so look upon it only because, otherwise, they must be impotent. It is to them that the compelling formula must come were the mass ever to come first.

The Mirror of the Times. Believing in architecture as essentially the greatest of all human documents and the most reliable record of time, place, and man, naturally I believe it to be good and great only when it is true to what is worthy in all these. And I believe that architecture should be an expression disciplined by ways and means peculiar to itself and to man, in its own time and place. That is to say, disciplined from within. I believe also that this discipline should reach the point in its development where, in any fair retrospect the buildings that compose it may be said definitely to belong to that era, and so, in the large, might be referred to as *a style*. But I still believe that this mass product would only be seen to have been "creative" were the effect of a style subordinate and subsequent to the individual perceptions that gave each building composing the whole its own great individuality. Good building, in itself unconscious of itself, is a feature of any style whatsoever. Style should be the architect's own, not imposed on him by *a style*.

Mass Production. I think mass production need be no bar to creative effort if creative effort could give direction and control to production. In the present circumstances of capitalistic production such might be the case were capitalistic control aware of the need and would be a fair judge of results. But the same condition now applies to any other form of society.

Style. A style is some form of spiritual constipation.

Wood. Good old-fashioned wood leaves nothing to be desired in the way of synthetic slabs or chromium plated pipe. Swift sure lines and clean planes in every way make a better background for living than lace curtains, figured wall paper, machine carved furniture, and elaborate picture frames.

Minorities. The minority report continues always to be the vital report. History has proved this. Where the report ceases to be "minority" be sure the truth it once held is only truism and the truth needed by the day and hour to keep life alive is off out in front somewhere unrecognized and alone.

Organic Architecture. Organic architecture includes all materials, accepts all forms so they be natural to purpose, considerate of ways and means and respectful to environment.

℞. I should say, from what I read and see in the magazines, that what the so-called "new" in modern architecture needs most at the moment is a good spiritual cathartic, perhaps even a number of first-class funerals.

The Plow. At last America has by way of the Resettlement Administration (and thanks to Tugwell) a remarkable documentary film. Soil erosion may seem a not very dramatic subject, but the talented young group who did the work on "The Plow That Broke the Plains" has made an unforgettable film that will take its place among great films anywhere. Pare Lorentz, Steiner, Strand, and Hurwitz: Smallen's direction with Virgil Thompson's music and Thomas Chalmers' resourceful story have given the country something of dramatic beauty and real social value. All great art is likely propaganda if you wish to look at it that way. And while all propaganda is not great art, all great art is, as surely, great propaganda.

This film splendidly dramatizes the sequences and ultimate consequences of bad farming on the future of this country of ours. For the first time the developed technique of American cinema has found a virtually useful theme dealing directly with the people in this future that is *now*.

Out of the vast dust bowl recently came devastation and death on a scale undreamed of. Other devastations ever more vast are imminent or proceeding unnoticed. These, too, might be (ought to be) dramatized and driven home on a par with this one. Timber destruction especially. "The Plow That Broke the Plains" makes it apparent that American cinema can be put on a plane of beauty and usefulness with Russian cinema. And Russian cinema leads the world just now in both. I see in this fine effort the beginning of the emancipation of our most popular medium of expression from Hollywood box office and simian sex.

Some of the best talent our country affords has been tied into the making of this film. When government takes a beneficent hand like this in looking ahead it is valuable teaching and deserves more than we ever give it by way of "politics." The administration seems, for once, to have overcome its prejudice in favor of mediocrity.

"The Plow That Broke the Plains" shows you that no more than a mere plow might break your country as this film all but breaks your heart.

"Real estate" may resent it. No one who loves the country will. A few of us, however, hate to see the little two-story Colonial hot box offered by Government as a pattern for living on the Great Plains as we see it here. But good architecture is not for government as things are except as mediocre may happen to be good.

1936-1940: At Taliesin

FROM THE *Capital Times,* MADISON, WIS.

Tucked into his busy days Wright found time to write a weekly column under this head in this liberal Madison daily newspaper edited by William Evjue. These selections are chosen from several typical columns as well as from some drafts which do not appear to have been completed or published.

The Horse and Buggy Doctor. Were I Governor of this State the country doctor of Wisconsin should have all the aid I could give him. But the Governor, I am afraid, would have to turn the job over to politicians in order to get anything done. Having just come through a serious illness, by choice at home with one of these rough diamonds, rather than be carried off to the latest and best in hospitals, I have the rural doctor on my mind with gratitude for his hard sense, his faculties sharpened by personal experience, faculties which proved right when precision instruments in more scientific hands went wrong.

Doctor Osler once said he never discounted the diagnosis of a country doctor. And no doubt all of you have read Ian MacLaren's tribute to "The Doctor of the Old School." Alex Woollcott includes it in his new "Reader."

What I would have the State do for him is no more than to endow every one of him with a small clinic of his own, including an oxygen tank, and the more indispensable modern instruments and free subscriptions to whatever scientific medicosurgical literature he might choose to subscribe.

And when he has grown less able to cope with the weather and finds himself no longer able to live on unpaid bills, then, to him, a modest pension from the State.

I think it more important to increase his initiative and characterful contact with the sick of his region than to further emphasize exportations to the big hospital. Yes, decentralization again instead of organized congestion. I believe American country doctors are the most valuable of America's shock troops and would like to see more power and greater opportunity for usefulness coming to them where sick folk are at home.

The big "institution" is drawing from him rather than building him up—just as the big manufactured newspaper has killed the crusading editor.

The kind of self-reliance that acting on his own judging in emergency on emergency breeds in the country doctor does something to his faculties "We, the People" can't afford to lose.

Let us give the doctor of our Wisconsin countrysides a break.

Limitations. The more one's own limitations are understood and respected the more the nature of the thing is revealed.

What to Teach. Do not try to teach design. Teach principles.

Architectural Education. The business of a school of architecture is not to organize and direct experience but to inspire interpretation.

Taste. Taste is a personal quality only coloring design. The design may be the better or the worse for it. It is relatively unimportant.

The Jefferson Memorial. Why waste more American tax-payer's substance on reactionary monarchical monuments? Our bureaucratic architecture is already hard enough for the growing spirit to bear without adding more.

I refer to J. Russell Pope's arrogant insult to the memory of Thomas Jefferson, a cultured democrat adored by many of us and honored by all. With Mr. Pope (he is apparently growing too fashionable in Washington) we are never safely on the firm high ground of fine sentiment but we must ever be in the traffic preening the fine feathers of sentimental affectation or be present with Pope at the morgue.

Thomas Jefferson? Were the gentleman alive today he would be first to scorn this stupid erudition mistaken in his honor and, abreast of the advanced thought of today as he was leader of the advanced thought of his own time, he would promptly condemn both the folly and the shameful waste. Life has changed, almost beyond belief, since Thomas Jefferson came to lend his abilities to our great experiment, bringing with him the clothes, furniture, and books on building familiar to the Georgian period he turned his back upon.

He was not an architect except as every gentleman of his day had a book smattering of the arts to whet his taste and abet his leisure. But he had a mind and would certainly have kept pace if he did not lead his country's growth. Had he lived until now we could not find *his* face turned toward the rear to encourage the gangrene of sentimentality, his fine mind closed to the superb advancement of the scientific art of building we call architecture. A hobby of his, and especially.

I imagine I see the sarcastic smile with which his shade must receive this official proposition to drag his mortal remains to the surface of the present to memorialize him to his own people in terms of the feudal art and thought that clung to him then, deliberately to make of him now a fashionable effigy of reaction instead of the character he was and is, appreciated by his own people as the noble spirit of progress and freedom. Were the great man living he might well say, What folly to spend our popular billions to preserve the letter of a man and not one cent to preserve his spirit!

Monuments. I, for one, am sadly familiar with the sterile results of officialdom where works of art are concerned. Yet I am astonished at the effrontery presuming to commit our people to one more world-famous miscarriage of grace to add to the disgraces already handed on to posterity by way of "government."

My earnest protest, as an architect and an American herewith: Government, my Government, let us up! Have we not suffered enough vain unreality because of cheap realism such as this? Take your unfeeling "realistic" bulk off our progress in architecture by showing us that American millions can now be spent to nobly characterize the immortal spirit of a noblest American and that you are, at last, able to respectfully allow his clothes, his book architecture, his furniture and utensils . . . his mere tastes of the period to remain with his mortal body in his tomb. They, too, are his mortal remains.

O Government . . . if you cannot yet learn how to pay honor to your bravest and best with true significance and grace as architecture—then pay it with green spaces, noble trees, and splendid masses of verdure and bloom. Or say it, in this case, by way of a great forum where Thomas Jefferson's own great people may find a voice or consciously be one themselves.

Exit Tombs. Similar blunders have made our official buildings in Washington a dead weight upon the spirit of our progress. Our official monuments are shameful waste betraying the future of our own architecture into the hands of cultural sycophant or politician or college boys educated far beyond their capacity. Meantime, indigenous creative art has gone begging for its life while the whole world where culture is concerned has laughed and laughs now at such erudite ignorance. Official America, alone, seems not to know it. Why, I ask, should easy money even if taken from too easily rich Americans be so wantonly spent to advertise to posterity that American authority is neither scholar nor gentleman? No scholar because unaware of the trend of honest advanced thought in the world of culture; no gentleman because willing to betray its own youth to senility or to deserved ridicule.

How many Americans living and loyal to Jeffersonian ideals, understanding and loving the spirit of the man, could tolerate this Johnny Pope masquerade, in his honor?

Name one capable of such treachery!

And "Government" would put this latest betrayal of our substance, this shameful mortgage on our future, beside other Government travesties of a great memory—for one, the Lincoln Memorial. Beside the two put the stupendous folly erected to caricature the Supreme Court of the United States and see what it all adds up to. It will total no more than provincial grandomania.

Sacrifice of the living spirit to the dead letter? Yes. But *more,* it adds up to a confession of impotence. Whatever can excuse this to the young America that will be taxed to pay the bills? Add to that tax, the tax still later generations will pay to get rid of it all as, even now, it would be glad were it taxed to get rid of the State Department building, the Congressional Library, the Union Station, the senseless "classic" and the General Grant Gothic conceits generally adorning the National Government's monumental seat at Washington.

Politicians. A politician is nobody until he has money to spend.

Money. The affairs of the people get hopeless to the degree that they become money affairs. There is nothing so timid as a million dollars—except two millions.

1937: Reply to Questions by *Architecture of the U.S.S.R.*

To show how the wheels go round in the creative mind of an architect would be none other than creation itself. But to answer your questions as may be.

1. An axiom: the solution of every problem is contained within itself. Its plan, form and character are determined by the nature of the site, the nature of the materials used, the nature of the system using them, the nature of the life concerned and the purpose of the building itself. And always a qualifying factor is the nature of the architect himself.

2. In integral architecture composition, as such, is dead. We no longer compose. We conceive the building in plan as an entity. Proceeding from generals to particulars by way of some appropriate scheme of construction we try to find the equation or the expression best suited, that is to say most natural, to all the factors involved as enumerated in above answer to question number one.

3. Drawing and sketching are merely a means to clarify and to record ideas. In themselves they should only play this minor part. As a means of communication between architect and client or between architect and builder they are necessary language and as such should say as simply and directly as possible what requires to be said and say no more.

4. The only way classical or modern monuments can be helpful is to study that quality in them which made them serviceable or beautiful in their own day and be informed by that. As ready-made forms they can only be harmful to us today. What made them great in their day is the same characteristics that would make great buildings in our day. But the buildings we should make would be necessarily very different.

5. It is seldom that collaboration can enter into truly creative work except as one man conceives and another executes. But, even so, the highest is not attained that way. In the art of architecture conception and execution should be a self-contained unit. An architect's assistants should be like the fingers on his hands in relation to the work he is to do. The "committee meeting" at best never produced anything in architecture above the level of a compromise. Nor has a public architectural "competition" ever resulted in anything above the averaging of averages. Competitions are devastating where creative work is concerned.

6. Sculpture and painting are integral features of architecture and the architect himself should be sufficiently master of both to enable him to visualize and embody these features where and as they belong in his creation. Architecture, sculpture, and painting should be a synthesis as sympathetically executed as the composer's score is executed by the orchestra when directed by the composer himself.

7. Final work on any design should merely be completing the harmony of the whole by justifying all details, checking up on and changing such as may not be digested in the sum total of the project. Little "polishing" should be necessary if the project has been well conceived and is a natural solution well worked out and if it was properly recorded.

8. Work on construction at the site should be directly under the supervision of the man who conceived the building: the architect. And such organization and assistance should be given him as will ensure the completion of the work to his satisfaction.

9. Corrections, additions, should be few as possible. If sufficient study has been devoted to the development of the project many should be unnecessary. But sometime in the final construction of any work a better way of accomplishing the desired result may appear in the field and a better way which should not be lost. But the architect should be the final judge in any such event and he should be free to make the necessary changes to the best advantage of the whole work. Plans and specifications are made by the architect and his assistants in order to educate themselves. Progress in this educational process should not stop as experience goes on after the structure has been begun except insofar as the process may complicate the system executing the building. For this reason it is better to have flexible means of execution with as little financial penalty for changes as possible and as little confusion or waste as possible in the work itself. Nevertheless, and before all, any good building is the proper working out of a definite system of construction which should be fully grasped and understood, that is to say "mastered," by the architect before he begins to plan his building.

1937: Architecture and Life in the U.S.S.R.

FROM THE *Architectural Record,* OCTOBER, 1937

One of several discussions of the state of architecture in the U.S.S.R. written by Wright following his return from a visit to Russia.

Now that I am back at Taliesin again, my Moscow colleagues are far enough away for perspective to assert itself. I enjoyed them so much, was personally so much in sympathy with them while there, that appraisals made on the spot might easily have been overdrawn. They were not.

As I see across the Pole my friends in Moscow and their work appear the more extraordinary. I went to them intending to do what little I could to end the confusion I thought I saw among them. I disliked the Soviet Work Palace exceedingly, do so yet, hoped to change the minds entangled with its erection, but the foundations were in.

And I found that in Russia now, as in the United States long ago, the masses who had nothing and to whom the landed aristocracy appeared to have everything, had their turn to be pleased. Nothing pleases them so much as the gleam of marble columns under high ceilings, glittering chandeliers, unmistakable luxury as they had to look up to it when it decided their fate, when they ate out of luxury's hand if they ate at all.

But reassurance for me lay in the attitude of the Soviet architects themselves. I may mention Alabyan, Colly, Jofan, the Vesnins, Niklosky, Chuseff, and the editor, Arkin, as personal acquaintances in this connection. All of them took the present situation calmly with Russian humor and a touch of fatalism, characteristically Russian.

Just now is no time to offer the liberated ones the higher simplicity which repudiates the falsity of that sort of luxury. This is not the time to insist upon something they could not yet understand, the higher simplicity that has turned upon that flagrant artifice as the people themselves turned upon its possessors. So in the Soviet Union I saw the cultural lag again as I have seen it and have fought against it for a lifetime in these United States. With the Russians, as with the Americans, several more generations must pass away before a more natural way of life and building can take the place of the old order. The Russian people see viciousness in that old order where human rights are concerned, but the masses of the people are yet unable to see viciousness in the order in that higher realm of created things of which architecture is the highest.

The architects, however, at least those I have named, are men who do see and realize it. They are men who say, "Never mind, we will tear it down in 10 years."

"But it will take nearly that long to finish the Work Palace," I said. "Never mind," said they, "we may tear that down too, even before we complete it."

"But this popular rush to get into Moscow? Are you on the right road when you prepare Moscow to take in 5 million country people, instead of sending Moscow out to the 5 million?"

"But Russia needs a cultural center for her uneducated millions for years to come. Let the city be that cultural center for a time," said they.

That resignation would not be possible for me; I can understand it, perhaps sympathize with it, in a way envy it, but I cannot approve it, still less share in it. Notwithstanding the tragedy of the first essays in the direction of the new simplicity, I would see the Russian opportunity as a mighty incentive in no way diminished by a false start.

But the attitude of the Russian architects is sincere and, I am sure, far in advance of the social consciousness of our own American architects. I do not know one architect among us who looks so far into the future, able to smile indulgently at his own present effort; perspective given by a fine sense of humor in his idealism.

Said Alabyan of his new Theatre, "I thought I would put all the columns I would have to use the rest of my life into this building and have done with it."

Said Vesnin, concerning his Palace of Culture and Rest (a very desirable improvement on Le Corbusier *et al.*), "It lacks color. It is only a preliminary study. It is not yet Russian."

Said young Jofan, not yet quite disillusioned concerning his highly decorative Soviet Work Palace: "Never mind, Mr. Wright, it will improve as we go along. We are studying it continually."

And I saw proofs of that statement in Jofan's studio (Napoleon's old residence in Moscow by the Kremlin wall).

Who can help loving such liberal great-hearted fellows? What colleague would not do anything he could do under heaven to help them? The result might be help *from* them.

Said they: "We have faith in our people. We Russians are by nature artists. We love the beautiful. Our sense of life is deep and rhythmic. We will create a new Russia. You will see."

I believe I do see even now in their efforts a new organic Russia slowly entering into their buildings "through closed doors," and I see no necessity for Russia to die that the Soviet Union may live.

If Comrade Stalin, as disconcerted outsiders are saying, is betraying the revolution, then, in the light of what I have seen in Moscow, I say he is betraying it into the hands of the Russian people.

In Moscow the architects, by themselves, enjoy a large old palace complete, as academy. There are a gallery and supper rooms on the top floor, libraries, studios and collections below. Just before leaving we joined some of the architects I have named for retreat and recreation at their Suchanov, a 400 acre park, 30 miles from Moscow, where another old palace stands. There, their own herds and flocks around them, they are putting up new buildings. All stand in a beautiful forest with fine vistas of beautiful countryside. To this wooded retreat, whenever they will, they may and do go with their families and friends for recreation. The architects are about to build small studios for preliminary study and shops for technical experiments there.

There seems none but friendly rivalry among them. Why should there be other than willing cooperation? Worldly rewards cannot benefit them. They are economically independent for life and so are their loved ones. One man's success hurts no one else but is a stepping stone for his fellows. The sting has been taken out of competition and the road to culture of the noble sort is wide open to all who choose to follow it. There is no humiliation in today's defeat because failure today may be retrieved by tomorrow's triumph. The road is open. And their "tomorrow" is today in the sense that eternity is now. You will feel it so when you talk to them.

Good fellowship at Suchanov, as Olgivanna, my good wife and interpreter, and I found, is a fine unforgettable human experience. Have you ever known Russian hospitality? No? Well, then, be an architect and go to visit Russian architects. They will take you to Suchanov.

Being a farmer myself as well as an architect, I visited a collective dairy farm. The people were at their work in the fields and barns, sharing according to their contributions. They milk three times a day, at sunrise, at 10 o'clock, and at sunset. All live together in a village like the farm village of the old order except that now there is the "crèche" filled with scientifically cared for babies, while their mothers are at work. The babies are nursed by their own mothers. Nearby, there is a kindergarten, along modern lines. Both "crèche" and kindergarten are maintained by the Soviet itself. The Kolknotz is a nucleus characteristic of Soviet effort, but agrarian effort, so far, is less developed than industrial effort, as it still is with us.

The factory is better built and run than the farm. For one thing, the farm requires so much more. This is partly because the revolution first came from organized labor in the factories, and the farms resisted subsequent movement to collectivize their work. At one time the farmers destroyed their pigs and crops rather than turn them in to the collective. We well know how difficult it is to bring any cooperation to bear upon American farm life, or within it, even now. The grange came nearest to anything we had, but it does not flourish.

The agrarian hurdle seems taken by the Soviets, however. Cooperative farming seems likely to prove the same blessing that cooperatives prove to be in factory industry. The houses of the farm village range about a central square that might be a beautiful park with loudspeakers there connecting each group with the voice of their leader and the cultural efforts of urban centers. In time, these farm units are sure to become the most desirable of all places in which to work and live.

Plans for the new Moscow are far ahead of any city planning I have seen elsewhere. There is splendid opportunity to make the city over because no private property, nor sentimentality, can say no when the great plan requires the blowing up of whole sections of old buildings. Even sacred old landmarks are blown into the air to make spacious streets where dirty obscure lanes existed. The scope and liberal character of the proposed changes and extensions is astonishing. When completed, Moscow will inevitably be the first city of the world. But, to me, that can only mean something already dated and outlived by the advanced thought of our today.

All of the new city will be much too high, the same premium put upon congestion seemingly that landlordism places there. And I suppose this is partly because the industrialist, still clinging to his habits of congestion, is ahead of the agrarian in the U.S.S.R. He is still ahead in our own U.S.A. For some reason, there will be regimented areas, too, in the "classic" manner, where inevitable freedom should be. There will be four-story schoolhouses (knowledge factories) where two stories would be too high. And while the entire outer belt is a farm area, it should be the other way around. The best of the traditional and official buildings should stand in a big central park, buildings growing higher as they extended outward into the country. But much that is splendid is already done—wide avenues and park spaces. The ancient Moscow River is being walled with cut granite blocks, sweeping in a fine curve from the water to the upper levels. The ancient Kremlin walls and domes stand nobly above these new granite slopes.

The Moscow subway is a succession of well-planned palatial stations. I like the more simple ones, built at first, with columns containing lights, the shafts rising and spreading dendriform into the overhead. Later ones are richer and more spacious. The Moscow subway makes the New York subway look like a sewer when one returns to compare them.

But cutting across the road to culture is a barrier, the same barrier that is with us, the popular demand for spiritually unearned, luxurious grandeur. But in their case, no wonder nor reproach. The Russians outside the aristocracy and bourgeoisie had less than nothing. Now it is their turn. Millions looking toward Moscow as a mecca for a lifetime can go there at last! Of course, they go and want to stay, because the lash of unrequited toil or the ground has left its scars.

Concerning new construction: their buildings are no better nor any worse than the best work of other countries. As I have said, misfortune befell Moscow, and our modern movement in architecture too, when her architects took after the left wing. That mistake in direction left some very negative and foreign results indeed, drab, lonesome, technically childish. The popular reaction from that fiasco could only be luxurious picture making in the antique, the picture making which the older people learned as children to admire and covet.

Chuseff and I stood together in his great new Soviet Hotel, a great constructed thing, done in what I told him should be called "The Metropolitan Style" because you could see it with such virtues as it has and all its faults, in Philadelphia or any big city of the world. A comfortable hotel though, and I exaggerated a little because in many respects it was better done, more comfort provided for an occupant, but still the building was the type of hotel we Americans are learning to hate. Mere size seems to captivate the Russians as it seduced us earlier. Of course, all this is reaction in action.

The Work Palace, to be the crowing glory of the new construction, suffers likewise from grandomania of the American type in imitating skyscraper effects way up to the soles of the enormous shoes of Lenin, where the realistic figure of that human giant begins to be 300 feet tall. Something peculiar to the present cultural state of the Soviet is to be seen in the sharp contrast between thick shoes and workman's clothes and skyscraper elegances. These perpendicular skyscraping motives are surmounted at the characteristic New York set-backs by sculpture, pygmy by comparison, Lenin, enormous, treads upon the whole, regardless. Nothing more incongruous could be conceived and I believe nothing more distasteful to the great man Lenin, if he sees. And yet the young architect whose design was accepted for this work 7 years ago has this year built the more dramatic and successful exhibition building at the Paris Fair. The general motive of that building is not dissimilar to that of the Soviet Palace. It, too, is a building surmounted by gigantic and somewhat better sculpture.

But the Paris Fair building is a low, extended, and suitable base for the dramatically realistic sculpture it carries whereas the Work Palace itself is a case of thoroughly unsuitable, badly overdramatized base underneath realistically undramatic sculpture.

I admire Jofan's Paris building as much as I dislike his Soviet work monument, which is saying a great deal.

The idea of sculpture at the base of the Paris building and the over-elaborate entrance might have been better omitted. All else might well have been subordinated. But, here, on the whole, is a master architect's conception that walks away with the Paris Fair. The Soviet Work Palace was an earlier work, the result of competition, and probably Jofan and his colleagues, after working so long upon it, can no longer get a detached view of the whole.

I went with him to see a sanitarium he had done near Moscow and that, too, was a very well designed, very well built structure. Any Soviet citizen needing attention and care may come here to luxury seen only on our transatlantic liners. An ingenious arrangement of balconies and rooms gives outdoor enjoyment to indoor comfort. There were too many small things about the place for ornaments, but on the whole here is a performance that could not be, has not been, excelled anywhere.

Jofan! What do you say? Let's declare it off with the palace of the Soviets. Let's have another competition. I will gladly enter one myself and we shall see how much you have grown. I believe you could win a second time and save the Soviet Union future humiliation.

The building occupied by *Pravda* I saw as the more creditable of the left wing "modernistic" attempts by the Russians, but because of its negative and unconstructive precedents such is not for the Russians, too laborious stylization of too little spirit and small content. I see the Russians discontented with less than something profound, when culture catches up, say, in 10 years.

The extensive Palace of Culture, a recreational center for the studious or artistically minded citizen, was better in many respects. It contains as good a design for an auditorium as I have seen. The scope and extent of the whole is good in conception, not bad in execution. I liked the architects themselves. I will like their work better when it is more like them. That means more Russian in spirit and character. Both architects are capable men, invaluable to the Soviet, as are many others besides the friends I have mentioned. The Soviet sent 400 Russian architects to the Congress at Moscow.

Leningrad is to be (I take it) the Soviet showpiece in cities. Nikolsky showed me his designs for the new stadium at Leningrad. This stadium is spaciously monumental, a broad treatment employing masses of trees in an architectural way which I liked much. A sensible relief from ponderous masonry, it will be a fine piece of work on a grand scale, really noble.

The Russian cinema has made its buildings the finest good-time places for the people to be seen anywhere in the world. The Vesnins have designed some of them. Colly, my interpreter at the Congress, president of the Architects' Society, the AIA of the U.S.S.R., has a fine sense of proportion and style, at present leaning classicward. Alabyan, president of the Congress, shows himself a competent designer in the new theater, giving life to the old mode. And so it goes on in the stupendous social construction that is calling upon architecture for help and direction. Competent architects able to build great buildings are there. And alongside are sympathetic critics, editors like Arkin, the editor of *Pravda*, and many others, among whom the heads of their fine arts academies may be included.

What a pity that architecture in Soviet Russia is not as free as the man, so that the millennium might be born at once where the road is more open than anywhere else, instead of again wearisome temporizing with the old time lag and back drag of human ignorance where culture is concerned. It is hard for me to be reconciled to the delays Russia herself is experiencing, no matter how cheerfully, in getting architecture characteristic of her new life and freedom.

I saw the admirable models for Soviet Russia's new towns and cities in various places, all better than good but too many concessions to the time lag in culture. I suppose the marvel is that a country so backward as Russia was should have these fine things at all, at least, have them so soon, perhaps too soon. I grant all that and still regret.

But I saw something in the glimpses I had of the Russian people which overcomes the regret and makes me smile in anticipation. The Russian spirit! There is nothing quite like that spirit anywhere in the world today. I felt it in the air, saw it as a kind of aura about the wholesome maleness of her men and femaleness of her women; in this new gospel of work; in the glad open expressions of the faces of workmen and workwomen. Freedom already affects the unconsciously proud way they carry themselves. Especially the women. I could not help feeling "what a mother this new Russia is going to have."

A new kind of heroism, one more integral with humankind, is growing up in the world here in the Soviet Union where men are men and women are women; where God has ceased to be an expensive attraction to the people; where abortion is abolished; where there is no illegitimate child and the resources of the State stand behind the mother to reinforce her in the care of her sons and daughters. In Russia, there is a place in the sun ready for the little newcomer when conceived. Wherever and whenever he is born, he is really a citizen with rights that are guaranteed by the State, education and opportunity to work. There is no discrimination between the sexes.

All this is wise.

And how wise the premiums placed upon *quality* in work, integral rewards which build up the man in his effort, the "Stakhanov principle," they call it. Rewards of a social and substantial character are devised by a wise leader to develop an entirely new success ideal. It is so hard for us with all as it stands now in our society to even conceive this new freedom for the individual without grasping several fundamental things totally changed in the human objective. I find myself continually needing a more simple viewpoint than our complex order allows. Until we get that viewpoint, we can never understand Russia. We will marvel at her vitality and strength, heroic growth and richness of expression, especially her colorful individuality, and never know the secret of such happiness.

The secret is too simple for us because it does not consist in to have or to hold but in acceptance of a life consisting in neither except insofar as having or holding may have human benefits each to each and each to all. The relief of such release from ignoble fear, economic anxiety, and false shames, you may already see in Soviet faces, Soviet acts. Heroes and heroism are the glisten in the fabric of this new life.

Having been and sensed the Russian spirit, I should say that enemies interfering with the Soviet Union would not only have to reckon with the whole male population bearing arms, but with the women, too, and every child above nine years of age. Nothing less than total extermination could conquer Soviet Russia.

In Pekin (now Peiping), 1919, I made the acquaintance of a Chinese writer, Ku Hung Hing. An Oxford graduate, he had been the Empress-Dowager's secretary. He was then an old man. He showed himself a nonconformist by the fact that his greyish pigtail still curled up beneath his little Mandarin cap.

I went about sightseeing with the sage and I learned more from him than from any other man I have met. I treasured a book by him, "The Spirit of the Chinese People," until it was lost when my home burned in 1925.

A true philosopher, he had the faculty of thinking and speaking in "simples." One day, while sitting on the edge of an old stone terrace overlooking a lotus pool, he summed up and characterized the various races of the world with what seemed to me great insight and justice—especially with regard to America.

"Soul" seemed to him to be the element most lacking in all the nations—the French having a substitute, "delicacy." But, he said, it was Russia who would give soul to the world.

At the time, I knew Tolstoi, Dostoyevsky, Turgenev, Pushkin, and Gogol. I knew Russian music and theater, too, somewhat, and I thought I saw then what he meant.

Today I believe what he said.

It is true. Russia may yet give to this money-minded, war-minded, quarrelling pack of senile races that make up the world, the soul they fail to find within themselves; and, I hope, in time to prevent the suicide their nations are so elaborately preparing to commit.

1937: Broadacres at the Wisconsin State Historical Library

FROM *Taliesin,* PUBLICATION OF THE TALIESIN FELLOWSHIP, OCTOBER, 1940.

The time lag is too great. The back-drag is becoming too heavy. Somebody has got to do some thinking which is neither politics, borrowing or lending. Why not you, my fellow citizens? Our government is doing what it can, but politics, though too willing to do so, *can't* think for you, Mr. Citizen. As our government was planned, politicians dare not really lead. American politics is mostly a shrewd guess, with an eye on the politician's future. At their best, politicians can only read the writing on the wall! So the greatest good of which they are capable is to execute the will of the people—but, seemingly, the people have no will. "The people" seem only to desire that more money-miracles be worked for them so that they may go on eating and sleeping in order to work and sit, as usual. . . . If you think even a little you will see how all the forces we call modern (automobility and electro-communication) are inevitably destroying the conditions we are now seeking to live by. You will see that just as an industrial plant goes out of date overnight when a new and better machine is invented, so our whole reactionary social set-up goes out when machinery comes to be our way of livelihood. I think you will see, too, that the sudden liberation from toil, which the machine brought to so many was no unmixed blessing, and that machine-made efficiencies can be just as much a curse as they are a blessing to humanity. Outside of plenty to eat and wear and show off with, the rich man is not truly better off now than the poor man. The quality of his life is often inferior. Indeed, it is just this Quality that is lacking in our lives. Quantity is a poor substitute, as we are learning now.

I believe you will see that if our country is to become better worth living in, the United States of America Will Have to Go to Work! The white collarite, himself an enormous speculative commodity, has gone to wreck riding upon speculative commodities. You probably know what these "commodities" are. I believe you will come to see, as I have, that the ground itself is the true sociological basis, and, when rightly interpreted, the salt and savor of all good life. And you will see too that the true profit of our future life is bound to come more from a man's sense of his own ground in relation to all of life—if the machine and invention are to mean anything valuable to human beings. We need a new freedom, wherein a man can use and improve a plot of ground, thereby making the ground his own as long as he uses it. Neither land nor man should lie idle, a mere speculative commodity.

If our boasted "progress" means anything human, the advantages of the machine age Must have social correlation with the ground. It is here that drudgery is best conquered by the machine. We are having our ultra-urban days, our suburban reactions and our rural isolations. Now we need the rural action that will refresh and give new meaning to all of these. We must break down the artificial barriers that exist between the urban and the rural. If you will think about it seriously you will see that Out of the Ground into the Light comes everything of structure that is Beneficial to mankind. And neither money nor leisure, given to us by the machine, can permanently change this nature of wealth.

A human being, from the time he is born, is as truly entitled to a piece of ground with which he can identify himself by the use of it as he is entitled to the air he breathes or the water he drinks. If he will work on his ground, he should eat. But, barring physical disability, he should Not eat if he does not work—except when he can fairly trade his right to work for some other actual contribution which he can make to the welfare and happiness of those who do work. Money, today, is this immunity from work, a false privilege. And because of it there is insecurity, confusion, and loss of quality in all life-concerns.

1938-1940: Education and the Issues

1938: Frank Lloyd Wright

FROM THE *Architectural Forum*, JANUARY, 1939.

This special issue of the Forum *was entirely devoted to Wright's work with especial emphasis on the presentation of buildings completed during the preceding two or three years. For it Wright prepared special drawings, layouts and wrote much of the text, selections of which are reprinted here. This exceptional document contains a most complete presentation of the principal Wright buildings, chosen by the architect.*

Unity Temple: Space Enclosed. Let us go back, here, to the first self-conscious assertion of the "third dimension" in building, as it came to be called. The reality of the building is not in the four walls and roof but in the space enclosed by them to be lived in. Earlier than this I had been trying to bring the room through. But in Unity Temple (1904–05) to bring the room through was consciously a main objective. So Unity Temple has no actual walls as walls. Utilitarian features, the stair enclosures at the corners; low masonry screens carrying roof supports; the upper part of the structure on four sides a continuous window beneath the ceiling of the big room, the ceiling extending out over them to shelter them; the opening of this slab where it passed over the big room to let sunlight fall where deep shadow had been deemed "religious"; these were to a great extent the means employed to achieve the purpose. Since then the "new" concept of building (Laotse, 500 B.C.) has never slept. You will find it working in many different ways in all the structures shown in this collection, often seeming contradictory.

Sculpture and Painting. Sculptors and painters ask me: "What place has sculpture and painting in your building?" I reply: "My buildings are painting and sculpture. But painting and sculpture that is architecture could enter and carry architecture further where I am compelled to leave off for want of more highly specialized technique. . . ." To carry the building higher in its own realm is the rightful place of painting and sculpture wherever they or architecture are rightly concerned.

The Kaufmann House. This structure might serve to indicate that the sense of shelter, the sense of space where used with sound structural sense, has no limitations as to form except the materials used and the methods by which they are employed for what purpose. The ideas involved here are changed in no wise from those of early work. The materials and methods of construction come through them, here, as they may and will always come through everywhere. That is all. The effects you see in this house are not superficial effects and are entirely consistent with the prairie houses of 1901–10.

The Architect's Home. The blacksmith's horses, the shoemaker's children, the architect's home; all know a certain habitual "lag." Taliesin knows it, too. But its architect has here taken his own medicine in doses all but fatal.

St. Mark's Towers. This plan for a skyscraper, standing park free in the city, the only urban skyscraper fit for human occupancy, is as nearly organic as steel in tension and concrete in compression can make it, here doing for a tall building what Lidgerwood made steel do for the long ship. The ship had its keel. This building has its concrete core. A shaft of concrete rises through the floors engaging each floor slab as one passes through the shaft at eighteen levels. Each floor proceeds outward as a cantilever slab extended from the shaft. The slab, thick at the shaft, grows thinner by way of an overlapping scale pattern as it goes outward until at the final leap to the rectangle it is no more than 3 inches thick. The outer enclosing shell of glass and copper is pendent from these cantilever slabs. The inner partitions nest upon the slab.

Quadruple in plan (four double-decked apartments to each floor, each apartment unaware of the other as all are looking outward), the structure eliminates entirely the weight and waste space of masonry walls. The central shaft standing inside away from lighted space carries the elevators and entrance hallway well within itself. Two of the exterior walls of every apartment are entirely of glass set into sheet copper framing. But the building is so placed that the sun shines on only one wall at a time and the narrow upright blades, or mullions, project 9 inches so that as the sun moves, shadows fall on the glass surfaces.

The building increases substantially in area from floor to floor as the structure rises, in order that the glass frontage of each story may drip clear of the one below, the building thus cleaning itself, and also because areas become more valuable the higher (within limits) the structure goes. The central shaft extending well into the ground may carry with safety a greatly extended top mass. This building, earthquake, fire and soundproof from within by structural economics inherent in its nature weighs less than one-half the usual structure besides increasing available area for living purposes more than 20 percent.

It is a logical development of the idea of a tall building in the age of glass and steel, as logical engineering as the Brooklyn Bridge or the ocean liner. But the benefits of modernity such as this are not merely economic. There is greater privacy, safety, and beauty for human lives within it than is possible in any other type of apartment building.

Again the 1–2 triangle is employed, this time because in itself it has a flexibility in arrangement for human movement not afforded by the rectangle. The apparently irregular shapes of the rooms would not appear as "irregular" in reality; all would have great repose because all are not only properly in proportion to the human figure but to the figure made by the whole.

The building is a complete standardization for prefabrication. Only the concrete core and slabs need be made in the field. Our shop fabricating industrial system could here function at its best with substantial benefits to humanity. Owing to the unusual conformations the metal (copper) furniture would have to be a part of the building, as the furniture is designed to be. Here again is the poise, balance, lightness, and strength that may characterize the creations of this age instead of masonry mass which is an unsuitable, extravagant and unsafe hang-over from feudal times.

San Marcos. I have found that when a scheme develops beyond a normal pitch of excellence the hand of fate strikes it down. The Japanese made a superstition of the circumstance. Purposely they leave some imperfection somewhere, easily seen, to appease the jealousy of the gods. I neglected the precaution. San Marcos was not built. In the vault of Taliesin this completely developed set of plans now lies complete, every block scheduled as to quantity and right place. These plans are one of our prize possessions.

The Hexagon Unit. I am convinced that the pattern made by a cross section of honeycomb has more fertility and flexibility where human movement is concerned than the square. The obtuse angle is more suited to human "to and fro" than the right angle. Flow and movement is, in this design, a characteristic lending itself admirably to life, as life is to be lived in it. The hexagon has been conservatively treated, however. It is allowed to appear in plan only and in the furniture which literally rises from and befits the floor pattern of the concrete slab upon which the whole stands.

The Jacobs House. These drawings represent a modest house that has no feeling at all for the "grand" except as the house extends itself parallel to the ground, companion to the horizon. That kind of extension can hardly go too far for comfort or beauty of proportion. As a matter of course a home like this is an architect's creation. It is not a builder's nor an amateur's effort and there is considerable risk in exposing the scheme to imitation or emulation. This is true because it could not be built except as the architect oversees the building and the building would fail of proper effect unless the furnishing and planting were done by the architect.

Showing it to you thus briefly may help to indicate how stifling the little Colonial hat boxes, hallowed by government or not, really are where Usonian family life is concerned. You might easily put two of them, each costing more, into the living space of this one and not go much outside the walls. Here is a moderate cost brick and wood house that by new technology of a lifetime has been greatly extended in scale and comfort. $6,000 for a single house; imagine how the cost would come down were the technique familiar or if many were executed at one time, probably down to $3,500, according to number built and location. There is freedom of movement, and privacy too, afforded by the general arrangement here, unknown to the current treatment. Let us say nothing about beauty. It is an ambiguous term in the provinces of which our big cities are the most provincial. But I think a cultured American housewife will look well in it. The now inevitable car will seem part of it. Where does the garden leave off and the house begin? Where the garden begins and the house leaves off. Withal, this modest house seems a thing loving the ground with the new sense of space, light, and freedom to which our Usonian life has always seemed to me entitled.

Unfinished Work. Coming back from numerous meetings with young people in the colleges of most of our States, it seems to me that some kind of snubbing post for Usonian youth is urgently needed where reality is concerned in this "functionalistic" drift toward realism and the realistic. Neither realism nor the realistic is the stuff of which the universe is made. As a matter of fact, the universe is made of intense and lively personal matter asking only that the matter have individuality. For a moment, risking offense, let me be personal, as an individual.

Already the architectural matter of this issue will look out upon a modern fashioning more in the likeness of the buildings, their interiors, building, and ways of furnishing them, originally designed by myself as early as 1895, getting into their modern stride by 1901 and continuing to this hour.

The ideas taking fresh form then have gone into the twentieth century designer's mold, world-wide.

With a change of labels from a bewildering variety of sources, the forms and features of these original designs are now, with certain sterilizations to make them safe for academic consumption, become modern architecture, modern industrial design, "streamlining" in general, mostly administered by minions "joined up" with our great American advertising order. That order never sleeps.

At least enough success is, prematurely, the result to make it apparent that the new simplicity unpretentiously making appearance as early as 1896 may be *the* fashionable eclecticisms of 1938–40. Then God help us all. We shall have sunk beneath the surface of an eclectic's world. Perhaps it is the only possible world.

But to this possibility the matter of this issue still says *no*.

What disconcerts me is simply this: the early ideas and ways of planning buildings and building ways of furnishing them do not seem so much changed for the better. "Effects" have been slenderized and hardened, they have been cleaned up a little, now and then, by unwisely leaving off protective copings abolishing the sense of shelter by concealing it behind parapets; interiors and exteriors have changed superficially (they should have changed fundamentally) with the use of steel, glass, and synthetics; surfaces in general are smoothed out a little by omission of the articulation of materials and their logical protection from the elements. A severe negation of ornament is evident, not a bad negation when ignorance of the nature of ornament generally prevails, as it does. Reaction against that negation, however, is already visible. Sterilized, then, as the order that clings to standardization for life deems suitable, the work, internationally, has been counted sufficient for "new schools." Nothing radical has been done to carry it further afield.

Thus history repeats itself.

Negation is easy. Affirmation difficult.

The negation dubbed, by the Museum of Modern Art, "international architecture" could make no headway unless there were truth in my accusation, "more reflection of surface than substance." How pernicious the notion of "functionalism" as a style! Why turn superficially to a style instead of being deeply concerned with style? The words "integral," "organic," "principle," basic words concerning our ideal seem never to have occurred as necessary to such language as I have read trade-marking that device. Yes, "device," academic device at that, seeking to make a style when only style is needed. "No ornament"? That collateral fetish is the bastard begotten by intellectualists out of the dogma "form follows function"; begotten because the abuse of a noble thing was mistaken for the thing itself.

"Form follows function" is but a statement of fact. When we say "form and function are one," only then do we take mere fact into the realm of creative thought. I should say that in that difference of statement lies the real difference between organic work, and that of the professed functionalists.

Melodic structure is absent in modern music for the same reason that genuine ornament is absent in "functionalism." True ornament is the inherent melody of structure and functionalism to date is a bad builder.

Russia trying out "functionalismus" proceeded to kick it out. That she should have mistaken it for modern architecture was tragedy for the Soviets.

I have at least 10 years more (unless I get a Ford up my back, or something) in which to practice the basic principles of an organic architecture. Slowly but surely, often through closed doors, these principles are making way against badly ballyhooed, badly oversold practices of the unfunctional "functionalist" wing of our cause. For you who sympathize with this ideal of an organic architecture there is not only urgent need for real thought on our part to account for the deeper feeling behind it, but need also for the kind of technical knowledge in hand which only the application of actual principles by way of experience can give. Neither academic formula nor sloganized dicta can really serve the cause at this time.

Organic architecture is profound architecture. Premature publicizing in this circus era has some passing value but the fact appears that the deeper the matter, the more undesirable is premature publicity. Notwithstanding rescripts of university education every future architect must develop, in his own grasp, a technology of his own, his hands in work, however limited (the limitations will be his best friends), if technologies he employs are not to defeat the main purpose, a living architecture for our country as a free country.

We speak of genius as though it were the extrusion of some specialty or other. No, the quality is not there. Find genius, and you will find a poet. What is a poet?

"If he is a poet he bestows on every object or quality its fit proportion, neither more nor less.
He is the arbiter of the diverse, the equalizer of his age and land.
He judges not as a judge judges, but as the sun falling round a helpless thing."

How America needs poets! God knows, she has enough profit takers, enough garage mechanics, enough journalists, enough teachers of only what has been taught, enough wage slaves. Without the poet (man of vision wherever he stands) the soul of this people is a dead soul. One must be insensible not to feel the chill creeping over ours.

We have technology and technologies to throw away, technicians to burn, but still have no architecture. To show, for them all, we have only a multiplicity of buildings imitating many insignificant countenances or making caricature of the countenance of principle. We need an architecture so rich in the life of today that just because of it life will be better worth living—even though a reeling capitalistic "system" falls flat of its own idiotic excess. Antiseptics are not enough to grow an architecture. Profit taking as a motive for a civilization does not seem to be the ennobling basis for one.

But I believe, were the "system" aware of it, the capitalists especially would fortify themselves in architecture that is organic architecture.

Having myself had the best and the worst of everything as preliminary to the 10 years next to come, I hope none of the years will be wasted or thwarted where architecture, in what remains to us all of life, is concerned.

1938: In What Am I Most Interested in This Cosmopolitan World?

Usonian Culture. Our country's humor is her honor. Even her vulgarity is picturesque. But I look upon her pretensions to culture with a wicked eye.

1938: Myself

My Enemies. Friends too often doubt me. Enemies never do. So I trust my enemies most.

1938: From an Architect's Point of View

TO THE REAL ESTATE BOARD, CHICAGO.

Gas Station and Pylon. We have these modern improvements by way of the profit taker, but now, it seems, we must use the improvements in spite of him or give them up. If the profit takers intend to bet on electrification, bet on glass and steel and continue to bet on mobilization against the proper place of all these things in the lives of the American people, either they or the people must give them up. Guess who will give them up!

Meantime we, "the people, yes," continue to live amidst the scaffolding of a civilization, defacing every countryside: needless poles and wires, out-done tracks and sheds. We have billions of acres of stumpage and erosion, endless miles of barbed wire fences, everywhere sign boards and dumpage. How long will such blind illiberal uses of invention be used regardless of man or landscape to make money instead of used to make better men in better houses. Profit taking put the old scaffolding there where it is. Good enough purpose as I believe. But I believe, too, it's time for those who put it there to take it down. The finished work should appear. But what social sense have the profit takers ever shown. Probably the people themselves must take the scaffold down sometime soon, capital notwithstanding.

Decentralization of industry (and Education—capital E—is now our major industry) is the way they will take it down. Capitalist centralization has already reached the point where our Nation no longer owns its own ground, no longer owns anything in fact above some slight equity in the ground or what they put on it, or in an automobile, a radio, or some kind of machinery. Soon, these corporate "makers" of ours must face the fact that they can no longer sell, outright, anything they make. They can only rent it to you by way of installment buying and "repossession." Our average citizen has no valid buying power. The sources of wealth (mainly human labor and the ground) have passed into impersonal corporate control or ownership in some one of its many forms and together with national resources are held against the people.

Well, all are a headache now for corporate bodies and a heartache, as ever, for the body politic. Never mind, my realtors, every problem carries within itself its own solution. The very forces that once exaggerated centralization are working, naturally enough against it. See decentralization going on around you! See the motorcar at first exaggerating the city, now tearing it down; see the new agents of distribution springing up (the gas station is one of them); see electrification having aided congestion, scattering it; see glass and steel having given impetus to congestion by way of the skyscraper and its brood, now giving rein by way of organic architecture (you call it modern architecture) to the new sense of space. And because of modern improvements the modern city is going to be everywhere or nowhere, whether "real estate" likes it or not.

Housing. Capital at the moment seems to imagine that the safest place for it to be, after all, is in homes for those people who have little or nothing—and we are seeing the big reservoirs of capital being tapped for low-cost housing. Even the politicians, the more politic they are the better they see it, see their old political jobs in need of new parties; parties with fresh attitudes, making bigger and better promises with fresher names to give to the people for the same old things; as though parties and partisanship hadn't fooled the country long enough. Both are become now one of the things that is the matter with our kind of democracy.

The People—Yes. Perhaps, most of all, we, the American people, need to realize that *government* is necessarily "ipso facto" and that we can't look to government to *initiate* better ways of doing things. Government, in a democracy, is executive to the will of the people. We hear of constructive legislation, but when we get it, or anything like it, such legislation will first have been the idea and then the wish of the people. So "it is up to us" —and we seem to have run out of ideas, substituting for them a lot of useless wishful thinking.

How stupid to blame our troubles on our President when we made them ourselves and keep on making them by our own cupidities and stupidities! He has done a lot to enlighten our ignorance. But what can an executive do when the people run dry? Does this profit motive dry up the sources of inspiration? The answer would seem to be *yes*—so far as the American people are concerned.

Real Estate. If "Real Estate" were to go before some bar of judgment where human values were uppermost, it would be taken out and shot at sunrise as it stands. The good it has done is so little compared to the injustice and misery it has deliberately caused for its own profit.

If it has wisdom in its locker it should use it now to decentralize urban centers and reintegrate the people according to the new space measurements brought to all by motor, radio, and telephone. That new space measurement as it now stands is 100 to 1 what "real estate" has made it or would even now see it.

Any 50-foot lot is a curse upon life. Less than 1 acre to the person is even less than this country affords when it gets into its right mind and on its appropriate stride.

Practice Makes Perfect. The motorcar is yet only an overgrown horse and buggy in these United States, this specialist in motorcars.

Subdivision. The fluttering flag, the barbecue and the bull—take your narrow slice or leave it—well—we have *had* that. Or have we?

Somewhere, Some Day. In any democratic future these three things, from any human viewpoint, I am sure, will not be speculative commodities:

1. There will be no speculation in land.
2. No speculation in money.
3. No speculation in the ideas by way of which society lives.

1938: The Man and the Issue

F. D. R. What Franklin Roosevelt has had to put up with in working to enlighten the people who elected him concerning their own affairs sickens the American spirit of fair play.

1938: Federal Architecture

TO THE ASSOCIATION OF FEDERAL ARCHITECTS, WASHINGTON, D. C.

In the course of a visit to Williamsburg, Wright's opinion of the restoration of this Colonial city was asked. The answer reverberated in the press for the next few days and explains the references in the first part of this speech to the Association of Federal Architects. The last part of this selection gives questions asked at the conclusion of the speech, together with the answers.

Colonial Williamsburg. It is an admirable restoration, authentic replica of the setting of our early historic settler's life. As a museum piece it is invaluable to us because it places it where we can see it and see through it. We may read (as I read there) something of what really was the matter with our forefathers when they got here—the men who came here as rebels against oppression (later to become revolutionists) to find a new and better land. They came and lived within shooting distance of the Indians and brought that culture with them which we now see in detail at Williamsburg. We see that it is all just what they had there, back home. Of course, "back home" is what all Englishmen in foreign lands wish for. If you watch Englishmen conduct their lives as their lives run around the whole world you will find them doing just *what* was done and just as near as possible *as* it was done back home, whether they are doing it in India, Africa, Australia, or at the North Pole. Whatever they did at home, that same thing they do so far as they can do it—south, north, east, or west in the new land in which they find themselves.

There Williamsburg then ran true to form. We must say that the restoration *is* a fine museum piece and as such valuable to Americans if they would only let it be a museum piece and not an *illusion,* and would study it for what significance it has where our life is concerned, and not attempting to live in it still. As an object lesson to the Nation in architecture, it *is* valuable. Studying the exhibit at Williamsburg closely, from the inside, one may see why and how, now, this Nation was contrived by the moneyed man for the moneyed man by the money minded; see why property was the criterion by means of which this union was to survive, if it could survive at all. You can read in this persistent "search for the elegant solution" that the culture which the colonists had on them (or with them) when they arrived was French culture modified by a century or two of English "taste." England had little elegance of her own so turned to that of the French, imitated French culture and, inevitably, brought that imitation to these shores. That is plain truth concerning the culture of our colonists. Now, why not, indeed, have a fine restoration of that culture where we can look it in the face for what it is worth today, and see what the culture was that lay in behind as one element in the culture of a mixed Nation such as this one of ours?

That early culture, as you will see, had little of reality in it but did have a certain reticence, a fine cleanliness when in poverty and a finer simplicity in general than is generally practiced now. But when, later, modern devotees of English Colonial culture became rich and could spend money like drunken sailors it is easy to see how and why we got Queen Anne, Medieval Gothic, General Grant Gothic and "the 57 varieties," and easy to see why we have all these blind-as-a-bat Government buildings to work in; and why we got the kind of grandomania the Government always so generously provides for us; for official purposes and especially for its heroes.

Facing reality (as it soon did) how, in actuality, could that Colonial culture prove itself equal to the strain soon to be put upon it? You may see the consequences all around you here in Washington. Now, with deeper thought, ignoring Colonial *culture* you'll find something in the Colonial life of our forefathers that was clean, something sweet and straightforward, something out of the nature of the true liberal. The ideals of our forefathers were fine and high. And you will see that among them were great men—endowed with greatness and generosity, true native aristocrats. That older nation from which they came knew that they were worth having, but didn't know how to keep them.

But unfortunately for the future of the ideals of freedom and democracy only here the old feudal hang-overs from England came along with them. The Colonials brought in the feudal land system, the feudal idea of money, the feudal notion of property rights in everything on earth as a *speculative commodity*. Among these high-minded men was one Tom Paine who did know something of a technical basis for the practice of individual human rights. But not until long after the Colonial rebels had set up the Constitution for property owners in this democracy was anything at all written into it concerned with the nature of human rights.

Knowledge—for What? I think we as a Nation have now been educated far beyond our capacity; educated out of thinking for ourselves; educated away from the things that mean life to the American people. Of course we have unemployment and misery because we have no *ideas* by way of which to utilize our sciences and mechanical inventions; no *ideas* by way of which we might use these newer riches, glass and steel; no honest *ideas* by way of which these things could come into the possession of the life of the American people. No. Our American people today, being so badly overeducated, still lack, most of all, what we properly call *culture*. The same lack of culture, "the cultural lag," is here that exists in Russia today, which does not flatter us. Russia, a great nation, 91 percent illiterate (mostly serfs who had far less than nothing), is now free. Eating, during their life time, out of the hand of a superior "class"; seeing what culture the upper classes had; their tall ceilings, glittering glass chandeliers, sensual paintings, statues, with fountains playing on wide terraces; utter magnificence; now what? Can you talk to them of the things of the spirit and mind? You cannot. They want that which they did not have and were subject to when they were slaves, only now they want all of it twice as tall, want twice as many glittering chandeliers, even more sensuality, more and bigger statues; more "magnificence," in short. And today, in what we call culture, how much better are we where this cultural lag is concerned? May *we* look down on *them* do you think? Not while Williamsburg is the principal criterion.

Government vs. *Organic Architecture*. The cultural influences in our country are like the "floo floo" bird. I am referring to the peculiar and especial bird who always flew backward. To keep the wind out of its eyes? No. Just because it didn't give a darn where it was going, but just *had* to see where it had *been*. Now, in the "floo floo" bird you have the true symbol of our Government architecture—too, and in consequence, how discredited American culture stands in the present time. All the world knows it to be funny except America. What prevented us and still prevents us from knowing it? Armchair education, let's say. Now, all this has parallels in history. The Romans were just as incognizant as we of the things of the spirit. They, too, had no culture of their own. England had none of her own, and we, having none, got what we have as a substitute second, third, or fourth hand from them all. Roman culture, for instance, was Greek. The Romans, however, did have great engineers (you have all heard of the arch), but what did the Romans do with their greatest invention—the arch? You know well enough that for centuries they wasted it by pasting a travesty of Greek trabeation over it to conceal the truth of structure, until finally, some vulgar Roman, more "uncultured" than the rest, one day got up and said: "Hell! Take it all away! What's the matter with the arch? It's a genuine, beautiful and noble thing"; and finally they got it, got the common arch as indigenous architecture. We, the modern Romans, probably are going to get architecture something like that same way. We are going to have a true architecture of glass, steel, and the forms that gratify our new sense of space. We are going to have it. No Colonial Eden is able, long, to say us nay.

Culture, given time, will catch up and assert itself in spite of reaction. This thing which we call America, as I have said, goes around the world today. It is chiefly spirit but that spirit is reality. Not by way of Government can we find encouragement of any help. No, we can have nothing by way of official Government until the thing is at least ten years in the past. What can Government do with an advanced idea? If it is still a controversial idea, and any good idea must be so, can Government touch it without its eye on at least the next election? It cannot. I know of nothing more silly than to expect "Government" to solve our advanced problems for us. If we have no ideas, how can Government have any?

That is a sensible question to ask, and the answer is that Government as a majority affair should never have any. So I see the tragedy of entrusting to Government billions to spend on billions. Why should Government ever be entrusted to build buildings? Inevitably buildings are for tomorrow. That is the last thing Government should be expected or be allowed to do because in entrusting building to Government, we must go 10 to 100 years backward instead of 10 years ahead into the future. Tragic. But to talk against it is just so much water over the dam. The driver may not know where to go but he is in the driver's seat. So what?

Public Housing. You know something of the degradation of the cultural fabric of our Nation when you see our billions now being spent to give us human slums taken from the region of the body and poverty fixed as an institution in the realm of the American soul.

That is what most of this so-called "housing" means to me and what it will come to mean to America in future. I stand here and challenge our America to reflect that any honest, willing, *busy* workman of today with his family can own no home of his own at all unless by grace and beneficence of Government. That should make it time to sit up and raise hell with what made it that way. At least so I think and so you would think if you thought about it at all. Perhaps you feel, as I do, a burning indignation when I see desecration everywhere in the name of culture and realize it is all our own fault.

Hierarchy. Nevertheless, directly or indirectly, we are all eating out of the hand of a man higher up just as he is eating out of the hand above him until finally Government takes the hand. And we call it a system. Well, God knows it is no system. It is an adventitious hang-over from feudal times. Let's face it. If we had allowed ourselves to learn anything of culture, or if we had a genuine American culture on the way now we would now insist upon a more organic structure for our society.

Experiments. I am not talking to you like this out of any books at all. I am speaking here as an architect who has built more than 200 buildings for his own people. Every one of the buildings is an honest experiment in behalf of the man it was built for and in his interest. I am always building, professedly and openly out of my own experience better buildings with truer economy. To what end? That I might become famous as an architect? That I might make a reputation for myself which I might follow up with profit? No! Not that. I persisted with will and patience because there is something compelling in this country, and it is the people of the country. They are right-minded and sincere; at bottom, patient, long suffering, generous, and wonderful. I love my people as I love architecture. You put those two loves together and what will you get? You will get a way of building born that is an honest way of building, affording a more genuine life for the people by way of the building. You will see those things we call buildings blossoming into new forms, free patterns for new life and wider life for all.

Every decent design for any building should be a design for better living, a better design for a richer, fairer way of life instead of being a shallow hang-over from feudal times to please grandmother.

Public Buildings.

Q. Who should design Government buildings, private architects or Government employees?

A. Certainly not Government employees. Because no employee is free to do creative work. And I am not so sure about private architects as they stand on the ragged edge at present. I think if we could forget about "official" designing, allowing buildings to be built simply, naturally, by real builders, wherever found, their hands in the mud of the bricks of which the buildings are made, a lot would come out of the ground a little more simply for the honest purposes of life, forgetting entirely "architecture" as we have now come to know it from the books. Then, I think, something good might happen. I think we could somehow get many "traditions" off our necks in order that great tradition might live. And we would learn to see that in truth the cultural lag persists and obstructs our path by way of too many little traditions with no great sense at all of tradition. I think that what we call great building might live again among us. But what hope when building has been turned over lock, stock, and barrel to college boys who are now in training to the books?

From the Site. My prescription for a modern house? First, a good site. Pick that one at the most difficult spot—pick a site no one wants—but pick one that has features making for character; trees, individuality, a fault of some kind in the realtor mind. That now means getting out of the city. Then, standing on that site, look about you so that you see what has charm. What is the reason you want to build there? Find out. Then build your house so that you may still look from where you stood upon all that charmed you and lose nothing of what you saw before the house was built but see more. Architectural association accentuates the character of landscape if the architecture is right.

Now, if you want a diagram, just come in sometime.

1938: To Williamsburg

The New York Herald Tribune *printed November 6, 1938, a similar article under the title "Williamsburg as a Museum Piece."*

House and Garden. Were I allowed but a single criticism of Williamsburg I should say the attempt to create an "illusion" by way of the restoration is where the matter goes wrong and is likely to do harm as it has done to little Margie Hoskings (William and Mary campus) who says she wants white palings, a scantling roof, and white clapboards to surround her "yes," when the time comes. The New York *Herald Tribune* credits her with sagacity beyond her years because she said it, and rests the case for Williamsburg right there with her. But there is little Mary Jones, little Frieda Hof, little Gusta, little Olga, little Rosa Gallo and little Rachel Finkelstein, what about them? A Richmond editorial proposes cultural segregation, showing how far gone Thomas Jefferson's "liberality" can go. That is where I saw it going as I talked at the college and why I said many of the things I said.

Of course the situation confronting us in Williamsburg is not new. It is old as civilization.

Of It or On It? As a memory Williamsburg may well be sacred. As an illusion it is silly. I contributed my mite at Williamsburg in expounding there not the new aesthetic, but the truth that great art is *of* the life lived and not merely something *on* it; that the new forms our life needs so desperately much will be the result of no aesthetic whatever nor a continued search for the "elegant solution," but a brave and happier facing of reality; the evolution of principle mastering the ways and means of our mechanisms in terms of better patterns for life; free; finding the beginning of all expressive art forms proceeding from the nature of the within here and now rather than begging the whole issue by preferring what our grandfathers had, quite thoughtlessly at the time. Since that earlier time a finer honesty in the realm of the spirit has been born to find its way into the affairs of our time by way of architecture.

Hats Off! The remark, "I am less and less willing to take off my hat to our forefathers, seeing what a mess they left us," probably needs some explanation. To see how culture failed them because it was merely an aesthetic is easy enough and no cause for a lessening of respect, because they were of their time, and there was then, nothing else. But it is difficult to see by way of a deeper understanding brought about by an honest search for the organic structure of our state, or society, that the Colonial dream of freedom lacked the technique necessary to abolish the impositions that they, coming here, rebelled against only to allow these very feudal hang-overs to persist as the economic basis of their beloved ideal—Democracy. Then I feel myself a rebel against the consequences just exactly as they, my forebears, were rebels, but probably the hat should come off nevertheless, it is not much of a hat anyway, for how in the world could their foresight have equaled our hindsight?

1939: An Organic Architecture

In 1939 Wright was invited to London to deliver the Sir George Watson Chair Lectures for that year. The following five selections are taken from the stenographic transcription of these lectures and the questions and answers which followed each evening's lecture. These lectures have now been published in England without revision under the title An Organic Architecture: the Architecture of Democracy *(1939).*

Language vs. *Building.* In construction at least sophistry falls down whereas in tactful language it seems able to outlive itself.

Inhibitions. It is impossible to feel that aside from sanitation, hygiene, and mechanistic contrivances, western academic culture, characterized by its hard shoes, compartment suits and hard hats, has had more than a destructive influence upon the love that is beauty and the beauty that is love wherever that love sought *form.*

1939: The Philosophy of That Architecture

1893. We were doing fairly well in the States, going on toward an expression of ourselves as a people with an architecture of our own, when as luck would have it, we got our first big World's Fair, the Chicago World's Fair of 1893. And there for the first time the United States of America saw architecture as a great orchestration, and loved it without giving much consideration to its nature, not knowing that, all dated, it came on tracing paper from musty books, or that as "traditional" it all lay oblique against the grain of our indigenous effort.

Axiom. I think it was our great architect, Henry Richardson, who said that "the first principle of architecture was to get the job"!

Humane Expression. The time is here for architecture to recognize its own nature, to realize the fact that it is out of life itself for life as it is now lived, a humane and therefore an intensely human thing; the most human of all the expressions of human nature. Architecture is a necessary interpretation of such human life as we know if we, ourselves, are to live. The "Classic" made no such statement; the "Classic" was more a mask than an expression of life.

Modern Contrast. Modern architecture rejects the major axis and the minor axis of classic architecture. It rejects all buildings that would stand tall all dressed up in military fashion, heels together, eyes front, all front, something on the right hand and something on the left hand. Modern organic architecture now favors the reflex, the natural easy attitude, the occult symmetry of grace and rhythm by involving the ground, affirming the ease, grace, and naturalness of natural life. Modern architecture, let us now say organic architecture, is a natural architecture: the architecture of nature, for nature.

Educational Dilemma. I believe that architects are born. I much doubt whether they can really be made. I think that if an architect is born and you try to *make* him you are going to ruin him at the present juncture because there are not enough data on the tables with which you can indoctrinate him and let him live and work creatively. If you are going to teach him, if you are going to tell him, what are you going to teach him? And what are you going to tell him? What have you in the universities, the academies, and the schools to give the young architect that is really out of life experience in this deeper, more valid sense? What have you in architecture that is not something *on* life: some armchair aesthetic of some kind?

Malaise (1939). Realty is not new except as we are new to reality! How new we are to reality I think you can all see by looking about you in violent city streets, in tedious suburbs, in dead towns or ruined countryside. And you can see how far from it we are, not only in architecture; you can see it just as well in the state of the world at the moment—hysterical, uneasy, an unhappy sense of impending danger and loss. Everything material at sixes and sevens with anything spiritual. In short, life everywhere at a loss, not at a premium.

Albion. I know of no egotism quite so rock-bound as English humility in the second person, plural.

1939: Organic Architecture—the Method

The Expert, on Tap or on Top? There is no very great difficulty in creating an organism, and entity, in the way of a building in which all needed services are incorporated features of the building. But that type of building, call it creation, cannot be under any "specialistic" system. Such creation must occur by single-minded mastery on the part of the creator of the building, that is, if we mean *organic* building. We cannot in organic building have a group of specialists; we have to relegate the expert to the backyard of the building, or to oblivion.

Codes. The building codes of the democracies embody, of course, only what the previous generation knew or thought about building, and the ensuing generation finds the code a stumbling block.

Clients. No man can build a building for another who does not believe in him, who does not believe in what he believes in, and who has not chosen him because of this faith, knowing what he can do. That is the nature of architect and client as I see it. When a man wants to build a building he seeks an interpreter, does he not? He seeks some man who has the technique to express that thing which he himself desires but cannot do. So should a man come to me for a building he would be ready for me. It would be what I could do that he wanted.

London Buildings. All that is possible now in the buildings you do build in your city, is a kind of merciful mitigation. Nothing of strength and purpose and character can be city-born nowadays, but you can do something to ease off dying and make this old city quite comfortable while it approaches inevitable dissolution.

Iconoclasm. I have sometimes been called an iconoclast. No such term properly applies to me. I never wanted to destroy anything living, nor ruthlessly take even the dead away, unless I had a better thing in my hand in a better way to plant there and with the planting of which the dead thing interfered.

Authority. Nations have run out of ideas. Why? Because the individuals composing them have none. Schools have none for the same reason. Authority is dry!

When Adam Delved . . . I have said that it is quite unlikely that a man can be a gentleman and a good architect too, and that is probably true, if we take the accepted sense of the term "gentleman" and the accepted sense of the term "architect."

Learning by Doing. What should those boys—architects in embryo—be doing now if this movement toward organic expression of organic society is to grow? Where should they be? Not there at all. Having ground they should make a plan and working drawings for the work they want to do and the way they want to do it. Somebody should give them that piece of ground; there are so many splendid pieces lying waiting for that, or what? Here in England! The boys should go out on that ground and inspired by it, build. And during the building while scheming and scheming while building, meantime designing and drawing details, learn something actual with the sweat of the learning on their brows. That, I take it, might not be education, but it would be culture and that is much better. Today, I think, our educational system and the thing we ought to call culture are not even on speaking terms with each other.

The Disappearing City. We, as architects at least, perhaps last, should be able to realize that the door of this animal cage, the thing we call the great city, is, at last, open; the door is open and we can go out, we must go out of the cage, and it can go from itself, never to return. We should realize, too, that gathered together now in cities we are frightfully vulnerable; no matter how closed the gates, we can easily be destroyed in masses. We can no longer deal with the enemy by shutting the gates in the walls.

How Liberals Work. Someone has said, and I think very well said, that liberals do their work not so much by growing strong in themselves, as by making all others more liberal. That has happened.

Education as Corruption. We cannot blame young people who were brought up at the drawing board by book, by armchair precept merely studying precedent for precedent's sake, for getting no further than that with fundamental principle.

More Bad Education. Education, unfortunately for us in dire need, has produced only those who can do things by patterned precept; by election and selection, rather than by any creative impulse or instinct guided by tested principle whatsoever.

1939: The Practical Applications to Date

Youth in the Shallows. I go about somewhat among our youngsters, not more now than seven or eight times a year. I have gone on to our various universities to talk directly to them about this matter of a center line for indigenous culture and have tried to explain these fundamentals as simply as I could. The response, I may truly say, has been tremendous. One and all seem hungry for something, they do not know quite what, but many know they are in shallow now. They feel that what grandmother had and the way grandmother had it is not just the thing for them. And that applies to buildings just as much as to anything else. Still more does it apply to life itself.

Exit from the City. The young have begun to understand that the door of the cage we call a city has been left open for them and they can now go out as they are qualified to go. In our United States of America we are beginning to find practical realizations of our ideal of freedom in the fact that spaciousness is the great modern opportunity, that human scale is now entirely different—10 to 1 extended at least—and that we no longer need live on little plots of ground with our toes in the street and a little backyard behind us with a few plants in it, shaking hands out of the windows on either side with neighbors good or neighbors bad. I have said that an acre to the individual should be the minimum and if there are 7 in a family that family should have 7 acres. This approximation we are trying to bring home to the people of our United States of America.

Chicago. The greatest and most nearly beautiful city of our Nation is probably Chicago. Eventually as cities go I think Chicago will be the most beautiful great city in the modern world.

More Space Ahead. I do not believe in any "back to the land" movement; I think that any backward movement would be folly; but if, turning away from excess urbanization now, we can go forward with all that science has provided for us, going forward intelligently to the new free forms which must be made for the accommodation of life so that it may live more generously, more spaciously and more fully, we shall be dealing—practically—with the problem now on our hands. The future we see is our present.

Education, Youth, and the Land. What asset have we—actually—in education? We have only this traffic in impositions of thought and ideas from armchair to armchair to armchair, making other incumbents of armchairs, educated but no longer on speaking terms with culture, knowing nothing of the nature of life as it has outrun the past, never facing the reality of now. Our own country is filled—and this is incidental to my topic tonight—although it may not seem to be—with young but helpless white collarites all walking city streets looking for a job, and not knowing a job when they see it, unless it happens to be one of those particular perquisites of education such as selling bonds or stocks or being agents for a "turn-over" in something, somewhere. It has never occurred to these young men, our better born and educated young men at that, to go back to their own countryside, or go out to the old farms, to go again to the wide open spaces of the ground to make life there beautiful, as they might, making their native land and buildings and way of life there homely and lovely and fruitful in modern terms. And just that would mean the building of Broadacre City. There today in the countryside our young men and women could easily have on more liberal terms anything a great city has to give them except the gregarious pressures of humanity upon humanity, and such excesses of the herd instinct as are there inevitably. But, tragic as it is, we, at least, must face the fact that by and large the United States of America no longer owns its own new ground. Our ground has already by way of one, industrialism, mostly gone into the hands of brokers, banks, insurance companies, and other money lending institutions of our country, until today to find any real popular ownership of ground is rare indeed unless we can get it back again to the people by some such plan as Broadacre City presents: the most practical application of our ideal of which I can think. The drift toward urbanization is what stands in the way of what we want to do and where we want to go.

Hen and Egg. It is useless to attempt to free humanity by way of architecture organic so long as humanity itself is living a life inorganic.

Freedom vs. *Speculation.* We found that we must first have ground free in the sense that Henry George predicted free ground—I am not speaking of the single tax. We found that we must have not only free ground, but free money, that is to say, money not taxed by interest but money only as a medium of exchange, and ground not held by absentee landlords but free to those who could and would use it. Then we ran against another dark place, iniquity there too: we run into the fact that the ideas by way of which society lives, moves, and has its being, were all speculative commodities. A little farther on we began to realize that everything we had to live on (it was during the 1929–36 depression, remember) was some form of speculative commodity. We found that life itself had with us become practically *a speculative commodity!* The matter had, practically, gone so far as that! Of course having everything in life down upon the basis of a speculative commodity, you would have naturally a Nation of gamblers. You would have gambling not only as the principle go-getting, money-making device, but see it as the great romance of being. And that is what the system (call it capitalistic—it isn't really) became in America.

Free Buildings for Free Living. How as things are, are we to build great free buildings, buildings out of the ground into the light with a new fine sense of spaciousness for a free scientifically advanced people unless life is itself free? How as things are, are things economic and social to be able to free life and make it happy to live in modern circumstances, realizing the advantages modern science has given us—the enlarged scale of living, the beauty of speed, of quickened community contact and interest the world over?

The Franco-Georgian Tradition. Let us admit that cultural life has not gone very far forward with our scientific advantages when we are still back with the Franco-Georgian tradition, jamming in bathrooms and hanging plumbing pipes all over the outside of these great old Renaissance palaces of ours. (I have often admired the ingenuity that kept the water closets, bowls, and baths inside—with all else outside. . . .)

Architectural Corruption. I know, as every architect who thinks must know, that such buildings are no longer valid; that they are a mask upon life and in no sense revealing or evolutionary where life is concerned. We know if we care to know that they lack integrity in every sense except one, and what is that one? Merely this moot matter of a far too sentimental, unenlightened taste. No practical matter at all anywhere to be considered, even the money matter.

Community Life. A realization is growing that community life in the sense that it is now lived in small hamlets, villages, and cities is no longer necessary nor as charming when modern improvements reach it as it used to be.

The Law of Change. I would ask you all here tonight—why civilization is everywhere so jittery and miserable today? Is it not because there has been no great vision, no profound thought, which wisely accepted the law of change and went along with it, making patterns for life so free that to the life concerned the law of change need not mean unhappiness and torture? The time must come to take this inexorable law as a matter of course into the philosophy and the concrete forms expressing our era. I am one of those who firmly believe that time is here.

Vision and Parasites. Our present backward folly is the result of our education, I believe, which does not wish to change nor is able to allow for it. So the young man cannot enter life qualified to go with it. He is helpless. Knowing nothing of the life of growth he is a parasite. Not born a parasite perhaps, but if he is not so born he is made one to breed one. What then are we to do with community life, say, in a parasitic world for parasites? Well . . . nevertheless this community life of the future will surely take care of itself, given fairly amplified, enlivened, widened horizons and conditions. And for one I believe that the community life to come will be much more alive just because it will be less an escape from life (when it realizes upon today). I don't think you or I need know too many details —all we need to know is the general direction and after that what is coming next in sight.

"Romance." From my point of view (as a modern architect of course) the center of what we call romance has shifted; I find it lying no longer upon the periphery of things. So it is no longer much concerned with "taste." I find it as a new sense of reality, a new adventure thrilling in search for reality. If there is anything more romantic than that, it has not appeared in my life, and I do not think it will appear in yours—the hazards, the great rewards, the incomparable beauties, the unreasonable punishments, all go to make life romantic. No longer escapist gestures, no longer taste-built, taste-formed ideas, but an earnest life-long search for that thing growing out from within the nature of the thing . . . not from anything applied to that thing from without.

Architecture Makes the Site. No one noticed that it was a particularly beautiful site until the house was built. Then as the depth planes came into play they began to realize how beautiful it really was. When organic architecture is properly carried out no landscape is ever outraged by it but is always developed by it.

Swimming Pools. The average swimming pool looks to me like a glorified bathtub. There is less sense there of the water than of the basin it is in. With the pool sides undercut you see no walls in the pool but only the water and reflections.

From the Inside Out. There is no feeling of weight when you are in it, the sense of inert mass has vanished. There is no sense of being enclosed—shut in—either, as you have not been cut off from outdoor light and space anywhere.

Photographs of Architecture. Photographs are poor things at best, where architecture is concerned.

Escape to Reality. Really, I confess I don't know exactly what "escapist" in his sense of the term is, not what it means to be one. I might call him one if I knew. But if he means escaping from the oppression of the dead past into a life more suited to the living present, the accusation does not slander. The basis of the "escapist" accusation may be that at Taliesin we live a pretty self-contained life, devoting ourselves to a life of our own much in ways of our own. You have just seen something of the character of that life on the screen. And if that is escaping from life then I do not know what life is. We intend to head straight into it, all courting it, not afraid of it but eager to explore reality. In fact, I believe Taliesin to be a little research station on the way toward just that—*reality*. We at Taliesin see reality as romance today. We have already found that romance lies no longer on the periphery of life as we see it now man-made, but is something profound to be independently involved within life by living it. So I dare say that that is an escape too. If so, let's all escape!

Preservation of London. Since coming to London I have found, as I expected, that the cultured Englishman is the best comrade and most charming company in the world, and I find his dear old London full of pathetic charm and a lively antiquarian interest. I have not been through a museum for many years and I like it. As such I do not want to see the better old historic London changed much. And I should hate to see this museum piece of yours much patched up. Why not save it as it is? Why let architects or bombers destroy it?

Failures of Education. The young people whom I meet and talk with as I have gone about our country somewhat, young "educated" people now, are many of them bewildered, all eager to know direction as I am sure you are. They are sure there must be a better life if not security for them somewhere just as I hope you are sure. All of them are educated, or being so in the style of some facade or other, and far beyond their capacity, in Usonia no less, nor more so, than in older countries. And all for what? Surely it cannot be that they are being educated merely for financial gods to make just another cog on the wheels of a capitalist system which is really no system at all. I wish we had a capitalist system; I believe in a capitalist system which has its base broad upon the ground, its apex high as you please. But here we have one with its apex on the ground and its base up in the air. Something has been going wrong for democracy! For all the swift swarming there is no real potence. The potential forces of peace are far greater in their human appeal and charm than those of war, but they have never been marshaled in all their colorful beauty. Love for Joan of Arc will far outlive hatred of Napoleon.

Democracy. With democracy crying for constructive thinking—all our culture has been this poor attempt to escape from the actual reality of existence by way of taste created, superficial illusions. Education has expediently confirmed the illusions from generation to generation by book and by social order. Socially and economically, nearly everything with which we started to build the democracy of our United States, like our inherited cultural lags, was some feudal hang-over; a hang-over from feudal times. We began with the truly great idea of making life an even break for every man, giving every man an equal opportunity because every real man must want the prosperity for others that he wants for himself. But I think it must have been an error when it was written into the Declaration of Independence that every man was born free and equal, because that is pure nonsense. I think what was meant was that every man is born free and equal before the law. But it did not take long for the hang-overs of a feudal age, freshly set up as the economic basis for the new democracy, to allow the wolf, the fox and rat, in human form, to be the winners in that new set-up, and quite completely the winners. In such wise were we headed off from any expression of a democratic life, quickly; yes, even before we had begun to grow. We are now stalemate but beginning to realize it.

What Architecture Is. What is architecture anyway? Is it the vast collection of the various buildings which have been built to please the varying taste of the various lords of mankind? I think not. No, I know that architecture is life; or at least it is life itself taking *form* and therefore it is the truest record of life as it was lived in the world yesterday, as it is lived today or ever will be lived. So architecture I know to be a Great Spirit. It can never be something which consists of the buildings which have been built by man on earth . . . mostly now a rubbish heap or soon to be one. Architecture is that great living creative spirit which from generation to generation, from age to age, proceeds, persists, creates, according to the nature of man, and his circumstances as they change. That is really architecture.

Inadequacy of Science. Now in this broad sense the scholars and professors handling the subject for us do not know so very much about it, do they? We are talking about architecture now as something which has to come right again by way of fundamental principles, something we must have right side up on native ground or miss the vital best of the inner rhythms life has in store for us, lose something vital and valuable forever, something for which all that science has been doing so much to accomplish at such frightful cost to us cannot compensate. Science has done much to accomplish miracles which might bless our lives but which are now chiefly curses, because culture without creative architecture, cannot come along with them to make use of them. Without creative consciousness as the center line of all culture, we cannot utilize what science has done, nor can we show how to use scientific results intelligently in even a material way, to say nothing at all of a great art and architecture.

Fear of Life. I believe that what has done most damage to youth in current educational training in our cultural and economic system, is the fact that the "isms" of institutionalism have become habitual and we must fight the "istics" of the "ites" who are all solidly lined up against the vital laws of organic change, regarding all changes whatsoever as enemies. So indeed we all have become somewhat afraid of organic change and feel secure only if we know we can keep what we have as we have it. But the more power we have, the more we become stupid stand-patters rather than promulgators of the good life for its own sake. The law of organic change is the only thing that mankind can know as beneficent or as actual; we can only know that all things are in process of flowing into some continuous state of becoming. Heraclitus was stoned in the streets of Athens for a fool for making that Declaration of Independence, I do not remember how many hundreds of years ago. But today modern culture has not made much progress in that direction because, being so institutional, we took no heed; so limited in outlook; so filled with fear of life rather than willingness to trust it, that I am afraid deep distrust of life is stronger in the United States of America and in England today than ever before. It is so because we are too busy having and holding (or trying to) that we have not yet got hold of something which we must now find, or ourselves disappear as a civilization. It is that same something which we must find that I have kept on driving at in all these informal talks with you. It is that same something which organic architecture has found, integral structure . . . form and function *one*. No wonder we have so little of it to show, the world over.

Trust in Life. Except for these rare prophetic examples, what can we do with an organic architecture in general as the architecture of a whole people, so long as we have no whole people, but only a society so departmental, documented and superficial as ours has become; so ignorant of cause and effect as to be afraid of everything life really is! I have learned in my limited experience that there is only one trust worthy of any man and that is trust in life itself; the firm belief that life is (world without end, amen!) and that you cannot cheat it nor can you defeat it. So far as culture goes we have been trying all these centuries to beat life and to defeat it . . . pretty nearly succeeding. We have so seldom trusted life. Certainly we have not trusted it in our architecture, nor have we trusted it in such economics as we profess, and we have not trusted it in politics nor in statesmanship. We have not trusted it anywhere, no, not even in religion! We talk about God, and we have built all these great architectural sacrifices to God, God being anything other and elsewhere than the life we know and the daily life we live. No wonder we are as we are, and not as we must be in order to go on really alive unless one wants to go to heaven. And it is of no little significance that one must be dead to go there.

Ends and Means. I have seemed to belittle the human nature of our time and the great achievements of science, but I have intended to do neither because I believe human nature still sound and understand that science has done a grand job well; but well I know that science cannot save us. Science can give us only the tools in the box, these mechanical miracles that it has already given us. But of what use to us are miraculous tools until we have mastered the humane cultural use of them? We do not want to live in a world where the machine has mastered the man! We want to live in a world where man has mastered the machine!

Architecture as Revelation. What we call organic architecture is no mere aesthetic movement, but is the profound idea of a new integrity, the true basis of a democratic human life wherein art, religion and science are one, the only path out of chaos.

1939: To the 58th

FROM THE *Architectural Review,* AUGUST, 1939.

This omnibus answer to the many critics of the Sir George Watson lectures grouped the British modernists with other eclectics as the "58th variety." The attack or defense of Wright's ideas, as published in Focus, *the* Architectural Review, *the* Journal of the R.I.B.A. *and other British periodicals make very interesting reading. One late result of these lectures was the award to Wright of the Royal Gold Medal for Architecture, 1941.*

Adulation. Hero worshippers are sometimes pretty awful. That any of mine can now bear hide or hair of me, would surprise me.

Escape, Escape! Can they really believe Taliesin turning its face away from life because it refuses to see any pattern as "fit for the establishment of any contemporary vernacular" whatsoever, and lives out in the country instead of some urban backyard or city slum? Can they believe that we at Taliesin advocate a "back-to-the-land" movement? Do they really imagine that I build self-indulgencies for capitalistic parasites in the name of esoteric philosophy and work for the rich, that my buildings are expensive, etc.? I would like to compare the cost of them with the cost of theirs. Is the idea that good architecture must be, first of all, good building and the architect a master builder first and an aesthetician afterward heresy? Is the idea that good community life is the life of the individual raised to the "nth" power rather than the life of the individual reduced to the lowest common denominator, idealistic hallucination?

Slums. All great cities are slums now, communism or no communism.

Answers. I could only prove to them that today my building is as far in advance of my building, 1895–1911, as my building of that period was in advance of that round about it at the time, by teaching them to put two and two together so they will not make just *one* "four" but make *infinite* "fours."

Once and for all concerning this constantly repeated reference to my contribution to architecture as a kind of romanticism; because any attempt on their part to establish a "contemporary vernacular" is defied by the revelations of principle eternally fresh and now in every building I build—they drag in the term "romanticism" to conceal their own impotence whereas it really only explains it.

I love romance as I love sentiment. But just as I dislike sentimentality I would dislike their "romance." I suggest you put a gently sloping roof on any Le Corbusier or Gropius just to see what you have left of the so-called international style after proper deductions have been made.

Boys, you are all going knowing *why* but not knowing *where*. Then why do you speak so much and so surely of *how?*

Machinelike Building. The "international style," a style that could never be democratic because it is *the use of man by the machine.* Why thus fail to distinguish between the economies of living and the forces of life?

The Whole or the Parts. I began my work as architect by sensibly accepting the machine as the creative artist's inevitable tool, believing that only where such as he had it in control could it prove a blessing instead of a curse. I saw the consequences of machinery: standardization, extreme urbanization, human life becoming more and more vicarious and so more and more removed from the ground. I saw that life might be made dependent upon the push button and steering wheel, saw it without flinching. I saw human energy reduced to ohms and kilowatts, germs and glands, new life centralized until it was at the mercy of the push button and steering wheel, still believing salvation lay in creative artist control. I had faith in that.

I still have faith, but *where is that creative force today?* The man is not using the machine! *The machine is using the man;* using him so that he is losing himself; becoming a "thing" beneath his push button and steering wheel. Neither are *by* him or *for* him. Already he is started and steered by forces beyond his control, owing to feudal hang-overs, society will not yet give up.

I see now, as I saw then, that the only way man can use the machine (not let it use him) is to get it as a working principle into work by way of the great human force we used to call creative artist. Well, again, where is he?

If he exists now he will probably be found under another name, because as he stood, in no man's land, the machine has already wiped him out as any constructive element in society life today. I foresaw this possibility. I did not accept it.

Le Corbusier, Gropius, *et al.* are yet where I stood in 1900. I do not resent nor resign the position I then took but I have *experienced* my own philosophy. I have seen it taking partial effect by way of the generations following me. What I started to do with high faith, and confidence in human creative force, I see giving way to certain sterilizing factors in my original equation. Instead of mastering those factors on the side of creation, Europe has seen only a new aesthetic for academic consumption in a foolish effort to establish a contemporary vernacular. So, bid to England, I came with another "declaration of independence." This time one concerned, not with taxes, but with independence of any aesthetic whatsoever where this matter of *life as structure* is concerned, social, political, or artistic. I said that the only way man can use his machine and keep alive what is best in him is to go by means of it to the larger freedom the machine makes possible; go toward *decentralization* instead of continuing the centralization the machine exploits and, so far as any great human benefit goes, will soon explode.

Simple enough?

Do I continue to befog the issue? If so the machine itself will prove me right.

Meantime I can wait and work.

1939: Dinner Talk

LECTURE AT HULL HOUSE, CHICAGO.

Correlators. This task cannot be performed by painters. They paint. The same is true of sculptors. They sculp. True of weavers and potters. They weave and pot. All, long ago, took a little shovel full of coals and went off somewhere to start a little hell of their own. Painting, the universal favorite, no longer contributes much to environment. As representation it is prostitute, the camera disposing of it. Pictures are hung on walls or painted *on* them; they are not *of* them. The easel picture has become a kind of accomplished self-indulgence, sensual as eating or pessimistic as a Broadway wisecracker. Therefore, such correlation as we desire can come only from the architect.

New Forms for a New Environment. Vital new forms are needed for environment, new expressions of life as now changed and as it will change continually.

Gold Coast Slums. My work is done mainly in the real slums of our great country, the upper income brackets of the gold coasts, peacock alleys, and penthouses of our cities. You laugh . . . but no, really, I mean what I say. Their plight is tragic. I well know the real poverty-stricken America today, in any important sense, is our ultrasuccessful rich citizenry.

So . . . during the dreadful time when we all had nothing at all to do (the breakdown we politely call "depression" was severe for about 7 years, I think) I knew most of my friends, those I had worked with and learned to love, had blood running down behind their dress shirt fronts, all dying a thousand deaths when they needed die but one. Having pinned their faith to "having" they must now "hold" simply because to *have* in that sense means to *hold*. Holding was now agony and futility. The circumstances were pretty tough for rich and poor alike, but toughest of all for the rich. And yet, I lived to see at that time a number of my rich friends form a ring around me to keep me at work when "they" tried to drive me into the streets to get a worm's eye view of society. Then why shouldn't *I* go to work for *them?* I did. I went to work on Broadacre City. A way out for the rich as well as for the poor. But the funny thing is that having attained a cross section of our civilization and evolved a free pattern which would let my friends out of misery and uncertainty to enjoy and live in fruitfulness and peace, came their criticism: "He's just Communist," said some, or "He's a Fascist," said others, or "He's escapist," still others said. They said anything and everything except to say what the city really was—a true basis for trying out genuine capitalism. I believe that some day capital will be honest enough so that honest capitalism will really be tried to establish a sound basis for trying it out. So, after the models of the city had gone around the country for a while, exhibited first in Rockefeller Center (a wonder the Center didn't fall in on the model) I took it all back to Taliesin. But we are not through with it. Broadacre City is again going out on exhibition, soon, in important places with sharper, clearer explanations than before.

Wasting Our Improvements. But all around our Nation the other countries of the world are beginning to see the great modern improvements that have cost us so much, take effect in new cultural forms. We have mostly thrown them away because to use them has not been "historical" and to so use them "unbankable." *Authority* has allowed nothing to live in the way of culture that was indigenous except as this puny, silly little "Colonial tradition" might be so. And of course it is not so at all.

Always I have seen cultural progress within us up against that precious remnant of would-be aesthetic self-righteousness. As for government's share in all this, observe the buildings at Washington. Every one of them is without exception superficially, expensively, falsely traditional. A monument to Abraham Lincoln? Gone to Greece. To Thomas Jefferson, the radical of his time, give him the latest thing from Rome. But I like to believe that the grand picture *that* spurious monument to Tom makes is the last defiant grandomania of scholastic obstruction, the natural end of the aesthetician's waste of life and opportunity to which we are "officially" bound and must call "classic" or say "Colonial." Notwithstanding all well-meant official or educational abuse whatsoever I believe our national soul is our own but so far as culture goes I can see it only as way down underneath or in out-of-the-way places. The States are, of course, in point of culture still a little one-horse England, the more so the farther east we go. Hence this solicitude of a parent for a necessarily tender young effort such as this one dedicated here at Hull House tonight. Will it begin to be usefully felt, its enemies native, well intentioned, ubiquitous, government and education, notwithstanding?

Public Housing. In passing, since I have dealt at length on distrust of government, just for good measure here is one more occasion for distrust. [Mr. Wright here told of a conversation with Nathan Straus starting with an account of how Mr. Straus, indicating the progress USHA had made, marked off a corner of a very large director's table, saying that "what has been done was as that small corner to the whole table."]

I felt thankful. I felt thankful that it had gone no further, for this reason; because we, you and I, everywhere are called upon to pay a little more rent to unearned increment so these desolate people of the slums may have a shower, a flower box, and a patch of lawn. So far so good, but what I saw in Government housing was the skyscraper laid down on its side, that's all, ourselves invited to help the poor into it, to stay in it. I saw Government making a national *institution* of poverty, poverty so subsidized by us that impoverishment must go on paying rent, forever. Mr. Straus kindly asked me to have dinner with him that night to meet some dozen other architects, most of them working for him. At dinner he asked me what I thought about what I had seen of "housing" in his office that day. I hesitated. "Do you really want to know?" I asked. He did, so I told him the truth. "Out of the slums of today, you are making the slums of tomorrow." He didn't believe me nor like it. Pressed for reasons I said, "Flower boxes and tubs are good camouflage. Camouflage isn't really what the poor need." Now I believe that if you and I are going to pay this subsidy out of our own pockets, why should we continue to pay more rent to realty? Why not pay the money to *transportation?* Make it easy for poverty to escape and cease to be poverty. Why not break down this iron ring that urban realty throws around poverty? Why not take "the poor" out and set them down where they can come and go rent free someday and meantime learn to earn from the ground as well as at the bench?

Yes, USHA housing is (and Hull House should know it) just another basis for distrust of the Government where ideas are needed. The life of the people is here concerned and, of course, where the people should live their own lives in their own way. Personally, I do not believe Government should be allowed to spend one dollar for creative work like architecture, painting, music, sculpture, or the theater. My faith is that given the opportunity, having the sincere interior impulse, what we call "art" is best left to take care of itself, *if only we will get the artificial lets and hindrances like education and Government out of the way.* Or where they belong, somewhere in the background.

I say, let's stand back and give indigenous culture a chance to live on its own feet. Shame to say, nothing of the kind will soon have a chance to live that way in what we still consider our "free" country.

Government in Art. I am naturally enough suspicious of anything "governmental" in art. The reason is that nothing "ipso facto" can be helpful and Government must be "ipso facto" only if it is to survive, in other words, win the next election. For instance, Government won't lend money or anything that is today or tomorrow. "They" won't lend money or give a hand to the builder of a house which is to be "the" better house 10 years from now. Believe it or not, "they" will only lend to you upon yesterday, and then lend to you only in the middle of the road. Yes, our yesterday is their tomorrow. Now, lots of things can be done by way of Government. But you cannot do much that way in what we call creative art. So I fear it is going to be more than difficult to come through with the radical ideas which are the neutral basis of all creative endeavor by way of "official" aid. No . . . nothing "official" in our new national experiment has ever encouraged original thinking in any cultural situation. Government cannot speculate nor can it experiment except at peril. On the other hand, it can take hold and consolidate what gains have been made in spite of it. *But how to get on with it to where we must go from there?* As I have seen that necessity, that is no affair for Government.

The Beaux-Arts in Usonia. Invited to take the Sir George Watson chair for the year 1939, I have just lately been in England. At the first meeting in the new hall of the R.I.B.A., I said England had had a Declaration of Independence from us, July 4, 1776, concerning taxes and now England was going to have another, May 7, 1939, concerning the spirit. (A minority report I confessed), and I politely invited cultural England to get off our cultural chest. I declared we had been harassed long enough by English "old Colonial" and that I didn't think it was ever worth much even to them because it was the dwindling end of a decadent French culture when they got it and it was all certainly worth less than nothing to us when we were confronted with the building of a new nation. Well, strange to say, they readily agreed with me.

Another thing not so strange and that you should know, for reasons I will explain, is that Paris agreed, too. While I was still in England, the director general of the Beaux-Arts, the president of the International Society of Architects and the Mayor of Paris sent a delegate to London to invite me to attend a little dinner in Paris (in my honor, yes) . . . and lecture there. I declined the lectures because I will lecture in no language but my own, distrusting interpreters almost as much as stenographers. But I gladly attended the dinner and afterward spent 3 days in Paris going about with Beaux-Arts architects looking at recent architecture. I saw many extraordinary modern buildings there as I had also seen them in the Balkan cities. I don't think we have many as genuinely advanced as those. I was surprised because I was familiar only with reactionary Beaux-Arts attitudes in the schools of our country, I saw I would have to reverse my feeling about the Paris Beaux-Arts. Said I, "I have never thought much of the Beaux-Arts training in our country." Said the president and the director general, "We don't think much of it in your country, either." They probably didn't realize the brick they were handing me. I suppose it is ungentlemanly to throw it now . . . but, just for good measure I will tell you that the director general and the president said: "We have wanted to show you we are standing shoulder to shoulder with you."

Published Writings of Frank Lloyd Wright

The Architect. *Brickbuilder.* June, 1900.

The Art and Craft of the Machine. In *Chicago Architectural Club, Catalog of the 14th Annual Exhibition.* Chicago, 1901.

A Home in a Prairie Town. *Ladies' Home Journal.* February, 1901.

A Small House With "Lots of Room In It." *Ladies' Home Journal.* July, 1901.

The "Village Bank" Series. *Brickbuilder.* August, 1901.

Introduction to *Hiroshigi: An Exhibition of Collected Prints.* Chicago, 1906.

A Fireproof House for $5000. *Ladies' Home Journal.* April, 1907.

In the Cause of Architecture. *Architectural Record.* March, 1908.

Ausgeführte Bauten und Entwürfe. Berlin, 1910.

The Japanese Print: An Interpretation. Chicago, 1912.

In the Cause of Architecture. *Architectural Record.* May, 1914.

Antique Color Prints. *Catalog, Chicago Arts Club.* 1917.

Experimenting With Human Lives. Hollywood, Calif., 1923.

The New Imperial Hotel. *Western Architect.* April, 1923.

In the Wake of the Quake I. *Western Architect.* November, 1923.

In the Wake of the Quake II. *Western Architect.* February, 1924.

Louis Henry Sullivan, Beloved Master. *Western Architect.* June, 1924.

Louis Sullivan, His Work. *Architectural Record.* July, 1924.

In the Cause of Architecture: The Third Dimension. In *Frank Lloyd Wright: The Lifework of an American Architect.* Santpoort, Holland, 1925.

Introduction to Auction Catalog: Anderson Galleries, New York. The Frank Lloyd Wright Collection of Japanese Prints. New York, 1927.

In the Cause of Architecture I, The Architect and the Machine. *Architectural Record.* May, 1927.

In the Cause of Architecture II, Standardization, the Soul of the Machine. *Architectural Record.* June, 1927.

In the Cause of Architecture III, Steel. *Architectural Record.* August, 1927.

In the Cause of Architecture IV, Fabrication and Integration: the New World. *Architectural Record.* October, 1927.

Why the Japanese Earthquake Did Not Destroy the Hotel Imperial. *Liberty.* December 3, 1927.

In the Cause of Architecture I, The Logic of the Plan. *Architectural Record.* January, 1928.

In the Cause of Architecture II, What "Styles" Mean to the Architect. *Architectural Record.* February, 1928.

In the Cause of Architecture III, The Meaning of Materials: Stone. *Architectural Record.* April, 1928.

In the Cause of Architecture IV, The Meaning of Materials: Wood. *Architectural Record.* May, 1928.

In the Cause of Architecture V, The Meaning of Materials: The Kiln. *Architectural Record.* June, 1928.

In the Cause of Architecture VI, The Meaning of Materials: Glass. *Architectural Record.* July, 1928.

In the Cause of Architecture VII, The Meaning of Materials: Concrete. *Architectural Record.* August, 1928.

Fiske Kimball's New Book. A Review. *Architectural Record.* August, 1928.

Towards a New Architecture. *World Unity.* September, 1928.

In the Cause of Architecture VIII, The Meaning of Materials: Sheet Metal. *Architectural Record.* October, 1928.

In the Cause of Architecture IX, The Terms. *Architectural Record.* December, 1928.

Taliesin: The Chronicle of a House With a Heart. *Liberty.* March 23, 1929.

Surface and Mass—Again! *Architectural Record.* July, 1929.

The Logic of Contemporary Architecture as the Expression of This Age. *Architectural Forum.* May, 1930.

A Broadcast With Hugh Ferris. *Architectural Forum.* November, 1930.

American Architecture as a Profession. *American Architect & Building News.* December, 1930.

Modern Architecture. The Kahn Lectures for 1930. Princeton, 1931.

Two Lectures on Architecture. Chicago, 1931.

Principles of Design. *Annual of American Design.* New York, 1931.

Advice to the Young Man in Architecture. *Architectural Record.* August, 1931.

Headlights. *Architectural Forum.* October, 1931.

Hell-bent Is Eclecticism. *Tower-Town Topics.* 1931.

An Autobiography. New York, 1932.

The Disappearing City. New York, 1932.

Why I Love Wisconsin. *Wisconsin Magazine.* 1932.

Books. *Scholastic Magazine.* 1932.

Letter to the Editor. *T-Square.* February, 1932.

"For All May Raise the Flowers Now, For All Have Got the Seed." *T-Square.* February, 1932.

Of Thee I Sing. *Shelter.* April, 1932.

The Frozen Fountain. A Review. *Saturday Review of Literature.* May 21, 1932.

America Tomorrow. *American Architect & Building News.* May, 1932.

The House of the Future. *National Real Estate Journal.* July, 1932.

Caravel or Motorship? *Architectural Forum.* August, 1932.

What Does the Machine Mean to Life in a Democracy? *Pictorial Review.* September, 1932.

To the Students of the Beaux-Arts Institute of Design. *Architecture.* October, 1932.

The Taliesin Fellowship. Spring Green, Wisconsin, 1933.

The Chicago World's Fair. *Architects' Journal.* July 13, 1933.

Another "Pseudo." *Architectural Forum.* July, 1933.

In the Show Window at Macy's. *Architectural Forum.* November, 1933.

Taliesin. Spring Green, Wisconsin, 1934.

Architecture of Individualism. *Trend.* March-April, 1934.

What Is the Modern Idea? *Physical Culture.* June 24, 1934.

Kindergarten Chats. A Review. *Architectural Review.* March, 1935.

Broadacre City: A New Community Plan. *Architectural Record.* April, 1935.

Louis Sullivan. A Review. *Saturday Review of Literature.* December 14, 1935.

Skyscrapers Doomed? Yes! *Rotarian.* March, 1936.

Taliesin: Our Cause. *Professional Arts Quarterly.* March, 1936.

Recollections. United States: 1893-1920. *Architects' Journal.* July 16-August 6, 1936.

Apprenticeship Training for the Architect. *Architectural Record.* September, 1936.

Architecture and Modern Life (with Baker Brownell). New York, 1937.

What the Cause of Architecture Needs Most. *Architectural Review.* March, 1937.

Architecture and Life in the USSR. *Architectural Record.* October, 1937.

Introduction to *A New House by Frank Lloyd Wright on Bear Run, Pennsylvania.* New York, 1938.

Architectural Forum. January, 1938. Special Issue on Frank Lloyd Wright.

Nine Chains to the Moon. A Review. *Saturday Review of Literature.* September 17, 1938.

Williamsburg as a Museum Piece. *New York Herald Tribune.* November 6, 1938.

An Organic Architecture; The Architecture of Democracy. The Sir George Watson Chair Lectures of the Sulgrave Manor Board for 1939. London, 1939.

Frank Lloyd Wright Again. *Architect and Engineer.* March, 1939.

To the 58th. *Journal of the Royal Institute of British Architects.* October 16, 1939.

Taliesin. Spring Green, Wisconsin, 1939.

Chicago's Auditorium Is Fifty Years Old. *Architectural Forum.* September, 1940.

Index